THOMAS HARDY

The Writer and his Background

★

EDITED BY NORMAN PAGE

BELL & HYMAN
London

First published in 1980 by
BELL & HYMAN LIMITED
Denmark House
37–39 Queen Elizabeth Street
London SE1 2QB

British Library Cataloguing in Publication Data
Thomas Hardy – (Writers and their Background)
1. Hardy, Thomas, b. 1840 – Criticism and
interpretation
I. Page, Norman   II. Series
823'.8   PR4754

ISBN 0 7135 1091 9

Printed and bound in Great Britain at
The Camelot Press Ltd
Southampton

Contents

The Contributors

LENNART A. BJÖRK
Professor of English, University of Stockholm; editor of *The Literary Notes of Thomas Hardy*.

PHILIP COLLINS
Professor of English, University of Leicester; author of *Dickens and Crime*, *Dickens and Education*, etc.; editor of *Dickens: the Critical Heritage*, *Charles Dickens: the Public Readings*.

JAMES GIBSON
Principal Lecturer in English, Christ Church College, Canterbury; editor of *The Complete Poems of Thomas Hardy*, etc.

SAMUEL HYNES
Professor of English, Princeton University; author of *The Edwardian Turn of Mind*, *Edwardian Occasions*, *The Auden Generation*, etc.

NORMAN PAGE
Professor of English, University of Alberta; author of *The Language of Jane Austen*, *Speech in the English Novel*, *Thomas Hardy*, etc.; editor of *Wilkie Collins: the Critical Heritage*, *Jude the Obscure*, etc.

ROGER ROBINSON
Professor of English Literature, Victoria University of Wellington; author of essays on Fielding, Dickens, Butler; editor of *The Way of All Flesh*.

RICHARD H. TAYLOR
Lecturer in English Literature, University of London Institute of Education; editor of *The Personal Notebooks of Thomas Hardy*.

MERRYN WILLIAMS
Formerly Lecturer in English, the Open University; author of *Thomas Hardy and Rural England*, *A Preface to Hardy*.

RAYMOND WILLIAMS

Professor of Drama, University of Cambridge; author of *Culture and Society*, *The Long Revolution*, *The English Novel from Dickens to Lawrence*, *The Country and the City*, etc.

GEORGE WING

Professor of English, University of Calgary; author of *Dickens*, *Hardy*, etc.

Editor's Note

Since editions of Hardy's novels are numerous, it has seemed preferable to provide chapter-references rather than page-references. Where a novel is divided into books or parts as well as chapters, both references are given (e.g. *Jude the Obscure*, II, 3). Throughout, the place of publication is London unless otherwise indicated. The following abbreviations have been used:

Cox	*Thomas Hardy: the Critical Heritage*, ed. R. G. Cox, 1970.
DCM	Dorset County Museum.
Life	F. E. Hardy, *The Life of Thomas Hardy 1840–1928*, 1962 (single-volume edition of the work originally published in two volumes).
Purdy	R. L. Purdy, *Thomas Hardy: a Bibliographical Study*, Oxford, 1954.

General Editor's Preface

THE STUDY OF LITERATURE is not a 'pure' discipline since works of literature are affected by the climate of opinion in which they are produced. Writers, like other men, are concerned with the politics, the philosophy, the religion, the arts, and the general thought of their own times. Some literary figures, indeed, have made their own distinguished contributions to these areas of human interest, while the achievement of others can be fully appreciated only by a knowledge of them.

The volumes in this series have been planned with the purpose of presenting major authors in their intellectual, social, and artistic contexts, and with the conviction that this will make their work more easily understood and enjoyed. Each volume contains a chapter which provides a reader's guide to the writings of the author concerned, a Bibliography, and Chronological Tables setting out the main dates of the author's life and publications alongside the chief events of contemporary importance.

In spite of the amount of biographical and critical writing on Hardy which has appeared in the last few years, a synoptic view of his artistic achievement has remained as elusive as ever; greater knowledge of his life has made his personality seem only more complex, and evaluations of his work have often seemed only to reflect the critical fashions of the times or the vagaries of their authors. The essays brought together here by Professor Page, an acknowledged authority on Hardy, while drawing upon recent scholarship and criticism, are able by the balance they give each other to present a convincing portrait of Hardy and an impressive account of his work. The distinguished contributors to this volume have produced an important assessment of Hardy's art which will provide the reader with a clear guide to his writings and to the biographical and critical studies now in print.

R. L. BRETT

Editor's Preface

To invoke the notion of 'background' in relation to Hardy is more than a pious gesture to openmindedness or eclecticism of approach: it is to imply a rich variety of quite specific meanings. Taking the term at the most literal level, it may be claimed that no English novelist – and perhaps no English writer – has depicted more persistently and comprehensively the physical qualities, both natural and man-made, of a particular region. Hardy renders with loving and informed exactness the landscape of heath and pasture and woodland, hill and valley and coastline; he also documents the works of the human generations, from earthworks and tumuli to church, barn, manor-house and cottage. He may not have set out with the intention of becoming identified as the limner of the Wessex scene, but his production in 1895 of a map of Wessex was a recognition that that was what a quarter of a century's authorship had led to, at any rate in the minds of a large body of readers for whom he had reintroduced the term 'Wessex' into the current vocabulary. Countless energetic enthusiasts have tramped 'the Hardy country', and if (despite Hardy's own warnings) the identification of real with fictional landscapes has sometimes been pushed too far, the impulse ought nevertheless to be respected as constituting, among other things, a tribute to the power with which Hardy creates for each reader a region that henceforth exists in the mind as well as (more or less) on the map.

Secondly, 'background' has a temporal relevance. Hardy chronicles a particular stretch of English history as well as portraying a specific region, and a full reading of his work both requires and helps to provide an understanding of the one as much as the other. In conjunction this amounts to a rendering of a whole way of life: what Dickens does for the city in the middle years of the nineteenth century, Hardy a generation later does for the countryside. Just as he sometimes moves to the borders of Wessex and beyond, he often looks back from the vantage-point of his own adult life to his childhood and to the period of his parents' and even his grandparents' youth; and both spatially and chronologically the double vision thus gained is a source of strength – Tess's experiences at Flintcomb-Ash and Sandbourne cannot be fully apprehended except in relation to her life at Little Marlott and Talbothays; the redundancy of the Mellstock choir and the incompetence of Henchard's business methods gain poignancy from the conveyed sense of time's indifference. J. H. Buckley has written that 'the sense of . . . a perpetually changeful public time was central to the intellectual life of the nineteenth century' (*The Triumph of Time*, Cambridge, Mass., 1967, 12–13); central to Hardy's thinking and feeling is a sense of the implications of this public phenomenon for private lives. Like Dickens (and most other novelists), of course, he operates within certain social limits, though the complexity of the matter is increased both by the speed and scale of historical change and by the ambiguities and ambivalences of his own attitudes.

Next, there is the intellectual background – especially philosophical, theological and scientific – which, for Hardy as for George Eliot, is of unusual importance. It is impossible to read a Hardy novel – or even, it is not much of an exaggeration to say, a Hardy poem – without becoming sharply aware of a highly individual vision of life. Although the Hardyan vision is deeply coloured by the emotions, it derives its power also from the sense of intellectual explorations doggedly pursued and convictions courageously acknowledged. His creative life extended from the age of Darwin and Mill to that of Einstein; his work reflects the struggle of intellect and conscience not just of a generation but of a whole sweep of English mental life from *Essays and Reviews* to the Great War and after.

Yet again, the 'background' of a writer has specifically literary and linguistic dimensions. Hardy's work can be related back to existing traditions not only in fiction and poetry but in folk-narrative, Shakespearean drama, the Bible, ballad, song and hymnody; viewed from the other direction, the verse in particular can be seen as a major landmark in the English poetic tradition (a fact of literary history which, if not yet everywhere confessed, is becoming increasingly recognized). And, like any significant writer, Hardy inherits a language common to all and transforms it into an unmistakably personal instrument.

Finally, there is the practical and commercial background against which a professional author conducts his career: the changing historical context of writers, readers, editors, illustrators, publishers and reviewers of books and magazines (not to mention newspapers, dramatic adaptations, agents, copyright laws, public and circulating libraries, and, before the end of Hardy's life, radio and film).

It is obvious that no collection of specialized studies could, within reasonable limits, render full justice to all that has been summarily indicated: the fields for speculation and investigation opened up by Hardy's writings stretch well beyond the horizons of a volume such as this one, which certainly lays no claims to inclusiveness. It does, however, present essays on some of the most interesting and significant aspects of Hardy's background, and it is hoped that they may stimulate even those for whom the texts are familiar to think about them afresh, and may enable both old and new readers of Hardy to turn from background to foreground with an enriched sense of the multifaceted interest of his work and the centrality of its place in the literary recording of the modern consciousness.

Hardy is one of the English novelists who have always exported remarkably well: from the early transatlantic serializations, through the numerous translations, to the present-day readership (beyond the skill of statisticians) inside and outside the English-speaking world, Wessex has come to occupy a place in the global imagination which is (except for Dickens' London) hard to match. So it is appropriate that this collection should include the work of scholars of three continents. And, since Hardy was a versatile as well as a prolific author, it is natural that the contributors should have sought to illuminate their various themes by ranging widely over his fiction, non-fiction, lyric verse and poetic drama. When various hands work independently on the same corpus of literature, a degree of fortuitous overlapping in the choice of quotations and examples is inevitable. I have allowed these minor repetitions to stand, believing that there may be some interest in the fact that different minds have found the same material striking or important.

Chronological Tables

Main events of Hardy's life and career	Events of literary and intellectual importance	Events of historical importance
1840 (2 June) Hardy born in Higher Bockhampton in the parish of Stinsford, Dorset	Browning, *Sordello* Darwin, *Voyage of H.M.S. 'Beagle'* Dickens, *The Old Curiosity Shop*	Marriage of Queen Victoria and Prince Albert Penny postage introduced Attempted coup by Louis Napoleon
1841	Carlyle, *Heroes and Hero-Worship* Newman, last 'Tract of the Times' (No. 90)	Peel becomes Prime Minister
1842	Dickens, *American Notes* Macaulay, *Lays of Ancient Rome* Tennyson, *Poems* Comte, *Cours de philosophie positive*	Chartist riots Child and female labour underground becomes illegal
1843	Carlyle, *Past and Present* Dickens, *A Christmas Carol* J. S. Mill, *System of Logic* Wordsworth becomes Poet Laureate	Rochdale Co-operative Society established Annexation of Natal
1844	Barnes, *Poems of Rural Life in the Dorset Dialect* Disraeli, *Coningsby* Chambers, *Vestiges of the Natural History of Creation*	Factory Act
1845	Disraeli, *Sybil* Engels, *The Condition of the Working Class in England in 1844*	

1846		Newman joins Church of Rome	
		George Eliot, translation of Strauss's *Life of Jesus*	Repeal of Corn Laws
			Irish potato famine
		Grote, *History of Greece* begins publication	Lord John Russell becomes Prime Minister
		Lear, *Book of Nonsense*	
1847		C. Brontë, *Jane Eyre*	Dorchester–London
		E. Brontë, *Wuthering Heights*	railway opens
		Tennyson, *The Princess*	Ten-hour Factory Act
1848	Attends school at Lower Bockhampton	Gaskell, *Mary Barton*	Chartist petition
		Mill, *Principles of Political Economy*	Public Health Act
		Thackeray, *Vanity Fair*	Revolutions in Europe
		Pre-Raphaelite Brotherhood formed	
		Marx and Engels, *Communist Manifesto*	
		Beginnings of Christian Socialism	
		Natural sciences tripos established at Cambridge	
1849	Moves to school in Dorchester	Arnold, *Strayed Reveller*	
		C. Brontë, *Shirley*	
		Macaulay, *History of England* begins publication	
		Ruskin, *Seven Lamps of Architecture*	
1850		Dickens, *David Copperfield*	Public Libraries Act
		Hawthorne, *The Scarlet Letter*	
		Kingsley, *Alton Locke*	
		Tennyson, *In Memoriam*	
		Wordsworth, *Prelude*	
		Tennyson becomes Poet Laureate	
		Death of Balzac	
1851		Kingsley, *Yeast*	Louis Napoleon's *coup d'état*
		Melville, *Moby Dick*	Australian gold rush
		Meredith, *Poems*	
		Ruskin, *Stones of Venice*, Vol. 1	

		Death of Turner	
		Great Exhibition	
1852		Arnold, *Empedocles on Etna* Stowe, *Uncle Tom's Cabin* Thackeray, *Henry Esmond* Death of Wellington	Derby becomes Prime Minister (to Dec.); succeeded by Aberdeen
1853		Dickens, *Bleak House* Gaskell, *Cranford*, *Ruth* Wagner, *Ring*	
1854		Comte, *Système de politique positive* G. Eliot, translation of Feuerbach's *Essence of Christianity*	Working Men's College founded Crimean War begins
1855	Begins to teach at Stinsford Church Sunday School	Browning, *Men and Women* Gaskell, *North and South* Lewes, *Life of Goethe* Trollope, *The Warden* Whitman, *Leaves of Grass* *Saturday Review* founded	Palmerston becomes Prime Minister Fall of Sebastopol
1856	Enters the Dorchester office of John Hicks as architectural pupil. Friendship with Horace Moule and William Barnes begins	Froude, *History of England* begins publication Flaubert, *Madame Bovary* Freud born	Paris Peace Congress
1857		Buckle, *History of Civilization in England* begins publication Dickens, *Little Dorrit* Baudelaire, *Les fleurs du mal*	Indian Mutiny
1858		Carlyle, *Frederick the Great* begins publication	Derby becomes Prime Minister Emancipation of serfs begins in Russia
1859		Darwin, *Origin of Species* FitzGerald, *Rubaiyat of Omar Khayyam* G. Eliot, *Adam Bede*	Palmerston becomes Prime Minister War of Italian Liberation

	Lewes, *Physiology of Common Life* Meredith, *The Ordeal of Richard Feverel* J. S. Mill, *On Liberty*	
1860 (or earlier) Writes his first poem, 'Domicilium'	Collins, *The Woman in White* G. Eliot, *The Mill on the Floss* *Essays and Reviews* Bradlaugh starts the *National Reformer* Wilberforce-Huxley debate at British Association meeting in Oxford *Cornhill* founded Death of Schopenhauer	Garibaldi lands in Sicily
1861	Dickens, *Great Expectations* G. Eliot, *Silas Marner* Meredith, *Evan Harrington* Palgrave, *Golden Treasury* Müller, *Science of Language*	Death of Prince Albert American Civil War begins Victor Emmanuel becomes King of Italy
1862 Goes to London; works for Arthur Blomfield, architect and church-restorer	Clough, *Poems* G. Eliot, *Romola* Meredith, *Modern Love* Ruskin, *Unto this Last* Turgenev, *Fathers and Sons*	Bismarck becomes Prime Minister of Prussia
1863 Awarded essay prize by Royal Institute of British Architects	Huxley, *Man's Place in Nature* Lyell, *Antiquity of Man* J. S. Mill, *Utilitarianism* Renan, *La vie de Jésus* Death of Thackeray	
1864	Browning, *Dramatis Personae* Newman, *Apologia pro vita sua* Spencer, *Principles of Biology* begins publication Scott, Albert Memorial	
1865 'How I Built Myself a House' published in *Chambers' Journal*; attends French classes at King's College	Arnold, *Essays in Criticism*, 1st series Carroll, *Alice in Wonderland* Dickens, *Our Mutual Friend*	Death of Palmerston; Russell becomes Prime Minister Lincoln assassinated

		Ruskin, *Sesame and Lilies* Swinburne, *Atalanta in Calydon* Tolstoy, *War and Peace* Wagner, *Tristan and Isolde* Salvation Army founded	
1866		G. Eliot, *Felix Holt* Gaskell, *Wives and Daughters* Owen, *On the Anatomy of Vertebrates* Swinburne, *Poems and Ballads*, 1st series Dostoievsky, *Crime and Punishment*	Derby becomes Prime Minister
1867	Returns to Dorset and resumes work for Hicks; begins work on first novel, *The Poor Man and the Lady*	Bagehot, *English Constitution* Ibsen, *Peer Gynt* Marx, *Das Kapital*, Part 1 Death of Baudelaire	Second Reform Bill Factory Inspection Act Garibaldi marches on Rome Paris Exhibition
1868	Novel rejected by Macmillan, submitted to Chapman & Hall	Browning, *The Ring and the Book* Collins, *The Moonstone* Morris, *Earthly Paradise*, Vol. 1	Disraeli becomes Prime Minister; (Dec.) is succeeded by Gladstone
1869	Hardy meets Meredith; begins *Desperate Remedies*	Arnold, *Culture and Anarchy* Mill, *On the Subjection of Women* Girton College founded	Irish Church disestablished
1870	Visits Cornwall and meets Emma Lavinia Gifford. William Tinsley agrees to publish *Desperate Remedies* at Hardy's expense	Newman, *Grammar of Assent* D. G. Rossetti, *Poems* Spencer, *Principles of Psychology* Death of Dickens	Education Act Irish Land Bill Franco–Prussian War begins
1871	*Desperate Remedies* appears. Hardy writes *Under the Greenwood Tree* and begins *A Pair of Blue Eyes*	Darwin, *Descent of Man* G. Eliot, *Middlemarch* Swinburne, *Songs before Sunrise* Zola, *Les Rougon-Macquart* begins publication First Impressionist Exhibition in Paris	Trade Unions legalized Religious tests abolished at Oxford, Cambridge, Durham

1872	*Under the Greenwood Tree* published; serialization of *A Pair of Blue Eyes* begins	Butler, *Erewhon* Nietzsche, *Die Geburt der Tragödie*	
1873	Horace Moule's suicide. Hardy begins *Far from the Madding Crowd; A Pair of Blue Eyes* published	Arnold, *Literature and Dogma* Mill, *Autobiography* Pater, *Studies in the Renaissance*	Death of Napoleon III Ashanti War
1874	*Far from the Madding Crowd* published. Hardy marries E. L. Gifford; wedding trip to France	Stubbs, *Constitutional History* Thomson, *City of Dreadful Night*	Disraeli becomes Prime Minister Factory Act Public Worship Act
1875		Gilbert & Sullivan, *Trial by Jury* (first of the Savoy Operas)	Public Health Act Artisans' Dwellings Act Britain buys control of Suez Canal
1876	*The Hand of Ethelberta* published. The Hardys visit Holland and Germany, move to a house at Sturminster Newton, Dorset	G. Eliot, *Daniel Deronda* James, *Roderick Hudson* Spencer, *Principles of Sociology*, Vol. 1 First Bayreuth Festival	
1877		Ibsen, *Pillars of Society* Tolstoy, *Anna Karenina* Zola, *L'Assommoir*	Victoria becomes Empress of India Russo–Turkish War Annexation of Transvaal
1878	*The Return of the Native* published. Hardy moves to London; elected to Savile Club	Whistler–Ruskin quarrel	Congress of Berlin
1879	Pursues research for *The Trumpet-Major* in British Museum and elsewhere	Browning. *Dramatic Idylls* Meredith, *The Egoist* Ibsen, *A Doll's House*	Zulu War
1880	*The Trumpet-Major* published. Hardy meets Tennyson. Serious illness hampers composition of *A Laodicean*	Gissing, *Workers in the Dawn* Dostoievsky, *The Brothers Karamazov* Death of George Eliot, Flaubert	Gladstone becomes Prime Minister Bradlaugh becomes M.P.

1881	*A Laodicean* published	James, *Portrait of a Lady* Ibsen, *Ghosts* Death of Carlyle	Death of Disraeli Democratic Federation founded
1882	*Two on a Tower* published	Death of Trollope	Married Women's Property Act Municipal Corporations Act Phoenix Park murders
1883	'The Dorsetshire Labourer' (*Longman's Magazine*); moves to Dorchester; building of Max Gate begins	Trollope, *Autobiography* Nietzsche, *Also sprach Zarathustra* Death of Marx, Wagner	
1884	Begins to write *The Mayor of Casterbridge*	Fabian Society founded	Third Reform Bill
1885	Moves into Max Gate. Begins *The Woodlanders*	Pater, *Marius the Epicurean* Maupassant, *Bel Ami* Zola, *Germinal* Death of Hugo	Salisbury becomes Prime Minister Criminal Law Amend- ment Act Irish Land Bill Gordon killed at Khartoum
1886	*The Mayor of Casterbridge* published	Gissing, *Demos* James, *The Bostonians* Kipling, *Departmental Ditties* Ibsen, *Rosmersholm* Nietzsche, *Jenseits von Gut und Böse*	Gladstone's brief ministry defeated on Irish Home Rule Bill Dilke case Contagious Diseases Acts repealed
1887	*The Woodlanders* published. Visits Italy	Mark Rutherford, *Revolution in Tanner's Lane*	Victoria's Golden Jubilee Independent Labour Party formed 'Bloody Sunday'
1888	*Wessex Tales* published. Begins *Tess of the d'Urbervilles*	Kipling, *Plain Tales from the Hills* Moore, *Confessions of a Young Man* Death of Arnold	Local Government Act

1889	Opening portion of *Tess* rejected by various publishers	Booth, *Life and Labour of the People in London* Shaw, *Fabian Essays in Socialism* Yeats, *The Wanderings of Oisin* *A Doll's House* performed in London Death of Browning, Hopkins	London dock strike
1890	*Tess* completed	Frazer, *The Golden Bough* W. James, *Principles of Psychology* Morris, *News from Nowhere* Ibsen, *Hedda Gabler*	Fall of Bismarck Parnell case
1891	*A Group of Noble Dames* and *Tess of the d'Urbervilles* published	Gissing, *New Grub Street* Kipling, *The Light that Failed* Shaw, *Quintessence of Ibsenism* Wilde, *Intentions*	
1892	Hardy's father dies. First version of *The Well-Beloved* serialized	Kipling, *Barrack-Room Ballads* Zola translated into English Death of Tennyson	Gladstone becomes Prime Minister
1893	Visits Dublin and Oxford; meets Florence Henniker	Pater, *Plato and Platonism* Wilde, *Salome* Ibsen's *The Master Builder* performed in London	
1894	*Life's Little Ironies* published	Moore, *Esther Waters* *The Yellow Book* Webb, *History of Trade Unionism* Death of Stevenson	Rosebery becomes Prime Minister Dreyfus Trial Armenian massacres
1895	Prepares Uniform Edition of novels; *Jude the Obscure* published	Allen, *The Woman who Did* Conrad, *Almayer's Folly* Wells, *The Time Machine* Yeats, *Poems*	Salisbury becomes Prime Minister Jameson Raid National Trust founded
1896		Housman, *A Shropshire Lad* Alfred Austin becomes Poet Laureate *Daily Mail* started Death of Verlaine	

1897	*The Well-Beloved* published	Conrad, *The Nigger of the 'Narcissus'* Ellis, *Studies in the Psychology of Sex* begins publication James, *What Maisie Knew*	Workmen's Compensation Act
1898	*Wessex Poems* published	Shaw, *Plays Pleasant and Unpleasant* Death of Mallarmé	Death of Gladstone
1899		James, *The Awkward Age* Kipling, *Stalky & Co.* Ruskin College, Oxford, opened	South African War begins
1900		Conrad, *Lord Jim* Shaw, *Three Plays for Puritans* Wells, *Love and Mr. Lewisham* *Daily Express* started *Oxford Book of English Verse* English translations of Tolstoy Death of Ruskin, Wilde, Nietzsche	
1901	*Poems of the Past and the Present* published	Kipling, *Kim* Yeats, *Poems* Mann, *Buddenbrooks*	Death of Victoria Accession of Edward VII Taff Vale case
1902		Bennett, *The Grand Babylon Hotel* James, *The Wings of the Dove* W. James, *Varieties of Religious Experience* Gide, *L'Immoraliste* Death of Zola	Balfour becomes Prime Minister Education Act
1903		Butler, *The Way of All Flesh* James, *The Ambassadors* Moore, *Principia Ethica* Russell, *Principles of Mathematics* Shaw, *Man and Superman*	Women's Social and Political Union formed
1904	*The Dynasts, Part 1* published. Hardy's mother dies	Conrad, *Nostromo* Abbey Theatre founded	Anglo-French Entente

		Workers' Educational Association founded	
1905	Receives Hon. Ll.D., Aberdeen	Forster, *Where Angels Fear to Tread* James, *The Golden Bowl* Synge, *Riders to the Sea* Wells, *Kipps*	Campbell-Bannerman becomes Prime Minister
1906	*The Dynasts, Part 2* published	Galsworthy, *The Man of Property* Webb, *English Local Government*, Vol. 1	Trade Disputes Act
1907		Death of Ibsen Conrad, *The Secret Agent* Gosse, *Father and Son* Joyce, *Chamber Music*	
1908	*The Dynasts, Part 3* published	Bennett, *The Old Wives' Tale* Lodge, *Man and the Universe* Wells, *The War in the Air*	Asquith becomes Prime Minister
1909	*Time's Laughingstocks* published. Becomes governor of Dorchester Grammar School	Masterman, *The Condition of England* Pound, *Personae* Wells, *Ann Veronica* Death of Meredith, Swinburne	Old Age Pensions begin
1910	Awarded O.M.	Forster, *Howards End* Death of Tolstoy	Death of Edward VII Accession of George V
1911		Brooke, *Poems* Conrad, *Under Western Eyes* Lawrence, *The White Peacock* Pound, *Canzoni*	National Insurance Act Parliament Act Shops' Act Copyright Act Agadir Crisis
1912	(27 Nov.) Death of Emma Lavinia Hardy	Shaw, *Pygmalion* *Georgian Poetry, 1911–12* English translations of Dostoievsky begin to appear	
1913	*A Changed Man* published. Hon. Litt.D. Cambridge; Hon.	Conrad, *Chance* Lawrence, *Sons and Lovers*	

	Fellow, Magdalene College, Cambridge	Mann, *Der Tod in Venedig* Proust, *À la recherche du temps perdu* (publication begins) Bridges becomes Poet Laureate	
1914	Marries Florence Emily Dugdale. *Satires of Circumstance* published	Bradley, *Truth and Reality* Joyce, *Dubliners*	(4 Aug.) Great War begins Asquith becomes Prime Minister
1915	Death of Hardy's sister Mary	Ford, *The Good Soldier* Lawrence, *The Rainbow* Woolf, *The Voyage Out*	
1916		Joyce, *Portrait of the Artist as a Young Man* First *Wheels* anthology Jung, *Psychology of the Unconscious* Death of Henry James	Easter Rebellion in Ireland Lloyd George becomes Prime Minister
1917	*Moments of Vision* published	Eliot, *Prufrock and other Observations* E. Thomas, *Poems* Yeats, *The Wild Swans at Coole*	Russian Revolution
1918		Hopkins, *Poems* Lawrence, *New Poems* Strachey, *Eminent Victorians* Stopes, *Married Love* Death of Wilfred Owen	(11 Nov.) Great War ends
1919	*Collected Poems* published	Sassoon, *War Poems* Keynes, *Economic Consequences of the Peace*	Rail Strike
1920	Hon. D. Litt., Oxford	Eliot, *The Sacred Wood* Lawrence, *Women in Love* Owen, *Poems* Wells, *Outline of History* Einstein, *Relativity* Fry, *Vision and Design*	
1921		Huxley, *Crome Yellow* Strachey, *Queen Victoria*	

1922	*Late Lyrics and Earlier* published. Hon. Fellow, Queen's College, Oxford	Eliot, *The Waste Land* Joyce, *Ulysses* Woolf, *Jacob's Room* Yeats, *Later Poems* English translation of Proust begins to appear B.B.C. incorporated; radio broadcasting begins Death of Proust	Bonar Law becomes Prime Minister
1923	*The Famous Tragedy of The Queen of Cornwall* published. Prince of Wales visits Max Gate	Bennett, *Riceyman Steps* Huxley, *Antic Hay* Hitler, *Mein Kampf*	Baldwin becomes Prime Minister
1924		Forster, *A Passage to India* Hemingway, *In Our Time* Richards, *Principles of Literary Criticism* Death of Conrad, Kafka	MacDonald becomes Prime Minister (to Nov.); succeeded by Baldwin
1925	*Human Shows* published	Pound, *A Draft of XVI Cantos* Woolf, *Mrs Dalloway* Whitehead, *Science and the Modern World*	
1926		Faulkner, *Soldiers' Pay* T. E. Lawrence, *The Seven Pillars of Wisdom* Tawney, *Religion and the Rise of Capitalism*	General Strike
1927		Forster, *Aspects of the Novel* Fry, *Cézanne* Woolf, *To the Lighthouse*	Prayer Book revision controversy Trades Disputes Act
1928	(11 Jan.) dies. *Winter Words* and *The Early Life of Thomas Hardy* published (second vol. follows in 1930)	Huxley, *Point Counter Point* Joyce, *Anna Livia Plurabelle* Lawrence, *Lady Chatterley's Lover, Collected Poems* Waugh, *Decline and Fall* Woolf, *Orlando* Yeats, *The Tower* First talking pictures	

1: Hardy and Social Class

MERRYN AND RAYMOND WILLIAMS

I

THE LANGUAGE OF CLASS is the language of capitalist society, and contains at once its clarities, its complexities, its confusions and its contradictions. Instituted as a specific terminology in the late eighteenth century and intensively developed in the nineteenth century (R. Williams, 1976), it is readily associated, historically, with the development of industrial society; agricultural or rural society is often seen as marginal to or even exempted from it. Yet the class system, defined by differential relations to the means of production, is at least as clear in agriculture as in industry, and in fact is historically earlier. By the eighteenth century, nearly half of the cultivated land was owned by some five thousand families. Nearly a quarter of the cultivated land was owned by four hundred families, in a population of between seven and eight million people. In 1873, when Hardy was writing his first novels, four-fifths of the land of the United Kingdom was owned by less than 7000 persons.[1] The characteristic structure of social and economic relationships in agriculture, steadily extending its dominance from the late sixteenth to the early twentieth centuries, was a class of landowners, a class of tenant farmers and a class of landless labourers. These are the clarities.

The first confusion is inherent in the language of class. This replaced the earlier language of estate, order and rank. Essentially the change was due to the relatively increased mobility and the new sources of wealth of capitalist society. Class is an indicator of social position but primarily through the indices of adult economic activity. Estate, rank and order, always more rigid categories, had indicated social position through birth and inheritance. Necessarily, of course, there is a substantial overlap between the earlier and the later categories. What was ordinarily inherited was not only a rank but property. Acquisition of property or wealth often brought formal rank in its train. On the other side of the fence, to lose wealth or property was to lose the significance of rank. The conseqent confusion of categories is very marked in English society from at latest 1550; in the nineteenth and twentieth centuries it is still both a voluntary and an involuntary confusion. Hardy, as it happens, illustrates part of this process very clearly, in direct relation to the confusion itself. In *Tess*, the d'Urbervilles are a declined, indeed extinguished, family of 'rank'. Their local descendants have become the Durbeyfields. The family of Alec d'Urberville has made its money in trade and bought its way into landed property and the resumed title. The action of *Tess* makes it clear that the consequent confusion between the inheritance of categories (the 'rank', the 'family name') and both the actual physical inheritance and the decisive contemporary social relationships is profoundly damaging. For the real social classes are in flesh and blood; the inherited rank name is, either way, an ideology. More generally, however, there was a rough fit between the language of rank and the language of class: a rough fit because in general it was both assured and contrived. The decisive economic relationships carried the presence or absence of rank through the inheritance of property or of propertylessness, and where they did not they were, by a characteristic English process, eventually brought into broad alignment. This confusion persists.

Yet beyond it there is a complexity, based in the actual history. The rural structure of landlord, tenant and labourer – the matrix of capitalist agriculture – was indeed dominant but it was not exclusive. There were two substantial complications. First, there was the persistence of a class of smallholders and 'family farmers': in 1873 numerically as many as the tenant farmers, though characteristically on the smaller units, on the poorer land, or on both. The pressures of capitalist agriculture – the increasingly organized market economy, the rising level of capital investment in improved agricultural methods, the rising level of viability in size of units with the increase in mechanization – were intensely felt by this class and, as through the whole eighteenth and early nineteenth centuries, were continually diminishing its relative importance. Secondly, from an older kind of village economy and in part distinct from, in part overlapping with, the smallholders and family farmers, there was what Hardy called, in direct comparison with the agricultural labourers,

an interesting and better-informed class . . . including the
carpenter, the smith, the shoemaker, the huckster, together with
nondescript workers other than farm labourers; a set of people who
owed a certain stability of aim and conduct to the fact of their being
life-holders . . . copyholders, or occasionally small freeholders.
(Ch. 51)

It is significant that, describing this class in *Tess*, Hardy says that the
village had 'formerly' contained it. It would not be the case that by the
late nineteenth century all these individuals and trades had disappeared,
but they were under very great pressure, from two directions: first,
internally, in the dominance of orthodox capitalist agriculture
(lifeholders, entitled to their cottages for the duration of three lives,
were now increasingly dispossessed when the last life ended; Hardy
describes such cases in *The Woodlanders* and *Tess*); second, externally, in
the development of a manufacturing urban economy, which steadily cut
out the more localized craftsmen. It is in these senses that capitalist social
relations, while not exclusive, were dominant: that they exerted pressure
on all who did not belong to or fit in with them, dispossessing,
undercutting or effectively pauperizing a majority of this residual class.
This in its turn interacted with the altered relative economic position of
agriculture, in the now industrialized and free-trading (food importing)
national economy, to produce a relative 'rural depopulation'. There was
prolonged and substantial emigration to the cities and industrial towns,
and to the dominions, the colonies and the New World. Within this vast
process, in which the residual complexity of the English rural social
structure was being sharply reduced, Hardy especially regretted the
disappearance of the relatively independent and intermediate class. As he
put it, again in *Tess*:

Cottagers who were not directly employed on the land were
looked upon with disfavour, and the banishment of some starved
the trade of others, who were thus obliged to follow. These
families, who had formed the backbone of the village life in the
past, who were the depositaries of the village traditions, had to seek
refuge in the large centres; the process, humorously designated by
statisticians as 'the tendency of the rural population towards the

large towns', being really the tendency of water to flow uphill when forced by machinery. (Ch. 51)

Here a social and economic change is seen also as a cultural change, but not only (although crucially) as the expulsion of the carriers of traditional village culture. What was happening was also a political change, for it was from this relatively independent and intermediate class that, as it happened, most of the early trade-union leaders and organizers had come. Describing and analysing their displacement, Hardy was looking forward as well as back. 'Every one of these banished people', he wrote, 'imbibes a sworn enmity to the existing order of things.'[2]

II

Thomas Hardy was born into this relatively independent and intermediate class. His lineal and extended family shows all the confusions and precarious complexities of just this group. Thus his father's mother was a charity child and his mother had been very poor; his father, by energy as a builder and mason, came to employ as many as fourteen men. The mixed and precarious character of these 'intermediate' people can be seen in the number of his relatives who were workingmen and labourers; he is said, characteristically, to have been ashamed of them. At the same time, in the new mobilities of education and the professions, his cousin Tryphena went to training college and became a headmistress at twenty-one, while Hardy himself became an architect. This is, decisively, a world not of rank but of class, but because it is a world of class, its complexities, its new definitions of relations between destiny, energy and accident, its profound interactions of personal quality and social position, its often crucially determining intermixture of the personality and the sociality of sexual and marriage relationships, created for Hardy a rich, dense, moving world in which, in quite fundamental ways, human lives were always at stake.

The distinguishing quality of Hardy's treatment of class in his fiction follows, as we shall see, from this precise position: at once complex and self-conscious, precarious and mobile. It is because class is at issue, and at a doubtful issue, within the difficult consciousness of this intermediate group, that he is both intensely aware of it and that he handles it through a particular fusion of what are elsewhere often seen as 'external' and 'internal' characteristics. Yet, before we go on to establish this, it will be useful to look at this class 'intermediacy', and at the variations within it, in some examples from his novels.

The residual elements of this intermediate class, from an older rural order, are especially evident in *The Woodlanders*, where their fortunes are directly affected. Both Giles and Marty belong to the semi-independent class of copyholders, and are eventually dispossessed by Mrs Charmond. Marty and her father work at a range of odd jobs with trees and wood, dealing with the timber merchant Melbury. Giles, originally Melbury's partner, travels with his press to make cider, undertakes contracts to plant trees for timber, and within these enterprises employs a few workmen. After dispossession by the landowning Mrs Charmond, they lose crucial elements of their independence. They move, in effect, into the specific exposure of the dependent labourers. That the knowledge and more generally the wisdom of this productive woodland life are centred, by Hardy, in the persons of Marty and Giles, and that they are shown in the process of dispossession and downward pressure, is centrally significant.

The contrast of *The Woodlanders* with his first rural novel, *Under the Greenwood Tree*, is significant because the differences of mood and convention correspond to the different presentations and estimates of the intermediate class. The village tradition of church music, in *Under the Greenwood Tree*, is in the hands of this group: cobbler, mason, night-school teacher and so on. Dick is the son of a tranter (carrier). At this stage, in spite of the complexities of class structure in the village – shown clearly and characteristically in Fancy's possible marriages: to the vicar, to the farmer Shiner, or to Dick – the intermediate group is still independent and effective.

The implications of mobility begin to be seen, in more serious ways, in *Far from the Madding Crowd*. Quite apart from the semi-independent cottagers and the craftsmen and tradesmen there is an always ambiguous group at the edge of capitalist farming, and Gabriel Oak is an almost perfect example. The skilled shepherd, 'tending the flocks of large proprietors', can become a bailiff and then a small tenant-farmer. But, at the edge of capital viability and struck by a single disaster, he has to offer himself for any kind of labouring at the hiring-fair. Eventually becoming a shepherd again he moves through the same sequence, to bailiff and then farmer.

The residual is again marked in *The Return of the Native*. It is inherent in the processes of capitalist farming that the marginal occupations tend to be pushed back into the marginal land. Egdon Heath with its turf- and furze-cutting is the basis of this kind of marginal subsistence: the semi-independent life of the old commons, the marginal trades like Olly Dowden's besom-making. There is also the marginal case of Diggory Venn, son of a dairyman, now the garish reddleman, eventually moving back to the fertile land as a dairy farmer.

In *The Mayor of Casterbridge* the stress is again on mobility and its problems, but now in the county town and the corn trade rather than directly on the land and in the villages. Henchard begins as a skilled labourer, a hay-trusser, and moves up through petty dealing to become a substantial merchant. Farfrae is on his way to emigrate, but in his fateful stop in Casterbridge repeats the rise to prosperity as a dealer. Henchard, ruined, goes back to day labour as a hay-trusser, though his friends offer to set him up in a small seed business. This range of possibilities, within dealing rather than primary property, is a crucial factor in the intermediate group as a whole.

Tess, in *Tess of the d'Urbervilles*, has often been described as a 'peasant'. This is the class language of another class. It is interesting that after it had lost any precise meaning in English rural society, following the rise of capitalist agriculture, it was reintroduced to express a more totalizing view: one which suppressed the crucial actual relations and variations. The reintroduction was essentially political, in the reaction which followed the French Revolution. A crucial text is Cobbett, in 1830:

> Pray, my readers, attend to these things, and then (if you be Catholics) *cross yourselves* when you hear Peel and Knatchbull say, that the fires *do not proceed from the 'peasantry'*, a *new* name given to the *country labourers* by the insolent boroughmongering and loanmongering tribes. But if it be not the 'peasantry', who is it?

Cobbett's fine sense of the actualities of rural society is matched, half a century later, by Hardy's. The blocking stereotypes of an urban ruling-class ideology dissolve in his patient application of detail. Tess, quite apart from the d'Urberville-Durbeyfield complication, is the daughter of a haggler or small itinerant trader. The working capital of this extreme marginal occupation is a horse. When it is killed they have nowhere to go but the labour market; they have also lost the life tenure of their cottage on John Durbeyfield's death. Tess takes employment to look after poultry, within a double social irony: that it is on the 'little fancy farm' kept as a hobby by the merchant family (the new d'Urbervilles) who have bought their way into the 'landed gentry'; and that the poultry are kept in an old cottage formerly occupied by 'certain dusty copyholders who now lay east and west in the churchyard' and now 'indifferently turned into a fowl-house by Mrs Stoke d'Urberville as soon as the property fell into hand according to law'. Thus Tess, as a girl, begins at the nadir of this struggling intermediate class, and is forced through the relatively light wage-labour of poultry and dairy work to the heavy work of the fields. But then also, intricately enmeshed in the same process, she is in the special position of a woman labourer, that as a woman as well as a worker she is exposed to the market, with its range of possibilities in seduction, marriage, desertion, kept mistress. The limits and pressures of a declining intermediate group are then an intrinsic part of her history.

Jude, in *Jude the Obscure*, is another example of the history of this intermediate group. His great-aunt keeps a baker's shop; the intermediate again. He can get a trade apprenticeship and become a skilled mason. But, both as a result of his desire to get a university education (on a scale of mobility beyond the terms of the intermediate class) and because, in any case, of the changing position of craftsmen within the rural economy, he moves, like many thousands in the same general situation, into the urban working class: the actual future of the majority of the semi-independent craftsmen.

What is being charted then, in an exceptional richness and variation of material, is what Hardy saw as crucial: the flattening and in a sense (though this can never be complete) the extinction of the 'intermediate' people who had been not only a 'sector of the economy' but the bearers of a culture. This at once places and limits Hardy in the radical tradition which runs back to Paine and Cobbett but which at the end of the century had to encounter the more systematic rigidities of a fully developed capitalist system. The complexities of this encounter, in the transition from radicalism to socialism, begin to sound in his work, but his centre of gravity is in the earlier rather than the later process. This can be seen clearly in his essay on 'The Dorsetshire Labourer', from which we may complete the quotation given earlier:

> Every one of these banished people imbibes a sworn enmity to the existing order of things, and not a few of them, far from being merely honest Radicals, degenerate into Anarchists, waiters on chance, to whom danger to the State ... is a welcomed opportunity. ... But the question of the Dorset cottager here merges in that of all the houseless and landless poor, and the vast topic of the Rights of Man, to consider which is beyond the scope of a purely descriptive article.[2]

It is not only the scope of the article, it is the scope of the experienced social history, now at a point of critical transition, which checks Hardy. The explicit class struggles, like the more integral class formations, of modern industrial capitalist society are beyond and ahead of his world, though he could sense their shadows.

However, at the point of critical transition, and within the perspective of the problems of an intermediate class, he picked up and remarkably embodied one of the characteristic themes of the new social situation: that of mobility through education. This had been present, in minor ways, within an older structure, in the figures of Fancy Day, Grace Melbury and Swithin (in *Two on a Tower*). There it interlocks with the more general problems of the older intermediate mobility. It is again briefly present in *Tess*:

> Mrs Durbeyfield habitually spoke the dialect; her daughter, who had passed the Sixth Standard in the National School under a London-trained mistress, spoke two languages: the dialect at home, more or less; ordinary English abroad and to persons of quality. (Ch. 3)

But it is of course in *Jude the Obscure* that it becomes central.

Mobility through education is often described as if it were a simple functional passage from one class (type of work) to another. In Hardy's social perspective it could never be reduced to this, even if the mobility had been easier than it commonly was. Precisely within the terms of his 'intermediate' perspective, he asked questions about the relations between social position, social experience and social and personal qualities which necessarily supersede merely functional answers. This is already evident in a significant exchange between Clym and his mother in *The Return of the Native*:

'I am astonished, Clym. How can you want to do better than you've been doing?'

'But I hate that business of mine . . . I want to do some worthy things before I die'.

'After all the trouble that has been taken to give you a start, and when there is nothing to do but keep straight on towards affluence, you say you . . . it disturbs me, Clym, to find you have come home with such thoughts . . . I hadn't the least idea you meant to go backward in the world by your own free choice. . . .'

'I cannot help it,' said Clym, in a troubled tone.

'Why can't you do . . . as well as others?'

'I don't know, except that there are many things other people care for which I don't.'

'And yet you might have been a wealthy man if you had only persevered . . . I suppose you will be like your father. Like him, you are getting weary of doing well.'

'Mother, what is doing well?' (III, 2)

This is, exactly, the radical moral question of a pre-systematic class society, to which, for all its pressures, there appear to be alternatives. Clym's failure, in fact, is that in practice these alternatives are not there: 'In striving at high thinking he still cleaved to plain living . . . mentally, he was in a provincial future . . . a man should be only partially before his time; to be completely to the vanward in aspirations is fatal to fame' (III, 2). And here the structure of feeling of an intermediate class is precisely delineated: the sense of radical independence of personality, of radical moral questioning, in the very phrases of the intermediate tradition running back in this case to Wordsworth; at the same time, in the authorial commentary, the guarded and sceptical, 'realistic' caution, mediated by the irony – at once the belief and the scepticism – of the considerations of success ('fatal to fame').

But at least in the intermediate structure there was an attempt to negotiate the difficult relations between moral purpose, learning and teaching, on the one hand, and social position, financial betterment, on the other. When he came to observe the orthodox educated world, Hardy saw, by contrast, a dull and false congruity, in which learning and privilege were taken to be naturally interchangeable. As he puts it of Angel's brothers in *Tess*:

. . . he noticed their growing mental limitations. Felix seemed to him all Church; Cuthbert all college . . . Each brother candidly recognized that there were a few unimportant scores of millions of outsiders in civilized society, persons who were neither University men nor Churchmen; but they were to be tolerated rather than reckoned with and respected. (Ch. 25)

Here, at the point of arrival of the most ideal educational mobility, was a deep cancellation of the life of the mind by the specific limitations and perspectives of class.

This recognition is one necessary way of seeing the tragedy of Jude. The straightforward exclusion from established and orthodox learning is already a fact of social class. The contemptuous rejection of Jude is on class grounds alone, with no pretence of academic or educational judgement. This fact has to be set alongside the limited mobility made available at that stage of class relations: entry to the teacher training colleges, to staff the new elementary schools. What is permitted and indeed necessary at that level is flanked by a sustained impermeability of the higher class institutions. But the interaction of class and education functions also in deeper ways, which take it beyond the more negotiable, though still serious and urgent, problems of access and mobility. The forms of this class education, and especially the attachments to dead languages and to orthodox religion (Biblioll College), betray the ambitious scholar from outside the class: not only in denying him access but in directing his mind towards limited class forms which, because of the social dominance, pass for general learning. It is tragic that Jude is excluded. It is also tragic that his mind and energy are alienated by forms which belong not to his working world but to this other privileged world, in which the connection between the forms of ancient learning, the externals of a dogmatic religion, and the insistent and governing social superiority, is inherent. This is why the tragedy of Jude can never be reduced to a mere fact of period: a tragedy which would not now be necessary, which has been redeemed by subsequent legislation. As we read Hardy's prolonged meditations on the real relations between learning and humanity, between educated and customary ways of feeling and thinking, and between the harsh necessities of material production and the painful complications of every effort towards a higher culture,we find ourselves moved beyond the formulas of the more familiar arguments and returned always to the question which is either left unanswered or at best ironically or precariously answered: 'what is doing well?'. To most of the members of this intermediate group, and to the writer who speaks from within their specific structure of feeling, both the question and the difficulty of the answers are all too well known.

III

One decisive element must be added to this account: Hardy's deeply original and still exceptional emphasis on work. This is not, except superficially, the consequence of the developing idea of the dignity of labour. Hardy looked at actual work too closely to rest on that abstract formula. In *The Woodlanders*, *Tess* and *Jude* especially, his descriptions of the detailed material processes of labour have an intensity of feeling which in most fiction is reserved for interpersonal relationships or for landscape and scene. It is not, obviously, that Hardy neglects either of these; they are as important in his work as anywhere in fiction. But he provides a further dimension, in which being is expressed in labour, but then is also, in all the variations of social and physical circumstances, exalted or degraded, fulfilled or frustrated, sustained or broken up. This integral connection, as it becomes in the later novels, between the quality and conditions of labour and the quality and conditions of primary and effective being, is very remarkable. Moreover it begins to offer an emphasis which can transform social values. It is very striking that people who do useful work are always, in Hardy, positive characters; the most evident examples are Marty, Giles, Tess and Jude. At the other extreme, people who do no work, like Eustacia or Lucetta or Mrs Charmond, are characteristically negative and disruptive. Nor is this merely an ethic of 'productive values'. The capacity to work and the habit of working are directly connected with the ability to love, to care and to sustain. It is not that the exercise of any of these virtues brings happiness, as in the older formulas. For as unquestioned primary processes, the only true sources of value, they are cut across in two ways: by the sheer hardness and harshness of the material world with which this work is always grappling – a kind of pain which is seen as intrinsic; but also by the arbitrariness, the coldness, the irresponsible power of a social class system which is of course not intrinsic, but which eats into all the processes of life and labour. Both emphases are there: the often intractable world; the historically specific class system. Hardy did not often extricate them, one from the other. What was experienced in a single dimension was responded to in a single dimension. This also, it can be said, is the limit of consciousness of an intermediate class. Yet the emphatic linking of labour and value, with the corresponding detachment of value from property, is a remarkable exploration of a new kind of consciousness, beyond a class system. That he held to this exploration while at the same time recording, ironically or bitterly, its practical difficulties, its repeated frustrations, its terrible actual losses in the people who, consciously or unconsciously, were attempting to live in these new ways, is at once the paradox and the triumph of his work.

NOTES

(The above essay develops themes treated in the following earlier work by its authors: Merryn Williams, *Thomas Hardy and Rural England*, 1972, *A Preface to Hardy*, 1976; Raymond Williams, *The Country and the City*, 1973, *Keywords*, 1976.)

1. F. M. L. Thompson, *English Landed Society in the 19th Century*, 1963, 25.
2. 'The Dorsetshire Labourer'; *Thomas Hardy's Personal Writings*, ed. H. Orel, Kansas, 1955, 189.
3. William Cobbett, *The Political Register*, 70, i, 695 (13 November 1830).

2 : Hardy and Education

PHILIP COLLINS

ONE OF THE 'CONSIDERATIONS' informing his first novel *The Poor Man and the Lady*, Hardy told the publishers Macmillans, was 'that, nowadays, discussions on the questions of manners, rising in the world, etc. (the main incidents in the novel), have grown to be particularly absorbing'.[1] Its hero, 'the son of peasants', had risen to a level at which he could aspire to win 'the Lady', the squire's daughter, because his cleverness was fostered by the educational system: he 'showed remarkable talent at the village school, and was patronized by the people of the great house, who had him educated as a draughtsman' and thus he became (as of course Hardy was becoming when he turned fulltime writer) a promising young architect.[2] Throughout his career as a novelist he remained 'particularly absorbed' by 'rising in the world' and by the enlargement of marriage choice which such social mobility produced: and, in Victorian England, this process, and especially making the crucial jump from the working-class to the middle-class, was commonly a product of education. Thus education becomes an explicit topic in his characters' courtships. Stephen Smith, broaching with his beloved Elfride the likely difficulties ahead of them, asks her: 'Where do you think I went to school – I mean, to what kind of school?' (*A Pair of Blue Eyes*, ch. 8). Or Bathsheba Everdene, rejecting Gabriel Oak's advances early in the story, gives as one of her reasons: 'I am better educated than you.' – 'You speak like a lady – all the parish notice it', he acknowledges (*Far from the Madding Crowd*, ch. 4). Or fathers, having invested in their daughters' education so that they can 'marry well', try to fend off suitors who are insufficiently genteel (Fancy Day and Grace Melbury suffer thus): and another father, Michael Henchard, himself of ungenteel origins, is aggravated when his adoptive daughter Elizabeth Jane uses dialect expressions and in various other ways imperils her new social standing.

Not that Hardy's interest in education was confined to its connection with class and status. Referring to the classic fairy story instance of rising in the world and thus marrying above one's original station, he distinguished his Jude Fawley from the common ruck of young aspirants: 'He was a species of Dick Whittington, whose spirit was touched to finer issues than a mere material gain' (II. 1). George Eliot used the same Shakespearean allusion in the final paragraph of *Middlemarch* (Dorothea's 'finely-touched spirit had still its fine issues'), and it is one of the many affinities between her and Hardy that his Jude and Clym Yeobright recall her altruistic young men such as Felix Holt and Daniel Deronda and her 'anti-Cinderella' heroines. He regarded such young men as the men of the future: the 'Wilhelm Meister and Daniel Deronda class' were, he wrote, 'the type to which the great mass of educated modern men of ordinary capacity are assimilating more or less'.[3]

However representative, in this and other ways, Hardy's educated young men may be, his preoccupation with these themes is manifestly bound up with his own experience and personality. Edward Springrove, the hero of his first novel *Desperate Remedies*, and Stephen Smith, the hero of *A Pair of Blue Eyes* (a novel containing much autobiographical matter), resemble the 'Poor Man' of that first-written (and lost) story in being, like Hardy himself, architects of humble provincial parentage.[4] Another architect-hero is George Somerset of *A Laodicean*: and he, like Edward Springrove, further resembles their creator (and Jude) in not being set on material advancement. In the *Life*, Hardy writes of the evidence, from his childhood onwards, of 'that lack of social ambition which followed him through life' (p. 16); in *A Laodicean*, he shows Somerset's 'inherent unfitness for a professional life under ordinary circumstances' (I, 11) – an unfitness which was caused, not by incompetence or lack of zeal, but by complexity and elevation of character. The first jotting about the story which was to be concerned, more than any of his others, with education is explicit about the degree of his personal involvement, though later Hardy was to deny, vehemently and repeatedly, that *Jude the Obscure* had any autobiographical reference. In 1888 he wrote in his journal:

A short story about a young man – 'who could not go to Oxford' – his struggles and ultimate failure. Suicide. There is something [in this] the world ought to be shown, and I am the one to show it to them — though I was not altogether hindered going, at least to Cambridge, and could have gone up easily at five-and-twenty.[5]

But if, as he felt, he had special qualifications for writing on such a theme ('I am the one to show it to them'), it was a tale of general and not merely personal significance ('something the world ought to be shown').

Slow rises worth, by poverty depress'd,

Samuel Johnson had written, in the previous century: and also about Oxford — Jude's Christminster —

There mark what Ills the Scholar's Life assail . . .

Hardy, in this novel, is even less hopeful than Johnson; Jude, though in many ways worthy, never rises at all, and never experiences fulltime the Scholar's Life. But by the latter decades of the nineteenth century, Jude and his like had more notions of rising than — to cite one of Hardy's favourite poems from Johnson's period — their forefathers in the Country Church-yard:

Far from the madding crowd's ignoble strife,
Their sober wishes never learn'd to stray. . . .

In Gray's *Elegy*, as William Empson observes, 'Full many a gem' (etc.) means that 'eighteenth-century England had no scholarship system or *carrière ouverte aux talents*. This is stated as pathetic, but the reader is put into a mood in which one would not try to alter it.'[6] By Hardy's time, this state of affairs had been altered — if, as Jude discovered, not altered enough — though Hardy's fictional world still of course contains many rustics who would have gone contentedly to their respose in Gray's church-yard. The guests assembled at the beginning of 'The Three Strangers', for instance (though indeed that story was set back in the 1820s): men of 'a truly princely serenity' because of

. . . the absence of any expression or trait denoting that they wished to get on in the world, enlarge their minds, or do any eclipsing thing whatever — which nowadays so generally nips the bloom and *bonhomie* of all except the two extremes of the social scale. (*Wessex Tales*)

Hardy comments grimly in his essay 'The Dorsetshire Labourer' that it is 'among such communities as these' – in retired districts in the backward county of Dorset – 'that happiness will find her last refuge on earth, since it is among them that a perfect insight into the conditions of existence will be longest postponed'.[7] But Jude is a man of 'nowadays' (that recurrent Hardy word) in substituting for the 'sober wishes' of his rude Forefathers that 'modern vice of unrest' (II, 11), that 'ache of modernism' as Hardy puts it elswhere (*Tess*, III, 19), which is a recurrent topic of the novels – the *Zeitgeist* which Jude himself eventually comes to see as ' the spirit of mental and social restlessness that makes so many unhappy in these days!' (VI, 1). This again is a concern which Hardy shares with George Eliot – the gradual awakening, as she puts it (in *Felix Holt*, ch. 3), of 'that higher consciousness which is known to bring higher pains'. In particular, the Pursuit of Knowledge under Difficulties – the title of G. L. Craik's much-reprinted compilation of success-stories in this endeavour (1830–1) – was a common theme of the fiction and the popular lore of the century. Victor Neuberg's *Popular Literature* reproduces, from the same decade as *Jude*, an illustration from one such novel, showing an urban Jude, with the caption, 'The street lamps were his study-lights, while he read and re-read the books lent him by Mr. Danvers', the master of the National School attended by this industrious and happily-destined urchin.[8]

For, though the merit of Self-Help was much lauded, nineteenth-century Britain devised many new social mechanisms to enlarge educational opportunity and to improve the standard of professional training. The National Schools attended by this lad, and by Tess Durbeyfield and other characters in Hardy, are just one instance of this. With the one major exception of Christminster, all the educational institutions and processes to which Hardy refers in his novels are nineteenth-century inventions; most, indeed, are Victorian. The two great school Societies – the interdenominational British and Foreign, and its Anglican rival the National Society for the Education of the Poor – were founded in 1808–9; Hardy himself attended schools of both Societies. The pupil-teacher system and the Training Colleges which it fed, Theological Colleges, medical schools, Mutual Improvement Societies, competitive examinations – to mention some other institutions and practices which appear in the novels – are creations of the mid-century decades. The Royal Institute of British Architects was incorporated in 1837, and was one of a host of such professional organizations, almost unknown before the Victorian period. W. J. Reader's study *Professional Men* surveys the multiplication of the professions and the emergence of their Institutes, Societies and Associations, and provides evidence which explains, for instance, how lucky Hardy's Stephen Smith is to have become an architect, and why he must nevertheless remain sensitive about his social origins. As late as the turn of the century, Dr. Reader comments, 'Even the *Architectural Review*, the organ of a profession generally considered artistic and therefore eccentric, assumed as a matter of course that a young man looking for architectural training would have come from a public school.'[9] His book illustrates, too, the resentment against the new passion for formal training and paper qualifications felt by men who had entered the profession the old way: and this appears in the novels. Thus, in *A Laodicean*, George Somerset is a Fellow of the Society of Antiquaries and a Member — hoping soon to become a Fellow — of the Institute of British Architects. His rival, Mr. Havill, 'was not brought up to the profession — got into it through sheer love of it' (he says) and after miscellaneous practical experience: but, as he tells Somerset,

'. . . nowadays 'tis the men who can draw pretty pictures who get recommended, not the practical men. Young prigs win Institute medals for a pretty design or two which, if anybody tried to build them, would fall down like a house of cards; then they get travelling studentships and what not, and then they start as architects of some new school or other, and think they are masters of us experienced ones.' (I, 8, 9)

Hardy, a prizeman and silver-medallist of the R.I.B.A. in 1863, doubtless had to endure similar putting-down speeches from disgruntled old sweats in the profession.

Education was, during Hardy's years, changing outlook and life-style, as well as affecting class mobility, professional procedures, and much else, at every level of society. He puts this splendidly, in a context other than has been mentioned so far, after Mrs. Durbeyfield has been consulting the *Compleat Fortune-Teller*:

Between the mother, with her fast-perishing lumber of superstitions, folk-lore, dialect, and orally-transmitted ballads, and the daughter, with her trained National teachings and Standard knowledge under an infinitely Revised Code, there was a gap of two hundred years as generally understood. When they were together the Jacobean and the Victorian ages were juxtaposed. (*Tess*, ch. 3)

Folk-lore and superstitions are a frequent point of reference in Hardy; so too of course is dialect, an obvious indicator of class and education:

> Mrs. Durbeyfield habitually spoke the dialect; her daughter, who had passed the Sixth Standard in the National School under a London-trained mistress, spoke two languages; the dialect at home, more or less; ordinary English abroad and to persons of quality. (Ch. 3)

But even Mrs. Durbeyfield's traditional inheritance is 'fast-perishing'. Inevitably, the railway is Hardy's other main symbol, besides education, of change in the village. The 'fairly true record of a vanishing life' which, as he claims in the 1912 'General Preface', the Wessex Novels contain, presents 'a modern Wessex of railways, the penny post, mowing and reaping machines, union workhouses, lucifer matches, labourers who can read and write, and National school children' (1895 Preface, *Far from the Madding Crowd*). In 'The Dorsetshire Labourer', Hardy traces some of the economic and social consequences of labourers' being able to read and write, and of other such manifestations of 'enlightenment' after 'centuries of serfdom' (Orel, p. 181), and he comments on the 'transitional state' of such youngsters as Tess, mixing 'the unwritten, dying, Wessex English' with the printed tongue taught at the National Schools (p. 170). (As Orel points out, this essay is particularly relevant to *Tess*, which novel indeed incorporates some passages from it.) Another reference which helps to explain such changes in the village as Mrs. Durbeyfield's losing command of her store of old ballads is Hardy's famous (if probably over-emphatic) comment on the local harvest-supper which he attended as a boy:

> It may be worthy of note that this harvest-home [1850] was among the last at which the old traditional ballads were sung, the railway having been extended to Dorchester just then [1847], and the orally transmitted ditties of centuries being slain at a stroke by the London comic songs that were introduced.[10]

Over-emphatic, I suggested: that 'slain at a stroke' should not be taken literally (as the dates, indeed, indicate); but an erosion of traditional culture was certainly fast proceeding. 'With railways and a cheap press, in the second third of the nineteenth century', wrote Mrs. Humphry Ward, more cheerfully than Hardy, 'there came in, as we all know, the break-up of a thousand mental stagnations, answering to the old physical disabilities and inconveniences.' She was arguing that railways were the 'leading cause' of the emergence of the Women's Movement – another social and cultural development, associated with education, which is reflected in Hardy.[11] His sense of what the railway meant to Wessex is felicitously given in a passage in *Tess*, where the 'fitful white streak of steam' against the dark green background 'denoted intermittent moments of contact between [the girls'] secluded world and modern life. Modern life stretched its steam feeler to this point three or four times a day, touched the native existences, and quickly withdrew its feeler again, as if what it touched had been uncongenial' (ch. 29).

Uncongenial maybe, but the changes were (as Hardy recognized) irreversible, and were palpable to the meanest intelligence, such as Humphrey's in *The Return of the Native*: 'True: 'tis amazing what a polish the world have been brought to', he assents to Olly the besom-maker's observation that 'the class of folk that couldn't use to make a round O to save their bones from the pit can write their names now without a sputter of the pen, oftentimes without a blot' (ch. 3) – and this in a novel ostensibly set back in the 1840s, though there is not much in it to distinguish its social and ideological world decisively from its period of publication (1878). Hardy, born three years after Victoria's accession, and ceasing to write novels shortly before her death, was a witness of most of the Victorian period, but the circumstances of his birth and upbringing and early professional career predisposed him to be especially aware of certain educational and cultural developments during this time. His part of Wessex was – and still palpably is – heavy with history. Moreover, Dorset was a notoriously backward county, slow to take the impact of forces which had already transformed other parts of the country. It thus retained a rich folk-culture, still semi-pagan, as Hardy often observed. All this, however, he saw being challenged and changed. His first-published novel, *Desperate Remedies*, was being written in 1870, the year of Forster's Education Act, the measure which began the process, completed over the following decades, of free

compulsory elementary education for all children. And he himself
belonged to that favourite area of his novels, 'the metamorphic classes of
society' (*The Hand of Ethelberta*, ch. 39); he was subject to 'the
incongruities that were daily shaping themselves in the world under the
great modern fluctuations of classes and creeds' (*A Laodicean*, I, 4). Like
Ethelberta, one of the women through whom he dramatizes aspects of
his own experience, he had 'the subversive Mephistophelian
endowment, brains' (ch. 31). Born into a family of humble pretensions –
some branches and forbears were successful and respectable, but many
more were poor and obscure – he became a professional man and left the
village for the city, working in London from 1862 to 1867 and returning
there for periods during his literary career. He thus experienced the
social and cultural transformations which were becoming a common lot
at this time of increased mobility. So some account should here be given
of his childhood and education, and the more so because, like many
novelists, he is least inventive, more dependent upon personal experience, when writing about these topics. Novelists generally find it
much more difficult to imagine children unlike themselves in character,
sex and experience than to create a range of adult characters. Not that
Hardy specializes in children: and, as will be shown, he is much more
interested in the consequences than in the process of education. He offers
little that is comparable to the schools and child-minds explored in
Dickens's novels.

   With a symbolical aptness so excessive that even Hardy would not
have dared to use such an invention in his novels, his immediate ancestry
included families named Head and Hand; his paternal grandmother was
Mary Head, his own mother Jemima Hand. (Jude Fawley indeed was
originally named Jack Head, and was renamed England before Hardy
settled for Fawley, which was the name of the village from which Mary
had come.) Hardy's father was a self-made man, who had risen from
artisan status to being a master-mason employing sometimes as many as
fifteen men (usually around six, it would appear), but he was not too
proud or too affluent to send young Thomas, his first-born, to the new
National School ('for the Education of the Poor') in Bockhampton, at
the age of eight. Previously he had learned his letters – he could read, he
said, almost before he could walk – from his mother, a woman of
remarkably wide and discriminating reading, and he had briefly
attended a private school of the brutal Dotheboys Hall type while on a

lengthy visit to relatives in Hertfordshire. The new school in Bockhampton had been established by a local lady, Mrs. Julia Martin, who took a great fancy to Hardy (thus giving him his first experience of the 'poor man and the Lady' situation he was later to explore, for he grew very attached to her, too). It was, Her Majesty's Inspector reported, a 'very creditable' school – 'instruction sound; . . . Methods very fair; master takes great pains; . . . [he and his wife] very respectable pleasing people', and Hardy too asserted that it was 'far superior to an ordinary village school'.[13] His parents removed him, however, in 1850 to a British and Foreign Society school in Dorchester, despite its being Nonconformist; the reason Hardy adduces is that its headmaster, Isaac Last, was 'an exceptionally able man, and a good teacher of Latin' (*Life*, 18). Latin was an 'extra', which Hardy's father paid for him to acquire, and when in 1853 Last set up his own fee-paying Academy in Dorchester, catering for boys from more affluent homes and offering a more advanced education, Hardy went with him and stayed there until he began his apprenticeship to architecture in 1856. There had been some talk of his entering Christ's Hospital, the historic public school in London, but the Governor who, it was hoped, would present him to a place died, so the opportunity passed.[14] While still at Mr. Last's Academy he began French lessons under the French governess at his sister Mary's school, and had started to learn German from Cassell's *Popular Educator*, a teach-yourself compilation from which he also gathered much miscellaneous information that found its way into the novels. Some years later, in London, he attended French classes at King's College for a term or two. As he put it rather pompously later, when ruffled by a remark that he was self-taught, he had been 'taught Latin and French at School and College'.[15]

He was a 'born bookworm' – like Jude, 'crazy for books' (I. 2) – and during his apprenticeship, he said, 'often gave more time to books than to drawings', rising early to spend several hours at the Classics before walking to Mr. Hicks's architect's office in Dorchester (*Life*, 27–8). He loved being alone, and had rather resented his schoolfellows' pressing their company upon him. He was remembered locally as 'a solemn small boy, odd-looking and with a big head, carrying a full satchel of books'.[16] As Emma Clifford remarks in a suggestive essay, he was no ordinary child, and the children in his novels take after him in being, almost all, 'to some extent weird': 'Indeed, all we know about Hardy as a child is slightly fantastic' – he was dreamy, precocious, he preferred adult company to other children's, he did not wish to grow up; as he says in the *Life*, 'he did not want at all to be a man, or to possess things, but to remain as he was, in the same spot, and to know no more people than he already knew'.[17] Everybody, he recalled, said that 'Tommy would have to be a parson, being obviously no good for any practical pursuit' and he had indeed 'sometimes wished to enter the Church' before he accepted Hicks' offer to take him as a pupil: and this ambition recurred at later periods during his youth (*Life*, 15, 27). One other point about these early years: during his protracted calf-love period, he had further experience of playing the poor man to the lady. At fifteen, he fell in love with Louisa Harding (a girl he never forgot), the daughter of a substantial local farmer, but her family discouraged the romance. As a cousin of hers recalled, 'You see, to my family, Hardy was just a village boy, although it was recognized that he was an unusual type and different from the other village children in several ways: for instance he never played games, and was a quiet, studious child of a retiring disposition.'[18] Hardy, surely conscious of being 'different' in a superior way, must have felt a sharp sense of disprized love and of merit spurned for unworthy reasons.

During his years in Hicks's office (1856–62) and then as assistant in the office of the eminent London architect Arthur Blomfield (1862–7) he was not only very diligent in maintaining a serious programme of reading but also was exceptionally fortunate in the intellectual atmosphere which he there inhaled. Both his principals were very cultivated men, and in both offices he found, as fellow pupils, young men of considerable intellectual strenuousness and vivacity. Also, while in Dorchester he became friendly with Horace Moule and his family, another highly intelligent and scholarly group: and biographers have stressed the profound influence that Moule, older and better-educated, exerted upon the young Hardy. Of these Dorchester years, he used to say that it was 'a life twisted of three strands – the professional life, the scholar's life, and the rustic life, combined in the twenty-four hours of one day' (*Life*, 32). In London, the rustic life was replaced by a horrified fascination with the great city, and by opportunities to pursue two artistic passions of this phase by frequent visits to theatres and art galleries. His strenuous reading continued, Greek having been added to Latin. He immersed himself in English poetry and began writing poems himself. He read the dominant 'Sages' of High Victorian Culture –

Newman, Mill, Carlyle, Ruskin – and soon afterwards he was studying
Herbert Spencer, Matthew Arnold, and such continental equivalents as
Fourier and Comte, who were to leave their mark upon Clym
Yeobright and Sue Bridehead. Reminiscing half a century later, he
related that 'he used to give little literary lectures as all the apprentices
did at Sir Arthur Blomfield's, instead of doing their work, and he said in
one of them that he would not have the reputation of Dickens for
anything' (an eventuality which, when he turned novelist, he avoided
with exemplary thoroughness).[19] At more relaxed moments, he and his
coevals deferred work to sing glees and catches in the office. Altogether
it was an admirable exercise in – to use the terminology of the age –
both self-help and mutual improvement, though earnest rather than
sophisticated. Hardy bridled when a commentator, writing in French,
described him as 'ce Saxon autodidacte', but Michael Millgate, in his
chapter using that phrase as its title, argues convincingly that this
judgement is accurate (though we dons who write about Hardy must
beware of patronizing him, for, lacking the advantages which we have
enjoyed, he read and pondered much that it would do us good to
master). That warning noted, Millgate expresses precisely my sense of
the matter when he remarks of the commonplace books which record
Hardy's reading, that they can seem 'profoundly depressing. . . . There
remains . . . something disturbing and essentially sterile about this
methodical storage of miscellaneous information . . .' for, as he
continues, 'The mark of the autodidact is perhaps to be found not so
much in what he knows as in how he regards the world of knowledge.'[20]
Of this, Hardy provides evidence which can cheer no admirer, both by
his sad proclivity for firing off his popguns of knowledge indis-
criminately in the novels, and by such naiveties as his remark, late in
life, that he had been invited to Eton by the Provost, Montague James –
'said Monty had written him quite an ordinary letter and here [*sic*] he
had always thought that provosts were a little greater than deans and just
below bishops.'[21]

'Having every instinct of a scholar he might have ended his life as a
Don. . . . But this was not to be, and it was possibly better so.'[22] This is
the first of a series of references in the *Life* to the possibility that Hardy
might have gone to Cambridge, or perhaps to London University,
which made special provisions for 'self-taught students', to prepare
himself for Holy Orders. 'As a child, to be a parson had been his dream',

and at the age of twenty-five, yearning to be a poet, he had formed the
'highly visionary' scheme of becoming a clergyman and of combining
this vocation with writing poetry. Another version of this notion of
going to Cambridge, however, concludes: 'But in the end it was thought
unnecessary for an architect.' The references in the *Life* become more
positive, from page to page. His father's 'never absolutely refusing' to
lend him the requisite money (p. 34) becomes, by page 207, an assertion
that he 'could have gone up easily'; the 'highly visionary' scheme (p. 50)
becomes an 'intention . . . to go up for a pass-degree' (p. 361), Hardy
having 'begun reading for Cambridge with a view to taking Orders' (p.
376), an undertaking abandoned 'mainly' because he became a victim to
Honest Doubt. It remains uncertain how seriously these hopes were
entertained, and some commentators have cast doubt upon Hardy's
father's ability at this time to finance any such venture. Also uncertain is
the contention that Hardy applied for admission to Salisbury Theological College but was rejected. Some Theological Colleges accepted
non-graduates and thus provided a cut-price *faute-de-mieux* entry into the
ministry, as Jude, Phillotson and the egregious brothers in 'A Tragedy of
Two Ambitions' are aware. J. O. Bailey refers to the asseveration of the
Librarian of Salisbury Cathedral that she can and will produce evidence
of Hardy's desire to enrol at Salisbury.

Certainly Hardy's two sisters, Mary and Kate, received a higher
education in Salisbury, at its Training College for teachers – to which
institution Sue Bridehead briefly follows them, without completing the
course. (In *Jude*, it is called Melchester Normal-School, or Training-
School, these being alternative nomenclatures for a Training College.)
Both sisters did well and, never marrying, made a career in education;
as Hardy put it on the death of Mary, to whom he had been particularly
close, 'she had been doomed to school-teaching, and organ-playing in
this or that village church during all her active years'.[23] Another woman
close to Hardy who went through the pupil-teacher system, attended a
Training College (Stockwell, in North London), obtained – like Fancy
Day – a First Class certificate, and achieved success as a teacher, was his
cousin Tryphena Sparks, his romantic connections with whom have
recently been the subject of much speculation. Whatever else may be
provable, it is clear that Tryphena was one of the figures behind Sue
Bridehead: and Stockwell was one of the Training Colleges which
Hardy visited in 1891 when thinking about *Jude*, the others being

Salisbury, where his sisters had studied, and Whitelands, the *doyenne* of the women's colleges.

One other family connection with education may be mentioned. Hardy's first wife Emma, illustrating the gentility of her origins, wrote: 'Trading was not adopted by the family – the scholastic line was always taken at times of declining fortune – school-keeping teachers or tutorships partly on account of ability for teaching and making things clear to other intelligences.'[24] Genteel characters in Hardy's novels, as of course in much Victorian fiction, take or try to take 'the scholastic line' when their family fortunes have declined, the father having died bankrupt: that, for instance, is how Ethelberta's suitor Christopher Julian became a music-teacher. The governess was a favourite character in Victorian fiction because, as *Jane Eyre* and *Vanity Fair* may remind us, the governess – cultivated and genteel, though penurious – has an outside chance of marrying her rich and grand employer, or his son. She has a 'romantic ubiquity of station', as Hardy puts it in *The Hand of Ethelberta* (ch. 13): Ethelberta, indeed, though of humble origins, was so greatly improved by education that she married Sir Ralph Petherwin's son (though Lady Petherwin sent her off to a finishing-school at Bonn). Other girls who offer themselves as governesses and marry satisfactorily include Cytherea Graye (*Desperate Remedies*), Avice the third (*The Well-Beloved*) and Lucy Savile ('Fellow-Townsmen'). Bathsheba, 'an excellent scholar', was going to be a governess once, 'only she was too wild' (*Far from the Madding Crowd*, ch. 4). Governesses who fare less well include Sergeant Troy's mother, a French governess seduced by Lord Severn, and Fancy Day's – 'A governess in a country family, who was foolish enough to marry the keeper of the same establishment' – but this parentage explains why Troy has such poise and dash and how Fancy, as her father says, has 'picked up her good manners, the smooth turn of her tongue, and her knowledge of books, in a homely hole like this' (*Under the Greenwood Tree*, III, iii).

Under the Greenwood Tree, though short and slight, is the first novel in which Hardy reconnoitres his characteristic territory, and it is noteworthy that its heroine is a newly certificated schoolmistress. The plot presents a variation on that favourite situation in Victorian fiction and drama – the village maiden with a faithful young lover of her own humble class and another, usually unprincipled, one from among the gentry – but here, because Fancy is educated and polished as well as pretty, her more prestigious and affluent suitors, Mr. Maybold and Mr. Shiner, want to marry her, not seduce her, and her father is anxious that she shall not marry the son of Reuben Dewy the tranter. Geoffrey is stinting himself to provide her with a good dowry, is waiting for her to attract some gentleman 'who sees her to be his equal in polish' (III, 2), and is so impressed by her achievement – top in the Queen's scholars examination which took pupil-teachers into College, and then top in the First Class for the qualifying Certificate – that he is on his guard against saying anything which might 'not agree with her educated ideas' (II, 6). A father so impressible will not stand out against Fancy's getting her own way eventually, though she allows her vanity and ambition to deflect her momentarily from the course of true love (Maybold offers her a piano, that recurrent symbol of respectability). At her wedding with Dick Dewy – no hobbledehoy, for, as his father reminds him, 'I . . . sent 'ee to a school so good that 'twas hardly fair to the other children' (II, 8) –

> The propriety of everyone was intense, by reason of the influence of Fancy, who, as an additional precaution in that direction, had strictly charged her father and the tranter to carefully avoid saying 'thee' and 'thou' in their conversation. . . . (IV, 2)

It is the first of Hardy's many dramatizations of the status of dialect.

Fancy Day is a shallow, if engaging, figure, and the novel makes no pretensions to a serious engagement with the issues it touches upon. Fifteen years later, in *The Woodlanders*, the same situation is much more fully realized and developed by Grace Melbury, her father, Fitzpiers and Giles Winterborne. And these themes endure: in his penultimate novel *The Well-Beloved* Hardy twice-over repeats this between-cultures situation of clever attractive young women educated above their parents' level. Thus, about the first of the three girls named Avice, Hardy writes one of his best attacks on standardization, but adds his frequent point that *Naturam expellas furca, tamen usque recurret*:

> . . . every aim of those who had brought her up had been to get her away mentally as far as possible from her natural and individual life as an inhabitant of a peculiar island: to make her an exact copy of tens of thousands of other people, in whose circumstances there was nothing special, distinctive, or picturesque; to teach her to forget all the experiences of her ancestors; to drown the local ballads by songs

purchased at the Budmouth fashionable music-sellers', and the local vocabulary by a governess-tongue of no country at all. . . . By constitution she was local to the bone, but she could not escape the tendency of the age . . . but underneath the veneer of Avice's education many an oldfashioned idea lay slumbering. . . . (I, 2)

'How the old ideas survived under the new education!' her fiancé discovers – but Hardy interjects to ask the reader to remember that this was 'more than forty years ago' (I, 4). Two generations on, the first Avice's granddaughter, having received a 'very thorough education – better even than her grandmother's', is described as 'a girl who with one hand touched the educated middle-class and with the other the rude and simple inhabitants of the isle. Her intensely modern sympathies were quickened by her peculiar outlook' (III, 1, 3). But, though 'a still more modernized, up-to-day edition of the [preceding] two Avices', she receives just the same parental admonitions as Fancy Day and Grace Melbury: 'Your expensive education is wasted down here!' says her mother, urging her to accept an elderly suitor who owns a mansion (III, 1, 4).

The story of Fancy Day includes some minor registrations of what was expected of certificated schoolmistresses then, a matter doubtless fresh in Hardy's mind in 1872, since both Tryphena and his sister Mary had recently, like Fancy, emerged from College into their first teaching posts. Fancy's ability to play the church-organ, which chimes with the new parson's notions and thus disrupts the time-honoured ways of Mellstock parish, was an accomplishment commonly expected of or required in National School teachers.[25] Hardy also notices well the proprieties incumbent upon a National schoolmistress, a mixture of acquired middle-class respectability and of humble deference to her more socially secure employers. Thus Fancy is conscious that she shouldn't wear her hair in curls or indulge in tête-à-têtes with young men, though she does contrive to mitigate such conditions, and even to commit 'an audacity unparalleled in the whole history of schoolmistresses' – wearing a hat and feather instead of a bonnet at church – partly because her 'papa's respectable accumulation of cash' enables her to feel somewhat independent, but also because of her well-founded belief that, being pretty and spirited, she can 'manage any vicar's views about me if he's under forty' (IV, 5; II, 7). A few years earlier, Dickens had given a much grimmer account of the exactions of 'respectability' in his presentation of the certificated schoolmaster Bradley Headstone and the pupil-teacher Charlie Hexam in *Our Mutual Friend* (1864–5); Hardy, years later, was to show Sue Bridehead losing her place at College, and Phillotson losing his headmastership at Shaston (having 'all the respectable inhabitants' against him [IV, 6]), for just such reasons. One other point about Fancy Day: Hardy, answering someone's question, years later, about what kind of wife she made, made the curious reply: 'I don't quite know . . . and yet I have known women of her type turn out all right, some of those early examples of independent schoolmistresses included.'[26] Why the surprise about schoolmistresses' turning out all right? Maybe he felt that they risked becoming too 'independent' for matrimony, like Sue Bridehead, who could be regarded (he noted) as typical of the new 'bachelor' girl 'who does not recognize the necessity for most of her sex to follow marriage as a profession' (1912 'Postscript' to *Jude*). Certainly, in a plan for a short story about this time (1871), he noted what strength of character it betokened, at that period, for such girls to live by themselves, away from home. The story was to concern a girl who 'goes to be schoolmistress' and gets caught in the familiar triangle ('leaves her village lover: loves a school-master') – 'In opening, the description of schoolmistress's arrival, or house. State the government requirements – and that it argues well for the courage of English maids that (so many) are every year drafted off to lonely residence, etc.'[27] No wonder that, the first time we see Fancy, her bright eyes bear 'an uncertain expression, oscillating between courage and shyness' (I, 5). At least she suffers no disadvantage from being a woman teacher (rather otherwise indeed); contrast the fact that Arabella Donn became Phillotson's pupil in Marygreen, walking there from her own village because, as she explains, 'we only had a mistress down at our place' (*Jude*, V, 8) – a nice example of the confident offhand social detail, relating to education as to much else, which give such 'solidity of specification' to the novels.

Fancy Day has no cause to regret her education, and it has qualified her to earn her living (a striking new Victorian development, for this was the first career open to respectable wellspoken girls, with the doubtful exception of the stage). Grace Melbury's education is explicitly an investment in the marriage-market; her father keeps brandishing the figure about ('near a hundred a year'), to impress neighbours, to bring the girl to heel, and to encourage Fitzpiers to snap up this bargain. 'We've done it!' he exults, when Fitzpiers agrees, and he tells Grace to 'make it all smooth for him' when he comes courting:

> 'You mean, to lead him on to marry me?' [she replies].
> 'I do.
> Haven't I educated you for it?' (*The Woodlanders*, ch. 22).

It is characteristic of Melbury's infatuation with social values that he respects Fitzpiers not for being a physician but for his genteel lineage, and that he is willing to sacrifice personal dignity, family feeling and friendship, as well as cash, to marry his daughter well. As he tells her:

> '. . . If you should ever meet me then, Grace, you can drive past me, looking the other way. I shouldn't expect you to speak to me, or wish such a thing – unless it happened to be in some lonely private place where 'twouldn't lower 'ee at all. Don't think such men as neighbour Giles your equal. He and I be good friends enough, but he's not for the like of you. . . . .'
>
> So much pressure could not but produce some displacement . . . (Ch. 23)

But Grace has already been corrupted by her schooling – though she had then been a victim of snobbery herself, 'always a little despised by the other girls' because they knew that her parents 'were not in so good a station as theirs' (ch. 30). She had been 'so trained socially, and educated intellectually, as to see clearly enough a pleasure in the position of wife to such a man as Fitzpiers' (ch. 23) and she agrees with her father that life with Giles Winterborne would have been 'too rough' for her (ch. 25). Later, disillusioned in Fitzpiers and abandoned by him, she discovers what really matters – has 'widening perceptions of what was great and little in life' (ch. 30) – and, meeting Giles again,

> Her heart rose from its late sadness like a released bough; . . . the veneer of artificiality which she had acquired at the fashionable schools [was] thrown off, and she became the crude country girl of her latent early instincts. (Ch. 28)

Her education, she now thinks, has done her harm. As she tells her father:

'I wish you had never, never thought of educating me. I wish I worked in the woods like Marty South. . . . Because cultivation has only brought me inconveniences and troubles. . . . I have never got any happiness outside Hintock that I know of. . . .' (Ch. 30)

Melbury, at first 'much hurt at what he thought her ingratitude and intractability', comes to the view that 'perhaps she's right' (chs. 30, 31) and strives, unsuccessfully, to restore her to Giles.

Fitzpiers is 'the only fully-fledged intellectual in the Wessex novels', writes David De Laura in an essay very relevant to my theme, '"The Ache of Modernism" in Hardy's Later Novels.'[28] Half-baked rather than fully-fledged, I would say, and I do not share De Laura's discomfort, that Hardy is 'curiously hostile to Fitzpiers from the first' and 'querulous and condescending to his intellectual pretensions'. Fitzpiers' pretensions are baloney, and his unprincipled egotism invites hostility; if anything, Hardy is over-impressed by him. But I agree with De Laura in seeing him as an *unfocused* first study of a less ethical Angel' (italics mine) and in associating him with Clym and Jude as intellectuals out of their element – as Grace sees him, before they meet, 'a tropical plant in a hedgerow, a nucleus of advanced ideas and practices which had nothing in common with the life around' (ch. 6). Unfocused, though: just as it is difficult to be sure that Hardy sees him as ludicrous as well as unethical in that preposterous scene when, visiting a lady-patient, he sucks the plaster off her luscious arm, so also one questions such narratorial phrases about him as 'his keenly appreciative, modern, unpractical mind'. What, for instance, is the force of 'modern' here? Is addle-pated Fitzpiers being offered as some kind of representative figure? And what is so 'modern' about his studies, mentioned the page before, of alchemy and astronomy? And why does Hardy quaintly term another of his studies 'poesy'? (ch. 17). Anyway, his non-professional studies do him little good; as he makes most clear in his *in vino veritas* maunderings in Chapter 35, their main effect is to give him a sense of overweening superiority to everybody around, and to feed his self-pity ('doomed to live with tradespeople in a miserable little hole like Hintock!'). It is a sign of merit that, when reunited to Grace, he burns many of his books. De Laura rightly generalizes about him and the other intellectuals in the novels, that Hardy's eye 'is consistently on the *painful* exigencies of modernism, its human cost, and not on its liberating effects.' Contrast Mrs. Humphry Ward, quoted above.

So education in *The Woodlanders*, as the two very different cases of Grace and Fitzpiers show, has caused more peril than benefit. This is indeed generally so in the novels: education becomes one more of the abundant causes of unhappiness in the Hardy world. The fiercest presentations of the social divisiveness and corruption of spirit caused by education occur in two sardonic short-stories, 'A Tragedy of Two Ambitions' (1888) and 'The Son's Veto' (1891), collected in *Life's Little Ironies*. In the former, two brothers are cheated out of their modest birthright by their father, a master-millwright, who drinks away the money which was to have taken them to the university, and thus into the ministry: so now they can only hope to advance by the hard slog of proceeding through Training College, a National School mastership, and then Theological College – and, these being socially inferior routes to preferment, they can never 'rise' far in the Church. Embittered but ruthlessly self-seeking, they make it that way, and are helped by their prudent investment in their clever and personable sister; they have her well educated, and she thus marries a rich man who can present them to good livings. But they are dogged by their father, now grown thoroughly disreputable, who threatens to disgrace them just as they are consolidating their gains. On his way to gate-crashing his daughter's wedding, he falls into one of those weirs which provide an extra hazard in the Hardy country. The softer son makes to rescue him, but his brother dissuades him; they leave him to drown, and the tougher brother has to conduct the funeral service over his (happily unrecognizable) body. Education, and the careerism or concern for social status which it can foster, makes another son 'lose natural kindness' (to use Yeats's phrase) in 'The Son's Veto'. He is first seen in familiar Hardy territory, vetoing his mother's substandard English grammar ('Surely you know that by this time!'). The son of a deceased clergyman who, in a characteristic cross-class Hardy alliance, had for improbable reasons married his parlour-maid, Randolph is at 'a well-known public school' in London (Harrow presumably, for it has a cricket-match with another public school at Lords), and he not only corrects his mother's grammar but also prevents her demeaning him by marrying her faithful first love, a man who progresses from being a gardener to market-gardener and prosperous fruiterer. She dies unfulfilled. The boy, needless to say, becomes a High-Church clergyman; Hardy's childish antagonism to the Established Church can provoke the mildest agnostic to rejoice in G. K. Chesterton's description of Hardy as 'a sort of village atheist brooding and blaspheming over the village idiot.'[29] But the moral is stated clearly enough: 'His education had . . . ousted his humanity' (Ch. 3), 'Those wide infantine sympathies . . . with which he, like other children, had been born' had been narrowed — by a schooling of, indeed, the most exclusive character — to encompassing only

> . . . a few thousand wealthy and titled people, the mere veneer of a thousand million or so of others who did not interest him at all. He drifted further and further away from . . . a mother whose mistakes and origin it was his painful lot to blush for. (Ch. 2)

The tale ends with the neatness of its *genre* — Hardy thought this his best short-story — the mother's funeral procession passes the wet-eyed black-suited fruiterer, outside his shop, 'while from the mourning coach a young smooth-shaven priest in a high waistcoat looked black as a cloud at the shopkeeper standing there.'

'Mother, what *is* doing well?' Clym Yeobright asks. In this novel it is the parent who is ethically inferior: 'What better can a man wish for', says Mrs. Yeobright, 'than success in the jewel-trade?' (*The Return of the Native*, III, 2).[30] Clym, another exotic like Fitzpiers (though he does know and love the countryside), is also akin, as was noted above, to Hardy and several of his heroes in rejecting conventional ambitions and material rewards. Many characters in Hardy are or have been or contemplate becoming teachers of some kind, but Clym is the only one with an educational idea and a zeal for the task. He announces his plans soon after his return to Egdon: he has determined to

> '. . . follow some rational occupation among the people I know best. . . . I shall keep a school as near to Egdon as possible, so as to be able to walk over here and have a night-school in my mother's house. But I must study a little first, to get properly qualified. Now, neighbours, I must go.'
>
> And Clym resumed his walk across the heath.
>
> 'He'll never carry it out in the world', said Fairway. 'In a few weeks he'll learn to see things otherwise.'

' 'Tis good-hearted of the young man,' said another. 'But, for my part, I think he had better mind his business.' (III, 1)

His 'culture scheme' (IV, 2) includes adult education (that night-school), and is anti-élitist and idealistically unconcerned with worldly success. People need 'knowledge of a sort which brings wisdom rather than affluence', he thinks, and he wishes 'to raise the class at the expense of individuals rather than individuals at the expense of the class'. Clym is 'in many points abreast with the central town thinkers of his date' (the 1840s), having during 'his studious life in Paris . . . become acquainted with ethical systems popular at the time'. His missionary zeal and his spontaneous effort (outside the State system) are indeed – like Felix Holt's in George Eliot's novel – in line with the ideas of Comte and (later) Herbert Spencer.[31] His mother sees such notions as 'crochets', and in deference to her he modifies his views 'a little', he says; Eustacia 'would make a good matron in a boarding-school', and he will now establish 'a good private school for farmers' sons' in Budmouth, and can thus hope eventually to be 'head of one of the best schools in the country' (III, 3). He has 'a system of education' which, he claims, is 'as new as it is true . . . instilling high knowledge into empty minds without first cramming them with what has to be uncrammed again before true study begins', but his mother remains unimpressed – 'Dreams, dreams!' she says (III, 5). Then of course his eyesight fails, under the strain of working extra-hard to 'make up for lost time' expended on his honeymoon (IV, 1; this sounds more like Dr. Casaubon than Felix Holt). His eyesight never recovers enough for him to 'attempt his extensive educational project' but he is finally seen initiating 'all that really seemed practicable of the scheme that had originally brought him hither':

> Yeobright had, in fact, found his vocation in the career of an itinerant open-air preacher and lecturer on morally unimpeachable subjects; and from that day he laboured incessantly in that office. . . . He left alone creeds and systems of philosophy, finding enough and more than enough to occupy his tongue in the opinions and actions common to all good men. (VI, 4)

Clym, writes Douglas Brown, is 'a key figure for a right appraisal of Hardy's art' – which, if true, testifies to the ambiguity of that art, for

Clym – certainly in his educational ambitions – has been very variously interpreted. Should we, with Michael Millgate, see his reformist pretensions as flimsy, his attitudes as essentially negative, his plans as totally unsound and impracticable, and see the man as utterly self-absorbed, isolated, humourless, 'incapable of sympathetic communication with anyone outside himself'? Or should we, with Merryn Williams, see him as noble, 'a genuine popular teacher', if a lonely and misunderstood one – a man whom the people need more than they realize? and is Hardy, therefore, far from endorsing that neighbour who thinks 'he had better mind his business'? Should Hardy's attitude to Clym be described, cautiously (as by Lennart Björk), as 'ambiguous, *perhaps* sceptical'? (italics mine).³² I cannot feel sure: nor am I sure what degree of irony (if any) should be read into those phrases in the novel's final paragraph, 'morally unimpeachable subjects' and 'occupy his tongue'; certainly the predominant tone of that paragraph is sympathetic rather than ironic. Hardy, I think, wishes the reader to feel some respect for Clym's altruism and rejection of conventional getting-on. He explicitly regards Clym – as later Jude and Sue regard themselves – as, tragically, too far ahead of his time: 'In consequence of this *relatively advanced* position', Hardy comments (my italics; for Hardy conspicuously refrains from throwing any of Millgate's adjectives at this position), 'Yeobright might have been called unfortunate. A man should be only partially before his time: to be completely to the vanward in aspirations is fatal to fame' (III, 2). But what is that 'fatal to fame' doing here? A lust for fame has never been one of Clym's weaknesses. Here, surely, is a covert identification with the character whom Hardy, with characteristic obfuscation, described as 'the nicest of all my heroes, and *not a bit* like me' (*Life*, 358). Italics Hardy's: and the emphasis alerts anyone familiar with him to the possibility that untruth or self-deception is lurking hereabouts – that Hardy is, here in the novel, projecting onto Clym a concern for fame that belongs not to the character but to his creator.

But what worries me most about the presentation of Clym, in his reformist and pedagogical aspect, is Hardy's complete vagueness. Clym is studying – what? – to qualify himself – how? He has been influenced by 'the central town thinkers of his date' – which ones, and to what effect? Could Hardy have filled out, more specifically than Clym, what is contained in that system of education, 'as new as it is true'? – for

Clym's description stays at that unexacting level where *new* more or less rhymes with *true*. I think not. Hardy participates in, rather than sees round, Clym's imprecision. Not a book, not an author, not a specific idea is mentioned; contrast Hardy's procedure when he knows what he is talking about, in the presentation of Jude and Sue, and is then properly eager to identify the books they read and the intellectual forces that influenced them. In this area, *The Return of the Native* is simply too flabby to sustain the novel's tragic, or even its ironic, pretensions. As a final illustration of this, consider Clym's late-expressed description of his original hope 'to teach the people the higher secrets of *happiness*' (V, 1; italics mine). This – apparently offered without irony – is obviously at odds with Clym's, the novel's and Hardy's habitual sense of human fate – that 'thought is a disease of flesh', that 'a full recognition of the coil of things' is fatal to 'ideal physical beauty' and much else (II, 6), that – in Keats's words, which epitomize this central notion of Hardy's –

> . . . *but to think is to be full of sorrow*
> *And leaden-eyed despairs . . .*

so that, logically, educating people to a point where they may risk thinking cannot possibly promote their happiness. Recall my quotation from Hardy, above, about happiness finding 'her last refuge on earth' in those primitive rustics, untouched by enlightenment, among whom 'a perfect insight into the conditions of existence will be longest postponed'. Clym is doing a disservice to his clients, if happiness is to be preferred to 'a perfect insight . . .'; anyway, this juxtaposition of quotations – Clym's hope to teach 'the higher secrets of happiness' and Hardy's reiterated opinion that knowing is incompatible with happiness – suggests, to adopt Björk's locution, his 'ambiguity, perhaps scepticism' about the benefits of education. Given the way the dice are loaded in Hardy's fictional world, it is tempting to prefer to be one of John Stuart Mill's pigs or fools, despite that admirable man's – that hero of Hardy's – assertion that 'It is better to be a human being dissatisfied than a pig satisfied; better to be Socrates dissatisfied than a fool satisfied'.[33] Maybe so, on Mill's terms; doubtfully so, on Hardy's. If 'our nursery children' feel instinctively all that Aeschylus had imagined (*Return of the Native*, III, 1), if the new race of boys is permeated with 'the coming universal wish not to live' (*Jude*, VI, 2), all but the most heroically truth-facing of mankind may be forgiven for declining to be educated and preferring to be a happy pig or, like Arabella Donn, to associate themselves with that supposedly contented species. There is, arguably, a limit somewhere to the merit of discontent.

Education produces little joy in *Jude the Obscure* – but, before examining that novel, it may be useful to mention a few other references to education in the novels, which the reader may relate to the concerns of this chapter. The 'poor man and the lady' theme persists, with educational advance putting the humbly-born Swithin St. Cleeve in *Two on a Tower* in a position to meet and win the love of the lady from the local mansion. A similar situation occurs in 'An Indiscretion in the Life of an Heiress', cannibalized from the unpublished *Poor Man and the Lady*. Its hero, Egbert Mayne, is a village schoolteacher, instead of an architect as in the original story, but he is of genteel birth (his father died poor) and his romance with the local squire's daughter is forwarded by his saving her life.[34] Moreover he is only a temporary uncertificated teacher, with hopes of better things; he wavers between trying for the Church or becoming a writer, and succeeds, Hardy-wise, in the latter profession. *The Hand of Ethelberta*, as has been noted, reverses the sexes, being a story of 'the poor girl and the lord'. Ethelberta has been a teacher and governess, and her sister Picotee also is going through the pupil-teacher stage of this career. At one point, sickened by the prospect of the mercenary marriage through which she is making life comfortable for her family, she decides to become a village schoolmistress and thus see no more of the rich; but she has read enough of Mill's *Utilitarianism* to diddle her conscience, and Hardy ends the chapter with a question about the 'gradient' from her earlier 'soft and playful Romanticism' to 'distorted Benthamism. Was the moral incline [he asks] upward or down?' (ch. 36). Hardy might have mentioned her, and Paula Power in *A Laodicean*, another intellectually flighty lass, when he remarked in 1906 that 'the half-educated girl especially' was becoming much like Tess or Sue – this being an example of his contention that country people were increasingly resembling the characters in his novels.[35] Paula Power, 'emphatically a modern type of maidenhood' (I, 2), holds advanced views, we are told, about the higher education of women, 'talking a good deal about the physical training of the Greeks, whom she adores, or did'; so, being wealthy, she has built a private gymnasium 'in imitation of those at the new colleges for women' (II, 6). This prepares the reader for the extraordinary episode of her gymnastic display, 'a sort of optical poem' (II, 7), but her 'advanced ideas' remain unspecific, and Hardy fails to imagine adequately the intellectual mélange in this curious character – 'a Dissenter, and a Radical, and a New-light, and a neo-Greek, and a person of red blood' (IV, 3).

Tess Durbeyfield's Sixth Standard schooling was mentioned above. She was to become a teacher 'but the fates seemed to decide otherwise' (ch. 6). 'There was trouble in my family', she explains to Angel (ch. 29), and she is about to tell him of her further troubles, with Alec, but her courage fails her. A sentence deleted in the manuscript – 'To carry out her once fond idea of teaching in a village school was now impossible'[36] – makes it clear that Tess cannot revive her old ambition after her baby has died, for she has now lost the spotless character required in the profession: recall Sue's and Phillotson's tribulations. Had the fates been kinder she would have managed well in such a 'very mixed community' as Sue found in her Training-School – it included 'the daughters of mechanics, curates, surgeons, shopkeepers, farmers, dairymen, soldiers, sailors, and villagers'.[37] As it was, her relatively good schooling helped to make her the more attractive to Alec and Angel. Being 'better educated' as well as 'more finely formed' than the other girls, she obviously had the best chance of gaining Angel's heart (ch. 21); as Marian admits, 'You are best for'n. More ladylike, and a better scholar than we' (ch. 31). So education contributes to her tragedy – even when Alec returns and offers, as one of the inducements for her to rejoin him, that he 'will put the children to a good school' (ch. 51). This novel, incidentally, begins the critique of the ancient universities which is continued in *Jude*. Angel's brothers have been to Cambridge, and are therefore subject to 'growing mental limitations'; they are parochial, snobbish and custom-ridden, and are thus typical of their kind – 'well-educated, hall-marked young men, correct to their remotest fibre; such unimpeachable models as are turned out yearly by the lathe of a systematic tuition' (ch. 25).

Jude the Obscure, I remarked, inherits the 'Pursuit of Knowledge under Difficulties' tradition: and the fiction and memoirs of the Victorian period contain many such working-class intellectuals. *Alton Locke, Felix Holt* and *The Life of Thomas Cooper, by Himself* may serve as reminders.[38] But the *Saturday Review* was right to recognize Hardy's profound originality here:

For the first time in English literature the almost intolerable difficulties that beset an ambitious man of the working class – the snares, the obstacles, the countless rejections and humiliations by which our society eludes the services of these volunteers – receive adequate treatment. . . . [And, after quoting from the closing chapter –] That is the voice of the educated proletarian, speaking more distinctly than it has ever spoken in English literature. The man is, indeed, at once an individual and a type. There is no other novelist alive with the breadth of sympathy, the knowledge, or the power for the creation of Jude. (Cox, 281, 283)

Hardy was indeed justified in his conviction that here was something that the world ought to be shown 'and I am the one to show it to them'. Different though Jude manifestly is from him in many particulars (Hardy was not a lone orphan, his family circumstances were more favourable, he was not over-given to the bottle, he became a successful professional man without excessive difficulty, and so on), there was enough similarity in temperament and disposition between character and creator to help Hardy to imagine Jude with special thoroughness. This is the only Hardy character whose childhood and adolescence, as well as adult life, are shown, and it constitutes much his best presentation of childhood – very dependent, of course, upon introspection and memory, for almost every item of Jude's reading (and of Sue's too), besides many particular episodes and moods, can be traced to Hardy himself, as the *Life*, the *Literary Notes*, and other evidence, clearly show. (But though we see Jude at his strenuous private reading, we never see him, or any other Hardy character, actually at school; as I have said, Hardy is interested less in the process than in the results of education.) Jude's fatal attraction to Christminster certainly derives in part from Hardy's early notion of going 'at least to Cambridge' – a comically dismissive locution (given its period-reference) about one of England's two great universities and explicable only in terms of Hardy's having an *arrière-pensée* about the Oxford/Christminster to which Jude had aspired: so, willy-nilly, Hardy was recognizing the association. Jude was thwarted both by that 'something wrong somewhere in our social formulas' (VI, 1) and by those 'two Arch Enemies' within, 'my weakness for women, and my impulse to strong liquor' (VI, 3), and this combination of circumstances gave Hardy the materials for a much richer novel, in this area of its attention, than *Alton Locke* or *Felix Holt*. The educational theme is further enriched by its dealing with the aspirations and careers of Phillotson and Sue Bridehead. Hardy's own 'weakness for women', which induced him to describe Sue's intellect as having 'scintillated like a star' and 'played like lambent lightning' (VI, 3), does small damage to the novel, and he corrected this over-estimate a decade later when he described her as half-educated. Sue, it may be added, helps in the deployment of the two major concerns which interact with the educational theme (and the class-issues raised by it) — matters of sex and marriage, and of religion and doubt. These concerns replace the political enquiry common in earlier novels in this area (Alton Locke was a Chartist, Felix Holt a Radical). Jude had ample cause to resent 'our social formulas', but he does not become an activist seeking to change them and he confesses indeed that he cannot discover just what is wrong (VI, 1). Hardy was not much interested in politics; Clym Yeobright's earlier social reformism, one notices, fades away — as much, one suspects, because Hardy lost interest in it as because Clym's ideas and preoccupations change. I am unconvinced by Terry Eagleton's argument that Sue's bourgeois individualism, influenced by J. S. Mill, is intended to be seen as 'in conflict with Jude's more communal and collectivist ethic'.[39]

'My scheme, or dream, is to be a university graduate, and then to be ordained,' Phillotson announces in the opening chapter, which also contains warnings that Jude is 'romantic', 'enthusiastic', 'whimsical', and is over-estimating his departing schoolmaster. The novel, which began publication under the title *The Simpletons*, makes emphatic use of the imagery of *dream, mirage, halo, glow-fog* and the like. The adult Jude is attracted to Sue by a photograph of her 'in a broad hat, with radiating folds under the brim like the rays of a halo' (II, 1). Soon afterwards he calls on Phillotson, 'an obviously much chastened and disappointed man', and his appearance 'destroyed at one stroke the halo which had surrounded the schoolmaster's figure in Jude's imagination ever since their parting' (II, 4). But above all, of course, Christminster is seen — literally at first, when the boy Jude strains his eyes to see the city, miles away in the sunset light — under a halo: but also he is, very understandably in a lonely innocent village bookworm, idealizing this 'heavenly Jerusalem' or 'city of light'. There are phases in his adult life when Jude awakens from his dream:

He saw what a curious and cunning glamour the neighbourhood of the place had exercised over him. To get there and live there, to move among the churches and halls and become imbued with the *genius loci*, had seemed to his dreaming youth, as the spot shaped its charms to him from its halo on the horizon, the obvious and ideal thing to do. . . . Well, all that was clear to him amounted to this, that the whole scheme had burst up, like an iridescent soap-bubble, under the touch of a reasoned enquiry. (II, 6)

But he never frees himself of this dream: the point is made nicely when, long after he had abandoned hope of becoming a student, Jude exhibits at the Great Wessex Agricultural Show a model of Cardinal College, and three years later is selling Christminster cakes at Kennetbridge Fair. 'Just like Jude. A ruling passion,' Arabella remarks. 'What a queer fellow he is, and always will be' (V, 7), and Sue, who has never been under the spell of Christminster, echoes Arabella, and realizes that he will never escape it. As she sits in their dreary lodging where

> . . . the outer walls of Sarcophagus College – silent, black and windowless – threw their four centuries of gloom, bigotry, and decay into the little room she occupied, shutting out the moonlight by night and the sun by day . . . [she] thought of the strange operation of a simple-minded man's ruling passion, that . . . he was still haunted by his dream. Even now he did not distinctly hear the freezing negative that these scholared walls had echoed to his desire. (VI, 2)

The judgement and the view are Sue's, but the accents are very much Hardy's too, and it was he who had arranged for the family to lodge where the deadly-named College's walls shut out the light.

A dozen years after *Jude* there appeared a report crucial in the history and development of adult education, *Oxford and Working-class Education*. 'It is undeniable,' it stated, 'that in spite of the presence in Oxford of a considerable number of comparatively poor men, Oxford is in the main the University of the wealthier classes.' For various reasons, the chances of 'poor students' gaining admission had declined during the nineteenth century, but in the previous twenty or thirty years there had undoubtedly been a 'growing demand for a University education . . . among workpeople' ('new classes are pushing upwards with new needs') and the report made recommendations about how Oxford should respond to this demand, particularly by 'mature students' such as Jude.[40] 'We are a little beforehand, that's all,' says Sue, about their multiple difficulties (V, 4). The prospects of Jude and his like getting into Oxford, or any other university, were minimal in the 1860s (the period of the action), and they are still not good; moreover, as Jude recognizes, personal weaknesses which would have been merely 'wild oats' in those millionaires' sons who elbow him off the pavement (III, 4) are fatal to an aspirant as precarious as he:

> 'It takes two or three generations to do what I tried to do in one; and my impulses — affections — vices perhaps they should be called — were too strong not to hamper a man without advantages; who should be as cold-blooded as a fish and as selfish as a pig to have a really good chance of being one of his country's worthies' (VI, 1)

— should be, indeed, like the brothers in 'A Tragedy of Two Ambitions'. A 'tragedy of unfulfilled aims', Hardy called it in the Preface: but the dream/halo imagery alerts the reader to the fact that Jude's aspirations, like Phillotson's, are not only unlikely to be achieved but are also illfounded: Christminster is not 'the intellectual and spiritual granary of this country' (II, 6) and all the other fine things that Jude imputes. Even in the darkness, on his arrival there, he has an intimation of this; he fails to register it, but the reader does. He has been casting a professional eye and finger over the medieval mouldings and carvings, 'their extinct air . . . accentuated by the rottenness of the stones. It seemed impossible that modern thought could house itself is such decrepit and superseded chambers' (II, 1). Next morning, indeed, 'What at night had been perfect and ideal was by day the more or less defective real,' but he 'soon lost under the stress of his old idea' his momentary 'true illumination' that work in the stoneyard was an effort as worthy as scholarly study — though Hardy immediately qualifies this 'truth' by insisting that the mason-work on which Jude was engaged was a fossil-activity, imitation-medieval stonework being akin to this medieval university in its irrelevance to 'contemporary logic and vision' (II, 2). Jude did not see this at the time, Hardy comments. But Jude never does sort out these multiple ironies, nor does Hardy quite do so: and Sue, though an effective questioner of Jude's ideals, is too shrill and too inconsistent to perform this function. Christminster is blamed for being too snobbish and inflexible to find a place for Jude (the attack culminates in the Duke of Hamptonshire 'and a lot more illustrious gents of that sort' getting their honorary degrees while he lies dead [VI, 11]), but what Christminster teaches and stands for – its medievalism – makes study there a dubious benefit anyway. Perhaps, says Jude, reverting to the dream imagery, 'it will soon wake up, and be generous [to the Self-taught]. I pray so!' (V, 8), and he refers to new 'schemes afoot for making the University less exclusive, and extending its influence' (VI, 10) – but not for making that influence more relevant to the times. Hardy's earlier impulse to use 'the town life' of Christminster, its 'struggling men and women', as a critique of the University – they were 'the reality of Christminster . . . the real Christminster life' (II, 6) – is not developed. We see too little of it, or indeed of any of the life surrounding the protagonists; but anyway the notion of making urban proletarian life operate as a substantiated critique of traditional high culture is so radical that Hardy's imagination can only glance at it (and he deserves credit for that); he is incapable of pursuing this idea to the point where it might become interesting, let alone challenging.

Referring, in his 1912 Preface to *Jude*, to the difficulties 'down to twenty or thirty years back of acquiring knowledge in letters without pecuniary means', Hardy remarked that it had been suggested that Ruskin College – established only three years after its publication, to cater for working-class students – 'should have been called the College of Jude the Obscure'. In a conversation in 1906 he had gone further: 'He considered that the foundation of Ruskin College in Oxford was due to *Jude*.' But Mr. Paul Yorke, author of a recent study of the early history of the College, found no evidence that its founders were in any way influenced by Hardy; no one concerned seems to have mentioned Jude, the Librarian of Ruskin, Mr. David Horsefield, tells me. This is surprising, but it is an irony which Hardy, on reflection, might have preferred even to that flattering illusion of having prompted the foundation of an Oxford college. An essay on Hardy may appropriately end on a wry note. His last night away from Max Gate, in 1923, was spent in Oxford, where Queen's College had recently elected him to an Honorary Fellowship. 'He was obviously happy to be in Oxford, and happy, I think, to be of it,' recalled his cicerone. He called in at Christ Church, the most aristocratic of the Colleges, but not at Ruskin. The trip was otherwise quite a *Jude* occasion. On the way to Oxford he had revisited the Salisbury Training College which, according to the *Life*, 'is faithfully described in *Jude the Obscure*', and had then paused at Fawley (the Marygreen of the novel, and the village with Hardy family associations which had given Jude his surname). But when, in Oxford, he was asked about Jude's village, 'he spoke briefly and depreciatingly of "that fictitious person. If there ever was such a person . . ."' – a curiously defensive phrase to use about a character from a novel (*Life*, 419–21).

He spoke 'depreciatingly', no doubt, because he was always prickly when questioned about this character with whom readers most commonly identified him; also perhaps because he did not wish the balm of those gratifying days in Oxford to be fouled by reminders of harsher views from years ago. By now he had sweetened Christminster in retrospect. 'I had no feeling against Oxford in particular,' he wrote:

> Christminster is of course the tragic influence of Jude's drama *in one sense*, *but innocently so*, and merely as crass obstruction. By the way it is not meant to be exclusively Oxford, but any old-fashioned university about the date of the story, 1860–1870, before there were such chances for poor men as there are now [1926]. (*Life*, 433; italics mine)

And if by now he was somewhat dismissive of 'that fictitious personage' Jude, he also tended to treat children with little more cordiality than Farmer Troutham did Jude. 'He was not amiable,' recalled a Dorchester boy whose family did jobs at Max Gate; 'by golly, he frightened me.' He was gruff, if not hostile, to children – had indeed 'a strong dislike' of them, according to one of the Max Gate cooks: 'And during the whole time I was there he showed that dislike in a number of ways. . . . Hardy was very unpleasant to my little boy. . . . He said my [four-year-old] son might poison him. . . . . That finished me.'[41] A man so uncouth to children must be pitied: and Hardy the novelist had never specialized in the young. As often, one is reminded that the novelist is much larger-souled than the man who lived at Max Gate and wrote the *Life* and the Prefaces.

NOTES

1. Hardy, letter to Macmillan, 25 July 1868, in *Letters to Macmillan*, ed. Simon Nowell-Smith, 1967, 130.
2. Edmund Gosse, 'Thomas Hardy's Lost Novel', *Times* [London], 22 January 1928, cited by Terry Coleman, Introduction to Hardy's *An Indiscretion in the Life of an Heiress*, 1976, 12.
3. Letter to Havelock Ellis, 29 April 1883, cited in Ellis's *From Marlowe to Shaw*, ed. John Gawsworth, 1950, 7. Hardy was here gratefully adopting Ellis's suggestion (*Westminster Review*, April 1883) that Stephen Smith in *A Pair of Blue Eyes* was 'the first serious study of Hardy's favourite hero', whose ancestry Ellis traces to these Goethe and George Eliot characters (*ibid.*, 240–1; repr. Cox, 112). Clym Yeobright, in whose face 'could be dimly seen the typical countenance of the future' (*Return of the Native*, III, 1) is, as Ellis notes, such another.
4. 'Few men have used their own experiences so much as Mr Hardy,' argued a reviewer in the *British Quarterly Magazine* (1881), who correctly deduced from the novels that he was a man 'sprung of a race of labouring men' in Dorset, who had become an architect (Cox, 82).
5. *Life*, 207–8. For a useful survey of Hardy's relationship to Jude see J. O. Bailey, 'Ancestral Voices in *Jude the Obscure*', in *The Classic British Novel*, ed. Howard M. Harper, Jr., and Charles Edge, 1972, 143–65. Roger Sale, 'In Hardy Country', *New York Review of Books*, 23 June 1977, 42–4, offers some interesting further speculations about the experiences lying behind *Jude*.
6. William Empson, *Some Versions of Pastoral*, 1935, 4. When his secretary, May O'Rourke, suggested that Stinsford (the Mellstock of the novels) was 'a Gray's Elegy sort of place', his 'voice and face changed completely' as he said, 'It *is* Stoke Poges!' and she could 'never find words to convey what I saw in him then' (reported in *Concerning Thomas Hardy: A Composite Portrait from Memory*, ed. D. F. Barber from materials collected by J. Stevens Cox, 1968, 132). Michael Millgate notes echoes of Gray's 'Elegy' in *Jude* (*Thomas Hardy: His Career as a Novelist*, 1971, 318).
7. *Longman's Magazine*, July 1883, repr. in *Thomas Hardy's Personal Writings*, ed. Harold Orel, 1967, 169; hereafter cited as Orel.
8. Grace Stebbings, *Walter Benn* (c. 1890), cited in Victor E. Neuberg, *Popular Literature: A History and a Guide*, 1977, 191.
9. W. J. Reader, *Professional Men: the Rise of the Professional Classes in Nineteenth-Century England*, 1966, 206.
10. *Life*. 20. For a more dispassionate and more cheerful view see J. S. Bratton, *The Victorian Popular Ballad* (1975).

11. Mrs. Humphry Ward, *A Writer's Recollections*, 1918, 98.

12. See my *Dickens and Education* (1963) and, for general background, Peter Coveney's *Poor Monkey: The Child in Literature* (1957), revised as *The Image of Childhood* (1967).

13. 1850–1 report, cited by J. Stevens Cox, *Thomas Hardy Year Book*, No. 5, 1975, 12; *Life*, 18. Cox reprints there memories of Hardy as a child, by a schoolfellow ('P'), originally published in *Sunday at Home*, May 1915.

14. Edmund Blunden, *Thomas Hardy*, 1942, 8–9.

15. Robert Gittings, *Young Thomas Hardy*, 1975, 24.

16. *Ibid.*, 21. Gittings' biography offers the fullest reliable account of Hardy as a boy, and this essay owes much to it.

17. Emma Clifford, 'The Child, the Circus, and *Jude the Obscure*', *Cambridge Journal*, VII, 1954, 522; *Life*, 16.

18. Ernest Harding, in *Concerning Thomas Hardy* (above, note 6), 42. On Hardy and Louisa Harding, see Gittings, 26, 89, 215.

19. Elliott Felkin, 'Days [1918–19] with Thomas Hardy', *Encounter*, XVIII, 1962, 32.

20. Millgate (above, note 6), 39–40. Cf. *The Literary Notes of Thomas Hardy* (a major commonplace-book), ed. Lennart A. Björk, 2 vols., Gothenberg, 1974. Arnold Kettle, in a judicious discussion, remarks: 'Hardy was, for an artist, an exceptionally well-read man . . . ; but his sensibility was not at all that of the typical modern intellectual' ('Hardy the Novelist: A Reconsideration,' repr. *The Nineteenth Century Novel: Critical Essays and Documents*, ed. Kettle, 1972, 263).

21. Felkin (above, note 19), 28.

22. This paragraph is based upon *Life*, 33–4, 50, 207–8, 361, 376; Gittings, 45–6, 53, 90; Millgate, 37, 365; Bailey (above, note 5), 151–2. According to a nephew of Horace Moule's, Hardy did have a sense of inferiority about not having gone to a university (Timothy O'Sullivan, *Thomas Hardy*, 1975, 136). For an account of the establishment and status of Theological Colleges, see F. W. B. Bullock, *A History of Ridley Hall, Cambridge*, 1941, I, 9–19.

23. *Life*, 371. On Mary and Kate Hardy at college and as teachers, see Gittings, 55, 66, 73, 100, 122–3, 208. On Tryphena's career, see Gittings, 55–6, 72, 107–13, 120–2, 147, 156; Lois Deacon and Terry Coleman, *Providence and Mr. Hardy* (1966); F. B. Pinion in *Notes and Queries*, CCXVI, 1971, 255–6, and CCXVII, 1972, 430–1; Anna Winchcombe, 'Letters from Tryphena Sparks', *Thomas Hardy Year Book*, No. 3, 1972–3, 97–9.

24. Emma Hardy, *Some Recollections*, ed. Evelyn Hardy and Robert Gittings, 1961, 17.

25. Cf. Mary Hardy's 'doom' (above), and the short story 'Schoolmistress and Organist' in Dickens's magazine *All the Year Round*, XI, 1864, 154–6. Ability to

help the local church in this way was not expected only of schoolmistresses, as again fiction from these decades shows; Dickens's Bradley Headstone's 'great store of teacher's knowledge' includes the capacity to 'play the great church organ mechanically' (*Our Mutual Friend*, 1864–5, II, 1).

26. Gittings, 154.

27. Evelyn Hardy, 'Thomas Hardy: Plots for Five Unpublished Short Stories', *London Magazine*, V, 1958, 35–6.

28. *ELH*, XXXIV, 1967, 392–6; *'painful'*, in the quotation below, his italics.

29. G. K. Chesterton, *The Victorian Age in Literature*, revised edn., 1914, 143.

30. In one of his two stories written for children, 'Our Exploits at West Poley' (1883), a very moralistic adventure story, Hardy lectures his juvenile readers about 'success'. A leading, and heroic, character is the retired gentleman who calls himself 'the Man who has Failed', but the narrator explains that 'the losers in the world's battle are often the very men who, too late for themselves, have the clearest perception of what constitutes success; while the successful men are frequently blinded to the same by the tumult of their own progress' (ch. 1).

31. Hardy's *Literary Notes* (above, note 20) contain more from Comte's *System of Positive Philosophy* than from any other single work. For a discussion, see Björk's editorial comments, I, xxvi, and II, 286–8, 300–1.

32. Douglas Brown, *Thomas Hardy*, 1954, 59; Millgate, 137–9; Merryn Williams, *Thomas Hardy and Rural England*, 1972, 142–5; Björk, ed., *Literary Notes*, II, 300.

33. J. S. Mill, *Utilitarianism*, 1863, ch. 2.

34. The Fancy Days and Ethelberta Chickerels were more likely than the Egbert Maynes to rise socially through meeting and marrying their 'superiors'. An H.M.I. remarked in 1843: 'Although I have met with several instances of the schoolmistress being received at the clergyman's table, I scarcely recollect an instance out of London (except the dean of Bangor) of a clergyman's shaking hands with, or even talking familiarly with, the parochial schoolmaster' (quoted by John Hurt, *Education in Evolution: Church, State, Society and Popular Education 1800–1870*, 1972 edn., 110).

35. Conversation reported in Henry W. Nevinson, *Thomas Hardy*, 1941, 15.

36. End of ch. 15; see J. T. Laird, *The Shaping of 'Tess of the d'Urbervilles'*, 1975, 119.

37. *Jude*, III, 3. Hurt (above, note 34), ch. 5, gives a good account of the social origins of such recruits to teaching. 'A certain amount of attainment' was required of applicants to Whitelands Training College, 'but the principal point attended to in the admission or retention of a pupil is character or conduct'; success in teaching was found to depend less upon 'literary acquirements' than upon 'moral qualities' and 'religious principle' – two official statements by the Whitelands College Council, 1850, cited by Joyce Collins, 'Training Women

Elementary Teachers: Whitelands College 1841–1881' (M.Sc. dissertation, C.N.A.A., 1977, 43–4). Whitelands, as the most prestigious though not quite the first of the women's colleges, set the tone – though on this issue a consensus obtained.

38. I have discussed some of these figures in *Thomas Cooper the Chartist: Byron and the 'Poets of the Poor'*, Nottingham, 1969.

39. Introduction to the New Wessex edition of *Jude*, 1974, 15.

40. *Oxford and Working-class Education*, 1908 (rev. edn., 1909, repr. 1951), 21–2, 26–7, 41, 53. On Ruskin College, established in 1899 and featured in this Report, see below.

41. *Concerning Thomas Hardy* (above, note 6), 61, 117; see also pp. 111, 116, 153–4.

3: Hardy and Regionalism

GEORGE WING

WHEN WE LOOK AT *The Dynasts* and, with Hardy, take a god's eye view of the world, we gain an impression of some premonitory film, of spectacular effect, portraying extensive movements of history, people, and affairs, armies marching to and straggling back from Moscow, navies scattered about the oceans, the exoduses of tribes, nations. Hardy is always susceptible to drama and melodrama but mostly on a smaller scale than this:

> The nether sky opens, and Europe is disclosed as a prone and emaciated figure, the Alps shaping like a backbone, and the branching mountain-chains like ribs, the peninsular plateau of Spain forming a head. Broad and lengthy lowlands stretch from the north of France across Russia like a grey-green garment hemmed by the Ural mountains and the glistening Arctic Ocean.
>
> The point of view then sinks downwards through space, and draws near to the surface of the perturbed countries, where the peoples, distressed by events which they did not cause, are seen writhing, crawling, heaving, and vibrating in their various cities and nationalities.[1]

This description is taken from the Fore Scene of Part First of Hardy's epic-drama; it renders an apocalyptic view of the geographical features and the convulsion of nations of a warring Europe, and interprets the world as apprehended through the blurred vision and indifferent consciousness of the Immanent Will, the rapt Determinator, the Great Foresightless. We are immediately aware of an interesting departure. Writing, as he most often does in his prose fiction, within the microcosm of hamlet, pig sty or inglenook, Hardy is still conscious of the 'web enorm'. His exploration extends from rural corners to the macrocosm, not only of the physical world beyond, but also of the unmapped reaches of the mind and the heart and the spirit.

In his novels, then, Hardy wrote from the earth, the soil, generally some cottage or purlieu of Wessex. Even in *The Dynasts* this view from the 'Overworld', where there is exhibited 'as one organism the anatomy of life and movement in all humanity and vitalized matter' (p. 6), closes in to a scene of humbler proportions: 'The time is a fine day in March 1805. A highway crosses the ridge, which is near the sea, and the south coast is seen bounding the landscape below, the open Channel extending beyond' (p. 8). Through the cosmic mists we distinguish Wessex at the beginning of *The Dynasts*, and although admittedly we then move to the Office of the Minister of Marine in Paris, to the Old House of Commons in London, to the Harbour of Boulogne, to the House of a Lady of Quality in London, to the Cathedral in Milan, and to the Dockyard in Gibraltar, we shortly return to the Wessex base, the rock bed of the novels and stories. The scene now is Rainbarrows Beacon, Egdon Heath:

> Night in mid-August of the same summer. A lofty ridge of heathland reveals itself dimly, terminating in an abrupt slope, at the summit of which are three tumuli. On the sheltered side of the most prominent of these stands a hut of turves with a brick chimney. In front are two ricks of fuel, one of heather and furze for quick ignition, the other of wood, for slow burning. Something in the feel of the darkness and in the personality of the spot imparts a sense of uninterrupted space around. . . . (p. 48)

And a few pages later the 'stage direction' reads:

> The two men hasten to the hut, and are heard striking a flint and steel. Returning with a lit lantern they ignite a wisp of furze, and with this set the first stack of fuel in a blaze. The private of the Locals and his wife hastily retreat by the light of the flaming beacon, under which the purple rotundities of the heath show like bronze, and the pits like the eye-sockets of a skull. (p. 53)

I have made this brief excursion into the physical setting of Part First of *The Dynasts* with its rapid switches from a nebulous universe to a continent, to capitals, to a ridge, to a turf hut, in order to contrast the sequence with that in the novels. The novels generally begin with a turf hut, or an inn, a cart, a lane, a hedgerow, a wood. And at first all seems static, all but immobilized into rustic statuary. The primary concern is localized into petty domesticity and agricultural chores. Whenever there is action it is slow moving, slipping imperceptibly into the ponderous cycle of the seasons. Yet within the stability of the physical geography Hardy bursts out, *Dynasts*-like, to wider horizons, but not necessarily physical, and we find him charting the human heart, mapping the overspills of human bile and measuring the effects of grotesque consequences of chance.

To describe Hardy as a regional novelist is to utter a cliché. Yet Hardy, in adopting the word Wessex and seeking a geographical 'unity' for his novels, warns that his imaginative world is different from the existing Dorset and adjacent counties:

> . . . it was in the chapters of *Far from the Madding Crowd*, as they appeared month by month in a popular magazine, that I first ventured to adopt the word 'Wessex' from the pages of early English history, and give it a fictitious significance as the existing name of the district once included in that extinct kingdom. The series of novels I projected being mainly of the kind called local, they seemed to require a territorial definition of some sort to lend unity to their scene. Finding that the area of a single county did not afford a canvas large enough for this purpose, and that there were objections to an invented name, I disinterred the old one. . . .
>
> Since then the appellation I had thought to reserve to the horizons and landscapes of a partly real, partly dream country, has become more and more popular as a practical provincial definition; and the dream-country has, by degrees, solidified into a utilitarian region which people can go to, take a house in, and write to the papers from. But I ask all good and idealistic readers to forget this, and to refuse steadfastly to believe that there are any inhabitants of a Victorian Wessex outside these volumes in which their lives and conversations are detailed. (Preface)

Much of this passage is incontestable if we accept the mystery of creative process in literature; but, as is so often the case in personal reminiscence, Hardy, partly because of pedantic endeavour to identify artistic purpose, partly because of characteristic secretiveness, provides challenging ambiguities. The novels are 'of the kind called local' and they are set among 'horizons and landscapes of a partly real, partly dream country'. Yet informed Hardy cartographers, like Denys Kay-Robinson,[2] have drawn detailed maps of the novels and stories, and indeed, at the front of every novel, we find maps of the region, on which not all of the place names are fictitious, which are an exact reproduction of the maps of the south-west counties. Sometimes a house or church is moved a mile or so from its original site, but Dorchester (Casterbridge), Stinsford (Mellstock), Salisbury (Melchester) and natural features whose names Hardy does not care to alter – the River Frome, Bulbarrow, High-Stoy, Quantock Hills, Blackmoor Vale – are there and can be identified today, almost where you could 'take a house in'.

It is probably unwise to be too confident in the case of identification or derivation of character, but this also has regional implications. In the matter of characterization practically every novelist (that is, what used to be called the 'realistic' novelist – I am not concerned with writers of fantasy or science fiction) uses 'models' to some degree or other. These fictive superimpositions can, however, be taken too far. Mrs Nickleby is not Dickens's mother nor Mr. Micawber his father; Maggie Tulliver is not George Eliot as a young girl nor is Tom her brother. But there are elements of association in the above cases and, in reaffirming worthwhile truisms, I am convinced that certain intrinsicalities, a twist of behaviour, a particular of dress, a twinkle of eye or cast of mind in a 'real' person – or persons, in composite portraits – can contribute to the original firing of the imagined character. Such single and composite imaginings abound in Hardy's writings and, according to one's source, Tess is a farm girl from Puddletown, or Tryphena Sparks, or a cousin called Theresa and so on. So far as most characters are concerned, given the legitimate artistic miming of reality, they do in fact belong to the 'dream-world' of the Wessex region. But nevertheless they belong both to 'our' world in the matter of universal recognition, and to Hardy's in the matter of personal recall, in that aspects of many of them were suggested by certain idiosyncrasies of people of his acquaintance or knowledge – people who really walked the fields of Wessex.

Much of this is tentative and speculative ground but incidents and sequences of action can be more readily substantiated. Many are adapted from news items in the *Dorset County Chronicle* (Hardy's notebooks are full of reports of curious, often macabre, happenings he meticulously copied out from current or old issues), or based on country stories he heard at various times of his life, or on sights and happenings that he himself witnessed. There are, for example, a number of instances of a man selling his wife. In one of his notebooks in the Dorset County Museum – 'Facts – from Newspapers, Histories, Biographies, and other chronicles – (mainly Local)' – we read two entries from the *Chronicle* which were probably entered in 1883 or '84: 'Sale of wife at Stanford. Fellow sold her "for 2/wet and 2/dry" delivered her to the purchaser on the market hill on a halter; after which the trio retired to a p. house to quaff the heavy wet.' This was reported in the year 1826; and in 1827 we read:

> *SALE OF WIFE:* Man at Brighton, led a tidy looking young woman up to one of the stalls in the market, with a halter round her neck, and offered her for sale. A purchaser was soon found, who bought her for 30/–. Which he paid, and went off with this bargain amid the sneers and laughter of the mob, but not before the transaction was regularly entered by the clerk of the market book and his toll of 1/– paid. He also paid 1/– for the halter, and another 1/– to the man who performed the office of auctioneer. We understand then they were country people, and that the woman had two children by her husband, one of whom he consents to keep, and the other he throws in as a makeshift to the bargain.

Lennart A. Björk argues,[3] and I agree with him, that we cannot be too sure at what date Hardy made the entries in the notebooks or when in fact he read the items concerned, but it would be safe to assume that the beginning of *The Mayor of Casterbridge* had its source in some such story. Hardy, himself, frankly acknowledges sources:

> In December [1882] Hardy was told a story by a Mrs. Cross, a very old country-woman he met, of a girl she had known who had been betrayed and deserted by a lover. She kept her child by her own exertions, and lived bravely and throve. After a time the man returned poorer than she, and wanted to marry her; but she refused. He ultimately went into the Union workhouse. The young woman's conduct in not caring to be 'made respectable' won the novelist-poet's admiration, and he wished to know her name; but the old narrator said, 'Oh, never mind their names! They be dead and rotted by now.'

The eminently modern idea embodied in this example – of a woman's not becoming necessarily the chattel and slave of her seducer – impressed Hardy as being one of the first glimmers of woman's enfranchisement; and he made use of it in succeeding years in more than one case in his fiction and verse. (*Life*, 157)

A great friend and confidant of Hardy's, Hermann Lea, claims on the occasion of a sheep-washing: 'As I stood watching the operation I was taken back in thought to Weatherbury Farm – the sheep, the men, and most of all the conversation and remarks and exclamations. The utter realism of Hardy's writing forced itself upon one; only a writer who had actually watched and listened could have reproduced the scene in words. Later, I was to learn from Hardy's own life that he had ever striven to attempt description only of such things as he had actually experienced or learned by actual first-hand knowledge.'[4] This knowledge is a consequence, also, of hours of research in institutions like Greenwich Observatory and the British Museum as well as of an eclectic reading in literature, philosophy, art and science. But especially the oddnesses of human behaviour, reported in newspapers, related in taverns, gossiped about in the fields – and all collected and recorded diligently by Hardy – constitute many of the fibres of his fiction in the matter both of direct impact on the main action and of incidental appeal.

Places, people, stories, legends. Are we really 'to refuse steadfastly to believe that there are any inhabitants of a Victorian Wessex outside these volumes . . .'? The 'partly real, partly dream country' is obviously, at a primary level, identifiable with the Victorian Wessex outside the volumes in many matters of fact; in matters of extant landscape, of agricultural, pastoral, sylvan and coastal varieties; of the different settlements, each with local manners, local tongues, who inhabit the area from Reading, in the Thames valley, to Land's End; from Oxford – although I shall comment on the strict accuracy of this later – to Plymouth Sound; from Bristol to Portland Bill; from Barnstaple to Portsmouth. Hardy's Wessex comprises the fat peninsula of England lying west of the line Oxford–Reading–Portsmouth. It was the least urbanized and industrialized of Victorian England. Hardy's centre of it (as was indeed his own personal centre) was Dorset and Dorchester, and as you move into the idyllic centre from anywhere on the periphery, move into 'the Valley of the Great Dairies, the valley in which milk and butter grew to rankness', into the Valley of the River Frome, whose 'waters were clear as the pure River of Life shown to the Evangelist, rapid as the shadow of a cloud, with pebbly shallows that prattled to the sky all day long' (*Tess*, ch. 16); move into the market town of Dorchester itself which 'was the complement of the rural life around; not its urban opposite. Bees and butterflies in the cornfields at the top of the town, who desired to get to the meads at the bottom, took no circuitous course, but flew straight down High Street without any apparent consciousness that they were traversing strange latitudes' (*Mayor*, ch. 9) – you move not only to the lyrical centre of Wessex but also to the heart of Hardy's lyricism, for Hardy's fiction beats with poetic cadences which reflect the emotions and actions of his characters, his casual fortuities and his Wessex landscapes – whether they are presented in haunting or caustic, tender or aching, moods.

The Wessex novels, then (and I include the short stories), are set in a region where hamlets, rivers and hills can be identified even now. This is not to suppose that it is not also an imaginative land, preserved on printed pages, waiting to expand into the sensitivity of the reader. Hardy's imaginative Wessex belongs to a field of human activity different from that concerned with surveyor's levels and the mapping of configurations. As Hardy himself cartographically illustrates, his envisioned region can be geographically described on a map of the west of England but it can also be located on maps of heaven and hell and poetry – charts of subjectivity both to Hardy and his reader. The ordinance coordinates, whether of invention or reality, suggest an ambiguous propinquity in that they are obviously interdependent yet retain also their own spatial identity.

The Cliff without a Name, where Knight, in imminent danger of falling to his death, indulges in geological speculation and is eventually rescued by the shredded petticoat of Elfride, is invested with a peculiarly Hardyan aura of romance and drama and is certainly part of that intense dream world. The shed where they take Mrs. Yeobright and, in an attempt to save her, fry live adders after her fatal bite on Egdon Heath, is the scene of the culmination of a bitter mother-son relationship. The woodlands, where on Midsummer's Eve, Fitzpiers races after Suke Damson and seduces her, are alive that night with powerful charges of sexuality. And Farmer Troutham's ploughed field where the young Jude contemplates man's inhumanity to the birds is a place that afternoon of gloomy vision. But however much these places are vibrant with Hardy's imaginative eloquence, however much they belong to an intangible world of a special author's creation, they are still identifiable features in South-west England. There is also historical mirroring, as I have indicated, when the transplanting of the real into the invented is not so elusive of definition.

After having glanced, then, at the general disposition of the region of the two worlds, the real and the dream, in terms of geography and history, I think there might be value in any examination of these two worlds to notice what is static in them, what has movement, and the inter-relationship of the two states. In general the canon of Hardy's novels begins with what is entrenched, unprogressive and, as a consequence, seemingly untroubled, and then gradually there is more movement, more shifting of people and spirit – within the limits of the region – and this appears to mean progress towards discontent. Such an investigation will necessitate some proposals of trimming of attitudes, on Hardy's part, to character and place. I am aware that we cannot categorize satisfactorily in any work of art and so my arbitrary groupings will be seen to be interdependent and multidependent, however isolated the place, however self-sufficient the character, however removed the incident, I happen to select.

The novel which most obviously goes back to Hardy's family history is *Under the Greenwood Tree*. The time is the late 1830s. The place, Mellstock parish, is based on Stinsford parish, which includes the hamlets of Upper and Lower Bockhampton and it is presented as Hardy remembered it in his boyhood: 'This story of the Mellstock Quire and its old established west-gallery musicians . . . is intended to be a fairly true picture, at first hand, of the personages, ways, and customs which were common among such orchestral bodies in the villages of fifty or sixty years ago' (1896 Preface). The woods have moved in the intervening time. In the lane in which the instrumentalists of the quire are, at the beginning of the book, shambling in single file, where 'almost every species of tree has its voice as well as its feature', where 'the fir-trees sob and moan no less distinctly than they rock; the holly whistles as it battles with itself; the ash hisses amid its quiverings; the beech rustles while its flat boughs rise and fall . . .' (I, 1), there are now no trees. The once treeless Egdon Heath, on the other hand, less than a mile down the lane, is now covered with extensive woodland.

The majority of the inhabitants of Mellstock were rooted like the trees and were so for generations, although no doubt like the trees they were eventually dispersed. Hardy, however, establishes a little acre or two within the bigger region of Wessex and although Dick Dewy and his father, being tranters, are more mobile, the furthest Dick travels is to Budmouth Regis (Weymouth) and the furthest most of the characters travel is to Yalbury Wood (about two miles) for Dick's and Fancy's wedding assembly. There is also the business of the nutting expedition and Dick's journey to the next parish to the funeral of a friend. Given this very restricted mobility in and around the village, the setting of the novel is fixed practically in one spot. From not too far off the scene would look stationary, differing in overall dress only according to season, and in this lies one of the stabilizing faces of Hardy's regionalism. 'A Rural Painting of the Dutch School' is the sub-title of *Under the Greenwood Tree*. The paintings of this school are becalmed, fixed in space and time, and yet by their very rootedness they imply a reassuring serenity, the unhurriedness of peaceful routine. The positioning of Mellstock parish, then, with its seasonal doings, presents a 'fairly true picture' of Hardy's boyhood, pastorally contained.

In general, contentment lies in staying close to the village. Hearth and church and Mr. Penny's bootmaker's shop are centres of assembly – the last exclusively male. The functions of living are governed by the drama of the seasons, of births, marriages, deaths, and by recall of the past. Inward or outward movement mean intrusion, disturbance – at worst discontent and sorrow. Fancy Day (who is an early Grace Melbury) and Parson Maybold (who is not the kind of alien intruder I shall mention later) move into this long settled community, where custom has been ritualized for generations, and by their very presence interrupt the familiarity of routine, a routine marked by its tranquillizing repetitions. Their intrusion is eventually reconciled in this, the second published novel, but they are harbingers of greater turbulence, of the invasions of Bathsheba Everdene and Troy, of Eustacia and Wildeve, of Lucetta and Farfrae, of Grace and Fitzpiers, of d'Urberville and Clare, in their respective novels. Hardyan regionalism, then, in one of its identities, means, without any indication of atrophy, staying put, existence through generations in one spot. And to a large extent Wessex implies a scatter of such entrenched places where inside humour, recollection and ungarnished wisdom are jealously guarded.

As one novel follows another, mobility increases (the first published novel, *Desperate Remedies*, in some ways a frantic imitation of Wilkie Collins' plots, is an exception to my proposal). Characters and action move further and oftener from the centre of Wessex – occasionally outside of its borders as in the third novel, *A Pair of Blue Eyes* – and movement is often associated with an intensifying of sexual frustration and misapprehension. Yet in all the novels, even in *Tess* and *Jude*, there are fixed points of local geography and human reference. Although the ancient maltster, Jacob's father, has in his lifetime brewed ale and hoed turnips around the neighbouring villages and farms of Weatherbury, he has been installed in Warren's Malthouse for 'one-and-thirty years come Candlemas'. Here, in advanced age and having endured a span of generations, he has set up an island of alcoholic refuge and reminiscence and the minutest change anywhere he has visited in the neighbourhood disturbs him:

'Sit down, Shepherd Oak,' continued the ancient man of malt. 'And how was the old place at Norcombe, when ye went for your dog? I should like to see the old familiar spot; but faith, I shouldn't know a soul there now.'
'I suppose you wouldn't. 'Tis altered very much.'
'Is it true that Dicky Hill's wooden cider-house is pulled down?'
'O yes – years ago, and Dicky's cottage just above it.'
'Well, to be sure!'
'Yes; and Tompkins's old apple-tree is rooted that used to bear two hogsheads of cider, and no help from other trees.'
'Rooted? – you don't say it! Ah! stirring times we live in – stirring times.'
'And you can mind the old well that used to be in the middle of the place? That's turned into a solid iron pump with a large stone trough, and all complete.'
'Dear, dear – how the face of nations alter, and what we live to see nowadays. . . .' (Ch. 15)

Hardy has often been attacked on the grounds of the vulgar infelicity of his yokels. I am not too concerned in this essay with the flippancy or otherwise of phrases like 'the ancient man of malt', 'Ah! stirring times we live in', and 'how the face of nations alter', except to declare that we either warm to this kind of comic patronage or not. Much depends on whether the reader's perceptivity is such that it can accommodate everything that is implied here – artifice combined with sympathy, trust in an alleged pessimist's comic observations or wonder at the sheer invention of gerontic gossip. What is important, what bubbles from the well of seriousness, is the concern that the old man reveals over what appear to him enormities of change in the narrow world of his cognizance. This is an intentionally comic scene which masks acidulous undertows. The insult to the old maltster's memory occasioned by the installing of the solid iron pump screens the immediate losses of Oak's sheep and girl and future loss of Bathsheba's self-respect. But in Hardy's world change often means loss. The word 'tradition' is much repeated. In 'A Tradition of Eighteen Hundred and Four' Solomon Selby relates: 'My father, as you mid know, was a shepherd all his life, and lived out by the Cove four miles yonder, where I wa born and lived likewise, till I moved here shortly afore I was married.' Places, for the old maltster, ought not to change. And perhaps not for Hardy. In the short story, 'The Three Strangers', we hear the author's voice:

> Among the few features of agricultural England which retain an appearance but little modified by the lapse of centuries, may be reckoned the long, grassy and furzy downs, coombs, or ewe-leases, as they are called according to their kind, that fill a large area of certain counties in the south and south-west. If any mark of human occupation is met with hereon, it usually takes the form of a solitary cottage of some shepherd.

An elegiac note haunts this passage in which the indirect lament concerns those features of agricultural England which were being modified. It is the older people, those who work in the fields and on the downs and in the woods, who cling to their plain homes because they are part of their tradition, their being. And when they are evicted by uncaring landowners on Lady Day or because the leasehold has lapsed – as happened to the Durbeyfield family and to Giles Winterborne – little private worlds fall apart.

Sometimes their homes are lonely and isolated like the shepherd's hut in 'The Three Strangers' or like Geoffrey Day's gamekeeper's cottage; sometimes they are huddled together in hamlets; sometimes they are menial appurtenances of a farm or a manor. One such, in *Two on a*

Tower, is Haymoss Fry's, 'a homely barley driller, born under the eaves of your ladyship's outbuildings, in a manner of speaking . . .'. Haymoss is a rural 'original', in a Smollett sense, and, like the old maltster, is shaped along the swell of the countryside by wind and labour. At times he becomes part of the landscape, scarcely distinguishable from the fields he works. Lady Constantine meets him when returning from her first visit to the tower: 'When in the midst of the [ploughed] field, a dark spot on an area of brown, there crossed her path a moving figure, whom it was as difficult to distinguish from the earth he trod as the caterpillar from its leaf, by reason of the excellent match between his clothes and the clods. He was one of a dying-out generation who retained the principle, nearly unlearnt now, that a man's habiliments should be in harmony with his environment'. (Ch. 1)

There are many such enclaves of withdrawal in the novels where the central action travels about Wessex, and always we apprehend a regret at the need for shift and change. In *Far From the Madding Crowd* events start at Norcombe, though the story is centred in Weatherbury and events move from there to Weymouth, Dorchester and Bath. The narrative in *Two on a Tower* looks up to the immensity of the stellar universe and Swithin St. Cleeve journeys far overseas, but Welland House and its adjacent tower remain the fictional core. Yet static retreats like Warren's Malthouse and Haymoss's cottage, and acres of pasture and plough, persist stubbornly; and despite broadcast hints of imminent dislocation they represent a Hardyan mood of survival, as indeed he wrote in a poem as late as 1915:

> Only thin smoke without flame
> From the heaps of couch-grass;
> Yet this will go onward the same
> Though Dynasties pass.
>> (*'In Time of "The Breaking of Nations"'*)

Hardy did not maintain, either before or afterwards, this certainty of restoration to times past; but even in *Jude*, that novel of human anguish with its concomitant restlessness, the sites of human history, although they often carry harsh and sardonic suggestion, provide this sense of enduring:

The fresh harrow-lines seemed to stretch like the channellings in a piece of new corduroy, lending a meanly utilitarian air to the expanse, taking away its gradations, and depriving it of all history beyond that of the few recent months, though to every clod and stone there are really attached associations enough and to spare – echoes of songs from ancient harvest-days, of spoken words, and of sturdy deeds. Every inch of ground had been the site, first or last, of energy, gaiety, horse-play, bickering, weariness. Groups of gleaners had squatted in the sun on every square yard. Love-matches that had populated the adjoining hamlet had been made up there between reaping and carrying. Under the hedge which divided the field from a distant plantation girls had given themselves to lovers who would not turn their heads to look at them by the next harvest; and in that ancient cornfield many a man had made love-promises to a woman at whose voice he had trembled by the next seed-time after fulfilling them in the church adjoining. (I, 2)

At least this field, despite the sardonicism, is peaceful and on occasions a matter for pleasure. There is, especially later, variety in the concept of immobility, when immobility does not necessarily imply content. We read of another field, which also presumably has its durability of existence and on which humans work:

The swede-field in which she and her companion were set hacking was a stretch of a hundred odd acres, in one patch, on the highest ground of the farm, rising above stony lanchets or lynchets – the outcrop of siliceous veins in the chalk formation, composed of myriads of loose white flints in bulbous, cusped, and phallic shapes. The upper half of each turnip had been eaten off by the live-stock, and it was the business of the two women to grub up the lower or earthy half of the root with a hooked fork called a hacker, that it might be eaten also. Every leaf of the vegetable having already been consumed, the whole field was in colour a desolate drab; it was a complexion without features, as if a face, from chin to brow, should be only an expanse of chin. The sky wore, in another colour, the same likeness; a white vacuity of countenance with the lineaments gone. So these two upper and nether visages confronted each other all day long, the white face looking down on the brown face, and the brown face looking up at the white face, without anything standing between them but the two girls crawling over the surface of the former like flies. (*Tess*, ch. 43)

This desolate expanse, which gnaws into the fibre of Tess's resolution, is still nevertheless part of Hardy's extant region – one of the halts in his heroine's daunting journey from drunken father and feckless mother, through to the murder of her lover, through to execution at Winchester – an odyssey which is none the less heroic because it is taken through modest parishes. Naturally it possesses none of the aura of benevolence of *Under the Greenwood Tree*, nor for that matter of the Valley of the Great Dairies where Tess reopened her spirit and selflessness to Angel Clare (although the latter location can express subtle menace). Both Tess and Jude are wanderers about Hardy's region and both often stay at places where the harmony of rustic appearance is jarred and made ugly.

In the matter of regional variation it is interesting to consider the scenic composition of *Tess* and *Jude* (because they constitute a culmination of perplexity) and, equally interesting, the human imposition on the scene. Even at the very beginning of *Tess*, Hardy fashions contradictory faces of his region, a region, we must remember, for which he always had a deep affection. The village of Marlott, where the action opens, is situated in the beautiful Vale of Blackmoor, where 'the fields are never brown and the springs never dry'. Here 'the world seems to be constructed upon a smaller and more delicate scale; the fields are . . . so reduced that from this height their hedgerows appear a network of dark green threads overspreading the paler green of the grass' (ch. 12). This would appear to be a veritably idyllic country, a place for the beautiful and good to live in. And indeed when the village maidens appear in their white dresses ready for the ritual of club-walking this seems to be the case. Yet within a few pages the action moves to Rolliver's inn where village society is presented as furtive, hangdog, rotting. There is a certain overlay of comic behaviour and patter, shrewdly observed, but the fundamental compassion, the 'loving-kindness', to be discovered in Warren's Malthouse is missing. 'In a large bedroom upstairs, the window of which was thickly curtained with a great woollen shawl lately discarded by the landlady . . . were gathered on this evening nearly a dozen persons, all seeking beatitude' (ch. 4). It is in this seedy bedroom, where human penury and greed foul the Vale of Blackmoor, that Tess's parents plot, in their wretched ignorance, her visit to 'Mrs.

d'Urberville's seat, The Slopes'. It is also in the Vale of Blackmoor that the death of Prince takes place as Tess was taking beehives to market because her father is too drunk, and Tess reflects that, amid all the beauty, she lives on a blighted star.

Contrasts and contradictions persist. When she arrives at the d'Urbervilles, all around are colour and rustic adornment: 'Far behind the corner of the house – which rose like a geranium bloom against the subdued colours around – stretched the soft azure landscape of The Chase – a truly venerable tract of forest land, one of the few remaining woodlands in England of undoubted primaeval date, wherein Druidical mistletoe was still found on aged oaks, and where enormous yew-trees, not planted by the hand of man, grew as they had grown when they were pollarded for bows' (ch. 5). In this glory of present and past natural history only the two inhabitants of The Slopes, like their names, are counterfeit. And, of course, it was in this 'sylvan antiquity' that Tess lost her virginity to the son of the spurious aristocrat, Mr. Stoke, who had discovered the name d'Urberville in the British Museum in 'the pages of works devoted to extinct, half-extinct, obscured, and ruined families appertaining to the quarter of England in which he proposed to settle . . .' (ch. 5). And that quarter is Wessex, and apart from the juxtaposition of natural beauty and human worthlessness, the comment indicates, incidentally, another aspect of Hardy's regionalism: his concern with the decline into poverty and insignificance of erstwhile proud and wealthy county families.

Tess moves on, heavy in pregnancy, 'the pure woman', with a knifing mixture of plausible innocence, placid bitterness and native indomitability. Back to Marlott and an importunate family, to labour diffidently but defiantly in the fields, to the birth, death and gothic baptism of her baby. And then on again after two or three years to the Valley of the Great Dairies. This journey constitutes a shifting of the action towards the spiritual centre of Hardy's Wessex; and we anticipate the affirmation of place to be, and to some extent it is, more placable. Yet in this late novel there lies a festering of ambiguities in the lyrical hypostasis of Hardy's region. It is true that her abused spirit, vibrant to place and season, flourishes: 'Amid the oozing fatness and warm ferments of the Froom Vale, at a season when the rush of juices could almost be heard below the hiss of fertilization, it was impossible that the most fanciful love should not grow passionate. The ready bosoms existing there were impregnated by their surroundings' (ch. 24). In this, some of his most highly charged sexual writing, Hardy identifies humans with landscape just as much as he does in the case of Haymoss Fry. This is in July; but a month earlier, in June, in the same Vale, we read a cautionary description in which it seems that Nature herself (or is it the uncaring of the Great Foresightless?) is foretelling some perverse eventuality:

> The outskirt of the garden in which Tess found herself had been left uncultivated for some years, and was now damp and rank with juicy grass which sent up mists of pollen at a touch; and with tall blooming weeds emitting offensive smells – weeds whose red and yellow and purple hues formed a polychrome as dazzling as that of cultivated flowers. She went stealthily as a cat through this profusion of growth, gathering cuckoo-spittle on her skirts, cracking snails that were underfoot, staining her hands with thistle-milk and slug-slime, and rubbing off upon her naked arms sticky blights which, though snow-white on the apple-tree trunks, made madder stains on her skin; thus she drew quite near to Clare, still unobserved of him. (Ch. 19)

Clare, albeit innocently – 'innocent' in that he vacillates, despite a frequent charm of mood and manner, in a confusion of staid theology and immature thought – is a human extension, in both a symbolic and participating sense, of the threat and repulsiveness of this uncultivated garden. A weed of dazzling polychrome to Tess's untutored eyes, he is to leave cuckoo-spittle and slug-slime on her impetuous charity and madder stains on the skin of her youthful and 'inexperienced' personality. This quarter of Wessex, the setting for the intense, hauntingly tender, but foredoomed courtship, represents a Gethsemane-like staging point in the progress of Tess's story. As with stunted trees and rotting fungi in *The Woodlanders*, we peer into the undergrowth of Wessex where Nature imitates Man.

It would be superfluous to compile a prolonged catalogue of this kind of locational structuring, and suffice it to mention one or two more places crucial to story and person. Still in the Valley of the Great Dairies, we find a certain narrative peace in the general evenness and harmony of the dairy itself, where the serenity of work and reminiscence is shattered for Tess by the threatening gossip of Jack Dollop, 'a 'hore's-bird of a fellow', a primitive Alec. For Dairyman Crick and the maids he is a figure of fun, fun which is unappreciated by Tess. Nor is there much fun on her wedding night. The arrival at Wellbridge, on New Year's Eve, and at their lodgings lying out of the village 'over the great Elizabethan bridge'; the sudden horror of the 'life-size portraits' of the ladies of the d'Urberville family; the news of Retty's suicide; the exchange of pre-marital confessions; the placing of Tess in a stone coffin as Clare walks in his sleep: all these events taken place on the quiet, eternal banks of the River Frome. We chart the vain journey to Emminster (Beaminster) at the end of which is the baulking pomposity of Clare's brothers; we record the surrender of courageous human endeavour in Mrs. Brooks' boarding house, The Herons, where 'the front room – the dining-room' affords a view of 'the little lawn, and the rhododendrons and other shrubs upon it' (ch. 55) (Victorian sexual morality is beside the point here) in Sandbourne (Bournemouth); we witness the flight through the New Forest where there occurs a brief sardonic recapture of sexual happiness. What all these settings lead to is something like this. In Hardy's novels we discover corners of stability and tradition which are often refuges from the human storms outside. But if we take an overall view of the shifting Wessex scenes in *Tess*, we find very few such havens. The physical background is often a gross mockery of human dolour. The surface in these cases has apparently the same scenic dress that advertises the diurnal restraint and acceptance of *Under the Greenwood Tree*, but humanity reveals lacerating intolerance in the foreground, and the contrast between natural idyllicism and human intolerance is all the more wounding. At other times the background identifies itself with pain and vulgarity, and the region and the people become integrated. The corruption of man is reflected in the corruption of nature and Wessex becomes, despite Hardy's great love for it, a green and fertile hell.

Much the same can be seen in *Jude*, except that Hardy can be even more ruthless in the later novel about his region and about his people. 'Ruthless' here needs some further observation. Hardy strongly denies that he is a 'pessimist' and asserts that his pessimism is 'in truth, only such "questionings" in the exploration of reality, and is the first step towards the soul's betterment, and the body's also'. There is, too, a school of critical opinion which holds that it is invalid to relate the novels to any apparatus of supernatural forces as they are portrayed in *The Dynasts*. Whatever the case it is abundantly clear that so many characters in the novels – we could select randomly – such as Elfride Swancourt, Clym, Eustacia, Lady Constantine, Henchard, Winterborne, not to mention those of our immediate attention, Tess, Sue and Jude, are, whatever they may contribute by way of personal shortcomings, special victims of some antagonism whether it be the 'indifference' of the Immanent Will (which generally turns out to be hostile), the uncaring or sanction of society, or just plain ill-chance – the capacity for being or doing at the wrong time. Hardy puts his well-beloved characters in pitiless circumstances and to that extent he is ruthless (I am well aware that there are all sorts of other messages and epiphanies). His chosen region, too (and, except in crucial phases of *Jude*, the personages nearly always belong to the places), is an agglomeration of places of great affection for him, as is abundantly evident both in his fictional and non-fictional writing. Yet these too can be exposed as though hostilely.

I have referred already to Farmer Troutham's ploughed field, and I should first like to put these agricultural acres in relationship to the locational sweep of *Jude*. The narrative swings from the centre of Wessex to the extreme north-east corner of 'North Wessex'. The novel is divided into six parts each with a locational heading: Part First – Marygreen (Fawley), where the field is; Second – Christminster (Oxford); Third – Melchester (Salisbury); Fourth – Shaston (Shaftesbury); Fifth – Aldbrickham (Reading) and elsewhere; and Sixth – Christminster again. It seems there are a conscious distancing and isolating of events (although they do overlap occasionally) – Jude's boyhood is at Marygreen, his academic disillusionment at Christminster, Sue's teacher training at Melchester and so on. It remains a rural novel but one, as the part headings indicate, also very much concerned with towns.

Hardy describes Wessex as 'partly real, partly dream country'. If we accept this in the matter of fictional localizing, Christminster becomes one dream further removed from 'reality' in that it seems to be presented as a 'false' dream of Jude himself. We may need to consider this. After Jude prays at the Brown House, 'a weather-beaten old barn of reddish grey brick and tile', that the mist will lift so that he can catch a glimpse of Christminster, it miraculously does, and we read of what seems at first to be a glorious revelation but what, in the event, turns out to be another stroke of ill-chance: 'Some way within the limits of the stretch of landscape, points of light like the topaz gleamed. The air increased in transparency with the lapse of minutes, till the topaz points showed themselves to be the vanes, windows, wet roof slates, and other shining spots upon the spires, domes, freestonework, and varied outlines that were faintly revealed. It was Christminster, unquestionably; either directly seen, or miraged in the peculiar atmosphere' (I, 3). This sight, working on Jude's too immediate sensitivity, sets up the city as the promised land, his 'heavenly Jerusalem'. Jude 'had his outer being for some long tideless time' inside and around his old aunt's shop window but 'his dreams were as gigantic as his surroundings were small'. Even within the splendour of this urban vision of a boy, Hardy has to sow a characteristic irony. If we reverse the two subsequent paragraphs, the irony becomes more apparent:

> In sad wet seasons, though he knew it must rain at Christminster too, he could hardly believe that it rained so drearily there. Whenever he could get away from the confines of the hamlet for an hour or two, which was not often, he would steal off to the Brown House on the hill and strain his eyes persistently; sometimes to be rewarded by the sight of a dome or spire, at other times by a little smoke, which in his estimate had some of the mysticism of incense.

But in the previous paragraph the incense swirls around disillusions yet to come and one already being experienced:

> Through the solid barrier of cold cretaceous upland to the northward he was always beholding a gorgeous city – the fancied place he had likened to the new Jerusalem, though there was perhaps more of the painter's imagination and less of the diamond merchant's in his dreams thereof than in those of the Apocalyptic writer. And the city acquired a tangibility, a permanence, a hold on his life, mainly from the one nucleus of fact that the man for whose knowledge and purposes he had so much reverence was actually living there; not only so, but living among the more thoughtful and mentally shining ones therein. (I, 3)

The reference to Phillotson constitutes an intimation of special anguish at this point. It is in a little school outside of Christminster that Jude is next to meet him, a failure, embittered by the inaccessibility of the colleges. His wretchedness anticipates Jude's when the latter's ambition is broken against stone walls under 'the spires, domes, and freestone-work'.

We discover appropriate connections, which there could not be anywhere else, between the tale of four people and the place, Christminster, which make Christminster the most important urban focus in the novel, although we must remember that 'it stood within hail of the Wessex border, and almost with the tip of one small toe within it, at the northernmost point of the crinkled line along which the leisurely Thames strokes the fields of that ancient kingdom' (II, 1). It is true that, before he arrives at the city, Jude has already taken an adventitious diversion off his proposed route by his chance encounter with Arabella and later marriage to her. But it is at Christminster, or near it, where the essential entanglement of four people begins, and where for Jude it ends with his death. It is there that he meets Sue Bridehead and introduces her to Phillotson. The main narrative excursion of the novel is, I suppose, Jude's and Sue's uneven progress, with its inevitably disastrous ending; but just as vital to the story's integrity is the intermittent changing of partners, two of whom seem to belong to Hardy's flotsam. Arabella and Phillotson possess wry identities, both are wretched and curiously pathetic, are strongly contrasted but are certainly not mere narrative props. I make this general aside on these four characters because, although none of them belongs there, they are all associated with the city at critical times: Jude, still bewitched, wandering around at night listening to the spectral voices of the 'sons of the University' – Arnold, Peel, Browning, Newman, Keble and so on; his finding a job as a mason just as a start; Sue ludicrously working in Miss Fontover's religious shop; Jude's drunken bouts in the quarter where he finds 'the real Christminster life'; and so on until, late in the novel and after much journeying, the final destruction of his children, his return to Arabella and Mr. Donn's butcher's shop.

Hardy uses Christminster in this novel as he has never before used a town in Wessex or elsewhere. Casterbridge in *The Mayor* and even London in *The Hand of Ethelberta* are presented in a very different way. It may be significant that Christminster is perched on the edge of his region but the fact remains that it is a crucial centre of *Jude*. After the boy's visionary glimpses the reality of the city is hostile, often repugnant. There is no affectionate recapture of urban place as there is even in Mixen Lane in Casterbridge. In a drunken fit Jude thinks he has found the essential human Christminster: 'He began to see that the town life was a book of humanity infinitely more palpitating, varied, and compendious than the gown life. These struggling men and women before him were the reality of Christminster, though they knew little of Christ or Minster. That was one of the humours of things. The floating population of students and teachers, who did know both in a way, were not Christminster in a local sense at all' (II, 6).

The vision of Christminster as paradisiacal city has inevitably been extinguished. Yet, as Hardy fills in the final details of his map (Christminster is, of course, on the regional map), there are more ruthless and merciless proposals of the city still to come both in its college and 'real' districts. Neither Melchester nor Aldbrickham is interposed with any fundamental sympathy or affection, but towards the end of the novel Christminster is exposed as a city of moral prohibition and sensual degradation. For all sorts of reasons of integrity, no doubt, Hardy turns this part of the Wessex boundary away from the sun. As Sue begins her weird dialogue of death with Father Time – 'It would be better to be out o' the world than in it, wouldn't it?' 'It would almost, dear' – in the desolate lodging from which Jude has been banned, we are aware of a chilling scorn of academic life: 'Sue sat looking at the bare floor of the room, the house being little more than an old intramural cottage, and then she regarded the scene outside the uncurtained window. At some distance opposite, the outer walls of Sarcophagus College – silent, black and windowless – threw their four centuries of gloom, bigotry, and decay into the little room she occupied, shutting out the moonlight by night and the sun by day. The outlines of Rubric College also were discernible beyond the other, and the tower of a third further off still. She thought of the strange operation of a simple-minded man's ruling passion, that it should have led Jude, who loved her and the children so tenderly, to place them here in this depressing purlieu, because he was still haunted by his dream. Even now he did not distinctly hear the freezing negative that those scholared walls had echoed to his desire' (VI, 2). It is hard to find in this passage any tolerance of place.

As Arabella schemes to remarry Jude we record an equally compassionless contempt for the dregs of Christminster, for the adulterated taverns, for the ineffectual of the world, for both Mr. Donn's shop and the list of pre-wedding guests: 'Donn had only just opened his miserable little pork and sausage shop, which had as yet scarce any customers; nevertheless that party advertised it well, and the Donns acquired a real notoriety among a certain class in Christminster who knew not the colleges, nor their works, nor their ways. Jude was asked if he could suggest any guest in addition to those named by Arabella and her father, and in a saturnine humour of perfect recklessness mentioned Uncle Joe, and Stagg, and the decayed auctioneer, and others whom he remembered as having been frequenters of the well-known tavern during his bout therein years before. He also suggested Freckles and Bower o' Bliss' (VI, 7).

And so Jude has progressed in one sense from a pig's pizzle at Marygreen to a pig's innards in Christminster, as a contemporary American lady pointed out.[5] These over-simplified points of narrative reference can of course be made disproportionate, but in this case they show Hardy making his locale degrading. As writer and observer, he has moved a long way from the happy inevitability of seasonal cycles, of entrenched and felicitous community. Even what is an apparently cheerful prospect of Christminster is described in the final pages with authorial savagery, with what Hardy calls Jude's saturnine humour: 'On the opposite side of the river, on the crowded barges, were gorgeous nosegays of feminine beauty, fashionably arrayed in green, pink, blue, and white. The blue flag of the Boat Club denoted the centre of interest, beneath which a band in red uniform gave out the notes she had already heard in the death-chamber. Collegians of all sorts, in canoes with ladies, watching keenly for "our" boat, darted up and down. While she regarded the lively scene somebody touched Arabella in the ribs, and looking round she saw Vilbert' (VI, 11). Arabella has just come from the dead body of her husband.

Hardy was very resentful of the adverse criticism which *Jude* occasioned, and at a distance it is not difficult to appreciate the reasons for such disenchantment and for his resentment. In *Tess* and *Jude* he has moved too far and too fast for many of his readers although, again with hindsight, we can detect the acceleration of this movement throughout the course of the novels. What in one sense is happening is that he has moved away from the 'partly real' map of the south-west counties of England, which people 'can go to, take a house in', to the more imaginative one of his Wessex which belongs more and more to the reaches of human relationship, of domestic torment. The fine tensions persist but the emphasis has shifted. The 'reality' of Christminster is still there, as Jude, Hardy and perhaps even the modern reader can experience it, but the insistence on its ruthlessness is in keeping with the social and other less definable pressures on a 'simple-minded man'.

To adapt an Aristotelian proposal, Hardy reaches his greatest intensity, his greatest impact as a novelist, when he achieves total felicity of relationship among action, person and place; and these three are all constituents of what is generally defined as the regional novel. Hardy chose and delineated his fictional domain and for the most part stayed within its confines, and consequently the action takes place there. The persons either belong where the action is or come from areas within the outer boundaries, and a transparency of the south-west counties of England could be placed over and fit exactly his imaginary Wessex – so far as its physical features, disposition of hamlets and towns and so on go. There are some occasional exceptions which are just worth mentioning. Not all the action takes place in the selected territory, not all the personages belong. And when, as very infrequently happens, the action moves outside fixed regional limits, it often becomes melodramatic, caricatural, uncertain, at times reading like a guide book. The 'foreign' people we encounter are mostly bloodless. There are occasional brief excursions about the world which, far from reinforcing conviction, merely reveal Hardy's carelessness in plotting when the compulsion of the narrative demands the convenient removal of a character for a time. This may be one of the reasons why Henry James could never become attuned to Hardy's fiction. Such expatriations as Stephen Smith's to India, Clym's to a jeweller's in Paris, St. Cleeve's in pursuit of the Southern Cross, to South Africa, Susan Henchard's to Canada, Clare's to Brazil, and Arabella's to Australia, may well exhibit the colonizing potential of the natives, but the reader has no interest in other parts of the world, however far-flung, as he has in the reading of – say – Conrad's novels. And this probably uncovers the heart of Hardy's regionalism. Once the characters are removed from their native downs, or even from the inimical streets of Aldbrickham or Christminster, the integrity of their creation is exceedingly debilitated.

It is not quite the same when 'foreigners' move into the region, but before commenting on them – an important group with a crucial if stereotyped function – I should like to mention briefly instances, in the novels, of Hardy's shifting his scene outside of Wessex. Substantial parts of the action of *The Hand of Ethelberta* take place in London, and Hardy, despite an unusual knowledge of that city, writes uncertainly about it –

especially when he attempts to recreate fashionable dinner parties. But when the action moves abroad to Rouen, where Ethelberta and Lord Mountclere climb to the top of the cathedral, we are reminded, despite the usual descriptive sensitivity, of a travel brochure:

> Out of the plain of fog beneath a stone tooth seemed to be upheaving itself: then another showed forth. These were the summits of the St. Romain and the Butter Towers – at the western end of the building. As the fog stratum collapsed other summits manifested their presence further off – among them the two spires and lantern of St. Ouen's; when to the left the dome of St. Madeleine's caught a first ray from the peering sun, under which its scaly surface glittered like a fish. Then the mist rolled off in earnest, and revealed far beneath them a whole city, its red, blue, and grey roofs forming a variegated pattern, small and subdued as that of a pavement in mosaic. Eastward in the spacious outlook lay the hill of St. Catherine, breaking intrusively into the large level valley of the Seine; south was the river which had been the parent of the mist, and the Ile Lacroix, gorgeous in scarlet, purple, and green. On the western horizon could be dimly discerned melancholy forests, and further to the right stood the hill and rich groves of Boisguillaume.
> (*Ethelberta*. ch. 34)

This is reminiscent of Dickens's *Pictures from Italy*. There is no heart, no integration of place. This is not even like the Christminster of Jude's dreams.

Both Dickens and Hardy write with a greater certainty in the matter of telling substance when they stay within their imaginative lands. Besides *Ethelberta*, a certain amount of the story of *The Well-Beloved*, that curious work of fancy at the end of the line of the novels, takes place outside of Wessex, but on the whole narrative excursion beyond its limits is rare. It is a different matter when we consider the 'aliens' who move into Wessex, the 'Mephistophelean visitants' who have been pertinently noticed by J. O. Bailey and A. J. Guerard.[6] Hardy originally uses the phrase to describe Diggory Venn in *The Return of the Native*, and Bailey adapts it to categorize a sequence of disturbing intruders in the novels. Bailey's is one of the most illuminating pieces in the crowded field of Hardy criticism, and this squad of intruders must be noticed in any study of Hardy's regionalism; but what is extraordinary is that the reddleman, despite his satanic appearance, is a benign character and does in fact belong to Wessex. The others come from the world outside and bring their own special menace.

This invasion of the knowing, the cheats, the devious, the infiltrators into what seems at first an unsophisticated land, indicates an authorial concern with their capacity for making mischief but it is a concern which is modified as the regional canon is worked out. From Aeneas Manston in *Desperate Remedies* to Alec d'Urberville in *Tess*, the villains certainly threaten courtships, break marriages, violate pastoral sanctities. Yet during the progress of the novels Hardy discovers more and more causes for human distress already existing within his borders. Until we get to *Jude* the formula is admittedly repeated again and again. The lurchings and surges of the plot in *Desperate Remedies* make this novel unusual in respect of Hardy's early works (there are special reasons for this — advice from Meredith being one), but, for all the frenetic movement of mystery and murder, it starts a pattern (as to the machinations of Manston and his beguilement of Cytherea) which is to be sustained. Threatening visitors include Sergeant Troy, Wildeve (possibly Eustacia), William Dare, Farfrae (a benign stranger but one who, however unwittingly, overturns Henchard's world), Fitzpiers (and possibly Felice Charmond) and finally Alec. Yet in these same novels we discover distress belonging solely to the region itself and with increasing intensity. Two of Bathsheba's suitors belong to Wessex; Clym, a heathman, and his mother, Mrs. Yeobright, contribute to the sorrow and deaths on Egdon; Paula Powers is not guiltless; Henchard carries within him the seeds of much of his undoing; Clare is in many senses more frightful to Tess than d'Urberville; and in *Jude* all the protagonists belong to Wessex. All this relates to my earlier proposal of the region appearing in harsher lights as we move through the novels, but what it probably indicates essentially is that, while Hardy's novels contain a special flavour, particularly in regard to place and often in regard to inhabitants of place, they are at the same time concerned with the human story, unrestrained by Wessex limits.

I do not propose, in conclusion, to discard all the local proprieties, the faithful observation and recapture of scenes past, the rustic centres of attitude and action. Not even so far as *Jude* is concerned. These persist throughout the novels. But a blight — affecting place and people — seems gradually to spread over the region, and it is part of the fascination of enjoying and studying Hardy to try to analyse this scourge in all its complexities. Much has to do with what we might diffidently call Hardy's disenchantment, and we see from contemporary criticism how very disturbing this was to many late Victorians. And yet it has surely to do also with the enriching of his vision, with the maturing of his descriptive and human poetry which permeates his fiction. This, to my mind, is the essence of his regional manifestation which, throughout the course of the novels, becomes ever more richly textured.

NOTES

1. *The Dynasts*, *Parts I & II*, 1958, 6. Subsequent references in parentheses are to this edition.

2. D. Kay-Robinson, *Hardy's Wessex Re-appraised*, Newton Abbot, 1972. This book, together with B. C. A. Windle, *The Wessex of Thomas Hardy*, 1925; H. Lea, *Thomas Hardy's Wessex*, 1913; C. J. Weber, *Hardy of Wessex*, New York, 1940; and *Thomas Hardy: Materials for a Study of his Life, Times and Works*, ed. J. Stevens Cox, Guernsey, 1968–71, has been of particular assistance.

3. *The Literary Notes of Thomas Hardy*, ed. L. A. Björk, Gothenburg, 1974, I, xxxiii.

4. J. Stevens Cox, I, Monograph 20, 19.

5. Possibly Jeannette L. Gilder in a review in *The World*, 13 November 1895; *Thomas Hardy and his Readers*, ed. L. Lerner and J. Holmstrom, 1968, 113.

6. J. O. Bailey, 'Hardy's Mephistophelean Visitants', PMLA 61, 1946, 1146–84; A. J. Guerard, *Thomas Hardy: The Novels and Stories*, Cambridge, Mass., 1949, 96–7.

4: Hardy's Reading

LENNART A. BJÖRK

I

IN *Thomas Hardy: A Study of his Writings and their Background*, still one of the most useful books on Hardy, William R. Rutland aptly formulates a traditional premise which is fundamental to the present essay: 'the work of a great artist proceeds out of his inmost life; and . . . it can only be fully understood and appreciated in so far as we know and understand the living thought out of which it came'.[1] It is, however, one thing to accept the premise in theory, another to follow it in practice. Hardy's 'living thought' is not an easily accessible phenomenon. Our immediate concern here – his reading – is, of course, only one of several avenues of of approach.

There is a good deal of helpful scholarship both on Hardy's thought and on his reading. Rutland's original study from 1938 remains a standard work. As he enjoyed the rare privilege of being admitted to Hardy's library before it was scattered, he was able to study Hardy's marginal annotations and to offer precise documentation. There followed several studies of high quality, but the next most significant step in the research on Hardy's reading was not taken until 1967 with Walter F. Wright's *The Shaping of the Dynasts*.[2] Wright was the first to use Hardy's extant notebooks, which had then only recently become publicly available in the Dorset County Museum.[3] Since then the notebooks have been used with outstanding results in, among others, Michael Millgate, *Thomas Hardy: His Career as a Novelist* (1971) and Robert Gittings, *Young Thomas Hardy* (1975).

For primary sources *The Life of Thomas Hardy* is an obvious starting point, although it is far from being a complete record.[4] Hardy's notebooks in general, and the two volumes labelled 'Literary Notes' in particular, constitute the most important additional sources.[5] The 'Literary Notes' cover some sixty years of Hardy's reading and notetaking. As is clear from the reports of the deliberate destruction of his diaries, notebooks, and other papers, the extant volumes in no way give a full account of his notetaking. In view of the unfortunate loss of so much material, it is remarkable that the 'Literary Notes' should span almost his entire mature life, from his early twenties to the year before his death. It is tempting to see a great number of the entries in the preserved books as a carefully compiled collection of quotations from his now lost papers.[6] I draw special attention to the 'Literary Notes', because, as we shall see, they shed unusually revealing light on some aspects of Hardy's reading.

Since Hardy's religious and metaphysical ideas have received such ample – many think too ample – scholarly treatment, there is little need here to trace once again the influences that we now know guided or prodded him from his firm Christian beliefs via the 'purblind Doomsters' in 'Hap' to the 'Will' of *The Dynasts*, that is, to recount his studies in Darwin, Spencer, Huxley, von Hartmann, Schopenhauer, and others.[7] Instead, I shall concentrate on Hardy's reading in psychological and social matters. These areas are not often discussed in accounts of Hardy's intellectual background, but the records of his reading in them – and, of course, his own works – prove them to have been of particular interest to him. However, before considering these special areas with the help of his own notes, it may be useful to recall, though quite briefly, some more general aspects of his intellectual development by drawing attention to a few individual authors and books that he read before he embarked on his career as a novelist.

As has often been noted, there is nothing very remarkable about Hardy's childhood and adolescent reading. The romantic tales of Bernardin de Saint-Pierre, Dumas, James Grant, G. P. R. Scott, W. H. Ainsworth, Scott and others all give, in Webster's appropriate analysis, 'the same specious and paradisaic view of life'.[8] Nor is there any reason to believe that Hardy's regular reading of the Bible at this time was anything but devout.[9] His intellectual and spiritual life was, in fact, quite orthodox up to the age of twenty-five. The most conspicuous testimony to the stability of his traditional thought is the well-known fact that he still contemplated entering the Church in 1865, at a time, as we shall see, when he had read publications which were highly disturbing to the religious and intellectual views of so many of his contemporaries.

Despite the fact that Hardy's reading before 1865 does not seem to have had any immediately noticeable effects, it is nevertheless of significance, for it is possible to trace in it general stimuli for the orientation of his future reading as well as for some of the preoccupations in his own writing. To begin with, there are two general and not easily defined sources of influence. The first is classical literature in general and Greek drama in particular. For instance, Hardy read Aeschylus and Sophocles with great care in the early eighteen-sixties; as Rutland suggests, if Hardy's 'twilight view of life' can be attributed to any purely literary influence, that influence is likely to be 'that great and sombre art whose *leit motif* is "call no man happy while he lives"'.[10] The second general influence is found in Hardy's early reading of Victorian periodicals, especially *The Saturday Review*. As the 'Literary Notes' show, this reading assumes increasing importance in the eighteen-seventies, but it was already in 1857 that, under the tutelage of his older and intellectually more mature friend Horace Moule, Hardy was introduced to *The Saturday Review*. It is indeed probable that, as Gittings maintains, the 'corrective scepticism' that we find in Hardy's early novels is attributable to his almost weekly confrontation over many years with the criticism in *The Saturday Review* of Victorian social evils, hypocrisy and sentimentality.[11]

Of the most interesting individual items on Hardy's pre–1865 reading list some are well known, others obscure (the approximate dating of his reading within parentheses): Darwin, *The Origin of Species* (1859–60); *Essays and Reviews* (1860–1); Walter Bagehot, *Estimates of Some Englishmen and Scotchmen* (1862); Ruskin, *Modern Painters* (1862); and Charles Fourier, *The Passions of the Human Soul* (1863). All except Fourier are mentioned in the *Life*.

Since we are leaving the religious implications of *The Origin of Species* and *Essays and Reviews* aside, the point here about Hardy's knowledge of the works at the time is that he was subjected to the principles of inductive science and the 'historical method'. As Buckley has reminded us, the inductive method is *the* method of nineteenth-century research, and the 'Historic Method' was considered by John Morley 'the most important intellectual cause of the nineteenth-century thought and sentiment'.[12] It is, then, not only the ideas *per se* but the *modes* of thinking in these celebrated works that may have prepared the young, orthodox and provincial Hardy for his later assimilation of the radical thought of Comte, Huxley, Spencer and others.

In Walter Bagehot's *Estimates* Hardy may for the first time have been introduced to an extended and more formal discussion of the problems and ideas of writers whom he was later greatly to sympathize with. Thus he read that Gibbon in his youth was left on his own to wrestle with the old problems of 'fate, free-will, fore-knowledge absolute'; he learnt that Shelley was expelled from Oxford after having written a pamphlet on 'The Necessity of Atheism' and he got a vivid, if not altogether sympathetic, account of Shelley's social radicalism, idealism and intense emotional life; with his own articulation of similar views in *Jude* several decades away, he read Shelley's famous statement on love and marriage: 'Love withers under constraint; its very essence is liberty. . . . A husband and wife ought to continue united only so long as they love each other.'[13] In *Estimates* Hardy also found expressed with great fervour certain ideas that he was later to voice in his own statements on literary matters. Bagehot emphasized, for instance, the importance and integrity of an artist's, in Hardy's own words, 'idiosyncratic mode of regard' (*Life*, 225). Again and again Bagehot drew attention to the idiosyncratic visions of Hartley Coleridge, Cowper, Gibbon, Macaulay, and Shelley. In his psychological analyses of the authors and their works, Bagehot consistently stressed the essential role of the emotions. He deplored, for instance, the detached and cool personalities of Gibbon and Macaulay as mirrored in their works. This emphasis on the emotional rather than the intellectual life we shall find essential to Hardy's own psychological speculations.

In Ruskin's *Modern Painters* Hardy again found the historic method at work, but also, and perhaps more explicitly stated than before, the concept of the idea of progress, about which he was to think a great deal in the future. Ruskin also vented the view that the nineteenth century represented 'sadder ages than the early ones' – an opinion permeating Hardy's own works.[14]

The most radical book in this period of Hardy's reading is Charles Fourier's *The Passions of the Human Soul*, but it is better to discuss this in relation to the psychological and social subjects below.

In addition to the above works, Hardy may by this time also have been familiar with some of John Stuart Mill's writings. He claims in a letter that he knew *On Liberty* 'almost by heart' in 1865 (*Life*, 330). He may thus already then have embraced Mill's bold assertion that 'no one can be a great thinker who does not recognize that as a thinker it is his first duty to follow his intellect to whatever conclusions it may lead.'[15] But, to repeat, even though it would seem from his plans of an ecclesiastical career that Hardy's intellect had not reached any daring conclusions in 1865, his early knowledge of Mill and the other writers here mentioned is not to be neglected in the development of his thought. On the contrary, it is highly probable that the rationalist modes of thought in especially *The Origin of Species*, *Essays and Reviews*, and *On Liberty* significantly helped to prepare Hardy intellectually and emotionally for his later acceptance of new ideas, detrimental to the conventional views of his youth.

To date and specify this gradual acceptance is neither possible nor necessary here. There are, however, a few pieces of evidence of his reading in the mid-eighteen-sixties that are of interest. The earliest preserved notebook, a small volume dated 1865 on the front fly-leaf and entitled 'Studies, Specimens etc', contains a number of entries from two radical poets Hardy read in 1865–6, Shelley and Swinburne.[16] It is suggestive, for instance, to see that not long before Hardy started writing *The Poor Man and the Lady*, the views of which were 'obviously those of a young man with a passion for reforming the world' (*Life*, 61), he had had first-hand experience of the social radicalism of Shelley's poetry. He is also likely to have been absorbed by Shelley's idealism and Hellenism, especially since, at about the same time, he found the pagan theme reiterated in his almost idolatrously enthusiastic reading of Swinburne (see *Life*, 344–5). Although it is perhaps true that the influence from Swinburne was more emotional than intellectual, the mixture of anti-Christian and 'Hellenic' ideas in *Poems and Ballads* and *Atalanta in Calydon* are likely to have left a lasting ideological impression as well. Like Shelley, Swinburne drew for him a picture of ancient Greece as a country of intellectual and moral freedom. This may well be the origin of Hardy's own Hellenism, particularly as it seems to have been only a year or so later that he singled out Mill's famous celebration of pagan virtues: in his 1867 edition of *On Liberty* Hardy heavily marked: 'There is a different type of human excellence from the Calvinistic: a conception of humanity as having its nature bestowed on it for other purposes than merely to be abnegated. "Pagan self-assertion" is one of the elements of human worth, as well as "Christian self-denial".'[17]

In the following decade Hardy's intellect continued to grow more mature and flexible, no doubt with substantial help from, among others,

Leslie Stephen, Huxley, and Spencer, to mention only a few of the men to whose rational and scientific thinking and writing – their agnosticism not to be forgotten – Hardy openly acknowledged his debt. It is, however, from the mid-eighteen-seventies that we are in a position to establish with more accuracy some specific trends in Hardy's reading.

II

In the spring of 1876 Hardy seems to have entered on an ambitious course of study, directly designed for his career as a novelist.[18] It is from then onwards – when the intellectual and aesthetic pretensions of his writing, starting with *The Return of the Native*, become more conspicuous – that we can find his interest in psychological and social matters revealed in his notebooks.

Into the 'Literary Notes' volumes which he started keeping in 1876 he also entered notes which had been taken down earlier. Among these the most important is a sheet with charts and diagrams based on the French utopian socialist Charles Fourier.[19] The chart lists Fourier's system of 'the twelve passions'. There are also three tree designs and a graph, headed 'Diagrams shewing Human Passions, Mind and Character – Designed by Tho . Hardy 1863'. To summarize very briefly, the Fourier notes are here primarily interesting for the psychological vision, the view of human nature, that they project. The essence of this view is an 'affective' psychology, a psychology of feeling, with the simple dichotomy of head and heart. In drawing the diagrams – and Hardy's heading seems to indicate that he makes some claim of analysis on his own part – he obviously has assimilated a good deal of Fourier's view of man, that is, Fourier's anti-rationalism, his notion that it is not reason but passion that is the primary motive power in human life. It is also to be noted here that Fourier's psychological vision plays a central role in his social criticism; he argues that the greatest obstacle to human happiness is the inability of the modern social order to satisfy the claims of the passions. And in this context he expresses, as Hardy was later to do, a strong preference for the moral views of classical antiquity. It is, of course, difficult to assess the influence of Fourier, but the fact that Hardy saved the old charts and diagrams at all is suggestive in itself. And the importance of his early familiarity with, perhaps acceptance of, an 'affective' psychology is further accentuated in the light of later notes with related ideas from other writers, especially Auguste Comte and the positivists.

The evidence of Hardy's reading of Comte is perhaps less immediately spectacular than the charts from Fourier. It is on the other hand more extensive, and it is quite likely that Comte may have left more of a lasting impression on Hardy's thought. Hardy's familiarity with Comte was considerable. In the early eighteen-seventies, the *Life* reveals, he read Comte's *Positive Philosophy* 'and writings of that school' so extensively that his own vocabulary acquired positivist overtones. He was, therefore, not surprised, though perhaps nettled, at finding his anonymously published *Far from the Madding Crowd* attributed to George Eliot (*Life*, 76, 98). From this early reading there is no extant material. From 1876, however, there are some twelve pages of excerpts in the 'Literary Notes' from *Social Dynamics, or The General Theory of Human Progress* (1876), vol. III of Comte's *System of Positive Polity*. In 1880 he also entered some material (entries 1200–1) from Comte's *Theory of the Future of Man*, trans. R. Congreve, vol. IV of *System of Positive Polity* (1877).

Auguste Comte had both quantitatively and qualitatively more to offer than Fourier. In the two main works by Comte that Hardy studied he did indeed find ample support for an 'affective' psychology. In *Positive Polity* he read that 'the struggle between the Intellect and the Heart is the principal feature of all great revolutions whether in the individual or in society'.[20] And, in addition to the dichotomy of Head and Heart, Hardy noticed also in *Positive Polity* a pervasive emphasis on the instinctive and affective elements in human behaviour, and he quoted: 'Feeling – [is] the great motor force of human life' (entry 666).

In Comte, Hardy also met a more plausible scientific background for an 'affective' psychology. As is well known, Comte, in order to stay clear of theological and metaphysical speculations on human nature, divided psychology between the sciences of biology and sociology.[21] Hardy is likely to have found Comte's emphasis on biology especially acceptable, perhaps even Comte's extensive reliance on Gall's phrenology.[22] Hardy did go to see a phrenologist once in London, and he outlined Comte's analysis – based on Gall – of the human brain in entry 728. But, in view of his warm acceptance of Darwin, Hardy should particularly have welcomed Comte's assertion in the *Positive Philosophy* that the 'affective' and 'intellectual' functions are to be studied in relation to 'the various organic conditions on which they depend' (I, 461–2), and that, as Hardy quoted, 'Thought depends on Sensation' (entry 731). He found the idea repeated in *Positive Polity* and copied the sombre observation 'A Fatal Dependence – that of the cerebral functions on the nutritive economy' (entry 750), but he had then already given expression to the notion himself in *Far from the Madding Crowd*: 'Bathsheba was in a very peculiar state of mind, which showed how entirely the soul is the slave of the body, the ethereal spirit dependent for its quality upon the tangible flesh and blood.'[23]

The biological basis of Comte's psychology is shown with equal clarity in another entry: 'Biological Dependence – The nobler phenomena are everywhere subordinate to those which are grosser, but also simpler and more regular. . . . Man is entirely subordinate to the World – each living being to its own environment' (entry 730). The general idea of 'biological dependence' is central also to Hardy's view of man and his environment, as his description of the bond between Clym Yeobright and Egdon Heath alone indicates. Clym's very character is determined by the heath: 'he was permeated with its scenes, with its substance, and with its odours. He might be said to be its product . . . ; his estimate of life had been coloured by it' (p. 180).

Hardy may, however, have had more ambiguous feelings about an essential aspect of Comte's sociological psychology – the basic positivist idea that the social feeling is as strong as selfish aspirations, and that, consequently, social harmony depends on this social instinct and not on any social contract.[24] Hardy did write that 'men's lives and actions' are 'less dependent on abstract reasonings than on the involuntary inter-social emotions'.[25] The anti-rationalist note is unmistakable, but for two main reasons it is difficult to see this statement as an unqualified acceptance of Comte's optimistic speculations on man's social feelings. Firstly, Hardy did not, with the exception of a brief period (see *Life*, 346, 349), believe that any significant growth of altruistic feelings had taken place. Secondly, he is not likely to have sympathized whole-heartedly with the more pronounced anti-individualistic tendencies of Comte's social psychology. And, as Kolakowski has observed, Comte's '"organic" interpretation of society involves the most extreme anti-individualism'.[26] On this matter Hardy is more likely to have been attracted by J. S. Mill's individualistic standpoint, or by the romantic and radical individualism of Fourier.[27] Hardy's enthusiastic markings of passages celebrating individualism in *On Liberty* are well known; and, as Donald Drew Egbert has convincingly documented in *Social Radicalism and the Arts*, Fourier won much sympathy among avant-garde artists and romantics (with whom Hardy had many points of contact) partly because they found in Fourier's individualism support for their idea of the autonomy of the arts – of which Hardy's dislike for 'fiction with a purpose' is only one expression.[28] What perhaps particularly alienated Hardy from Comte's sociological psychology was the Comtean argument that 'altruistic feelings flourish in family life, [and that] hence the family must be the cornerstone of the collective edifice' and divorce impossible.[29] Hardy, no doubt, preferred Fourier's more radical notions about arranging the relationship between the sexes.

Hardy, then, is likely to have found acceptable the main elements of the 'statics' of Comte's analysis of human nature – the scientific orientation of his psychology and the emphasis on the instinctual and emotional life. Equally interesting Hardy must have found Comte's 'dynamic' or historical perspective on human psychology – that is, Comte's famous psychological law of the three stages. 'Seen in its full completeness the fundamental law of the Intellectual Evolution consists in the necessary passage of all human theories through three successive stages: first the Theological or fictitious, which is provisional; secondly, the Metaphysical or abstract, which is transitional; and thirdly, the Positive or scientific, which alone is definitive' (*Positive Polity*, III, 23). Unfortunately the various branches of thought are not in the same stage at the same time; consequently, despite its advanced scientific thinking, modern society still presents the following spectacle: '*Theological stage of social phenomena*, at the present day. Law in these phenomena, as in other phenomena, not being recognized, they are treated as if produced by arbitrary Wills, either divine or human' (entry 737). The essence of Comte's analysis here of modern thought is recognizable also in most of Hardy's criticism of contemporary ideas; that is, much of the suffering of his characters is due to the fact that traditional moral concepts and religious ideas have not kept pace with the general progress of human thought, or with each other. This is realized, for instance, by Angel Clare in Brazil: 'Having long discredited the old systems of mysticism, he now began to discredit the old appraisements of morality' (*Tess*, 433). Had his moral notions been as advanced as his theological, Tess and he would, of course, have been spared a good deal of suffering.[30] In view of

Hardy's lifelong preoccupation with religious and theological problems it is not surprising that, judging from the extant notes, Hardy should have paid most attention to the theological stage of Comte's tripartite division of man's psychological development. And of the three subdivisions (fetichistic, polytheistic, monotheistic) of the theological stage he seems to have been most fascinated by the first. He noted Comte's relatively favourable analysis of Fetichism as 'the most spontaneous mode of philosophizing' (entry 755), which looks 'on all subjects in nature as animate' (entry 754) and does not, like Theologism, exaggerate the differences 'between man and the rest of organic nature' (entry 760). Particularly commendable about this phase, Comte noted, is the fact that 'Fetichism alone kept emotional life directly in view' (*Positive Polity*, III, 355).

These psychological speculations are also perhaps most clearly reflected in *Tess*, the novel which, after all, to Frederic Harrison, one of England's leading positivists at the time, read 'like a Positivist allegory or sermon'.[31] Tess herself is a daughter of Nature, 'a mere vessel of emotion', and repeatedly in the novel she is made to see Nature as animate. She is thus – in philosophical and religious terms – at a very primitive stage of human development, and her singing one Sunday morning at Talbothays is described in a language which suggests the Comtean psychological law of development as a general frame of reference: 'And probably the half-unconscious rhapsody was a Fetichistic utterance in a Monotheistic setting' (p. 134; cf. also 'fetichistic fear', p. 23 and 'lives essentially polytheistic', p. 211; see entries 669n, and 754–60n).

On the basis of available evidence, however, it is not possible to draw any far-reaching conclusions as to the traces of Comte's law of psychological development in Hardy's thought. That it may have offered some specific stimulus is suggested by the echoes in *Tess* discussed above. It seems equally probable that it gave Hardy a general psychological/philosophical perspective on the uneven rate of development of different branches of thought, a phenomenon which is such a major source of tragedy in Hardy's writing.

Hardy's most complex reaction to Comte's psychology, however, relates to what is perhaps the single most important principle behind Comte's law of psychological development – the Idea of Progress. As an acclaimer of Darwin, Hardy believed, of course, in the general principle of evolution, and if he had not himself seen the close relationship between evolution and the teaching of Comte, he found it enthusiastically explained in J. H. Bridges' 'Evolution and Positivism', which he read and copied from in 1877 (see entries 1061–3). In this, as well as in *The Origin of Species* itself, of course, evolution is looked upon optimistically. But, as Bury reminds us, evolution *per se* is a 'neutral, scientific notion compatible with both optimism and pessimism' and the interpretation of it depends largely on 'the temperament of the inquirer'.[32] Whether or not Hardy's temperament was as gloomy as it is often held to have been, his general attitude seems to have been similar to one he copied from the *Examiner* in 1876: '*Science tells us that*, in the struggle for life, the surviving organism is not necessarily that which is absolutely the best in an ideal sense, though it must be that which is most in harmony with surrounding conditions' (entry 392). That is, moral criteria are irrelevant to the biological laws operating in the struggle for life in nature, and therefore the 'surviving organism' is not automatically best in 'an ideal sense'.

Despite the difficulty of determining the exact scope and ramifications of Hardy's debt to Comte's analysis of human nature and his law of the psychological development of man, there is, as has been argued above, considerable evidence both in Hardy's notes and his fiction to suggest that the overall influence from Comte is of consequence. Above all, Hardy found in Comte, as he had earlier found in Fourier, the belief that 'man is essentially an affective being'[33] – additional support, that is, for an 'affective' psychology. And, although he may have had reservations about Comte's optimistic belief in the growth of altruistic feelings and the anti-individualistic basis of positivist social psychology, Hardy was in accord with the general objectives of Positivism: 'The grand aims . . . are the amelioration of the order of Nature where that idea is at once imperfect and most modifiable, i.e. human society; and the triumph of social feeling (altruism) over self-love.'[34]

The evidence in the 'Literary Notes' of Hardy's interest in 'affective' psychology generally, and positivist social psychology specifically, is not limited to excerpts from Fourier and Comte. The notebooks reveal that Hardy was familiar with a wide variety of writers with positivist tendencies. There are, for instance, quotations from J. H. Bridges, George Eliot, Frederic Harrison, G. H. Lewes, J. S. Mill, John Morley, George Sand, and Leslie Stephen. In all of these Hardy found support for, and further exemplifications of, positivist social psychology and the

Idea of Progress *per se* as well as in relation to man's moral development.

Thus, in Frederic Harrison Hardy found, and quoted, a strong belief in the Idea of Progress in general: '*The 19th Century*. We are on the threshold of a great time. . . . "We shall see it, but not now". The Vatican with its syllabus, the Mediaevalists at all costs, Mr. Carlyle, Mr. Ruskin, the Aesthetes, are all wrong about the nineteenth century. It is *not* the age of moneybags and cant, soot, hubbub, and ugliness. It is the age of great expectation and unwearied striving after better things . . .' (entry 1272); and, in George Sand, the idea was applied to altruism: 'When the sight of the wretchedness and crimes of society break my heart and trouble my mind . . . I say to myself that, since all men have agreed to love nature . . . they will agree also, one day, to love each other. Patience the philosopher (in Mauprat) G. Sand' (entry 477).

Hardy also found ample manifestation of the Comtean emphasis on biology and sociology in various psychological speculations. From Leslie Stephen, writing on J. S. Mill, he quoted that 'the prevailing tendency to regard all the marked distinctions of human character as innate, and to ignore the irresistible proofs that by far the greater part of these differences, whether between individuals, races, or sexes, are such as not only might, but naturally would be, produced by differences in circumstances, is one of the chief hindrances to the rational treatment of great social questions, and one of the greatest stumbling blocks to human improvement' (entry 1190). From Morley he excerpted passages on biological determinism (entries 1065–6) and from G. H. Lewes the observation that 'Physiology began to disclose that all the mental processes were (mathematically speaking) *functions* of physical processes, i.e. – varying with the variations of bodily states; and this was declared enough to banish for ever the conception of a Soul, except as a term simply expressing certain functions' – a passage which at least partly reflects the positivist psychology which according to Lewes' definition is 'a combination of biology, mental physiology, and sociology'.[35]

The emphasis here on Hardy's reading is not, of course, intended to imply that Hardy's view of human nature derived from written material alone. It would be equally if not more misleading, however, to argue that his psychological vision was shaped exclusively by introspection or his own first-hand experience of his fellow man. The nature and the extent of the sources on psychology quoted in the 'Literary Notes' suggest that Hardy was eager to learn more about man's nature than he had himself observed, and it seems reasonable to assume that a great deal of what in the course of his reading he found interesting enough to write down he must also have absorbed as his own views. As argued above, his notes point towards an 'affective' psychology, with the term used in the broad sense of a psychology emphasizing the primary role of the emotions, not reason, in human behaviour, a psychology in harmony with the view that Hardy quoted from Disraeli, that a 'knowledge of mankind is a knowledge of their passions' (entry 1118). Equally important is the tendency towards a social psychology – found in both Fourier and Comte – towards a method of relating human psychology to the social environment. This disposition is, as we shall see below, a basic element in Hardy's brand of 'social' criticism.

III

According to his own description of it, Hardy's unpublished first novel, *The Poor Man and the Lady*, was a 'sweeping satire of the squirearchy and nobility, London society, the vulgarity of the middle class, modern Christianity, church-restoration, and political and domestic morals in general, the author's views, in fact being obviously those of a young man with a passion for reforming the world . . . the tendency of the writing being socialistic, not to say revolutionary' (*Life*, 61). If this is a true analysis, Hardy seems to have been a dedicated social critic at the time. There is on the other hand good reason to believe that his social radicalism was not as profound as his account of the novel suggests. Most importantly, there is the fact that he did not make a second attempt at such overt social criticism again until *Jude the Obscure*. Admittedly there can be several explanations for this, especially practical and financial ones. It also seems probable, however, that he may soon have realized that his interest in the human situation focussed more readily on emotional and spiritual than on socio-political aspects. This appears all the more possible in the light of his 'affective' psychology, whether this be derived from Fourier or Comte and the positivists. For whatever reason, the fact remains that there is a definite change of focus of Hardy's social criticism after his abortive first attempt. This change is gradual, for although the revolutionary and socialistic views of *The Poor Man and the Lady* have disappeared, there remains a strain of social criticism in the traditional sense in the early novels. The first noticeable change of focus comes with *The Return of the Native*, but it is not only a shift from socio-economic matters to spiritual and emotional. The novel also introduces 'Hellenism' as a criterion against which modern life is assessed.[36] Unfortunately, Hardy's 'Hellenism' cannot be said to be a clearly defined criterion, but it is at least a more explicitly stated criterion than is found in the early novels.

It seems possible to distinguish, then, two phases in Hardy's criticism. It is tempting to see the first one – up to 1876 when he started writing *The Return of the Native* – as primarily influenced by his reading of Fourier and Comte, as long as it is remembered that their influence continues to be noticeable in the clear inter-relationship between Hardy's psychological vision, his 'affective' psychology, and his criticism of modern civilization. The second phase probably owes a great deal to Hardy's reading about Ancient Greece in the mid-1870s and, as we shall see below, to his knowledge of Matthew Arnold.

In both phases there is a strong tendency to concentrate on spiritual and emotional values. I do not mean to suggest either that Hardy was unable to understand the importance of the overall situation of society to its intellectual or spiritual life, or to imply that he was insensitive to social injustice or inequality. On the contrary, his notes offer abundant evidence of his interest in broad social issues. From Disraeli, for instance, Hardy quoted: 'We owe the English peerage to three sources – the spoliation of the Church; the open & flagrant sale of its honours by the elder Stuarts; & the borough-mongering of out own times. . . . The House of Lords is a valuable institution for any member of it who has no distinction – neither character, talents, nor estate' (entry 1124). And from the radical Irish politician Max O'Rell, he copied a sharp assessment of the political power based on this kind of genealogy: 'The existence of the House of Lords is an insult to the common sense of the English nation.'[37] The ultimate form of subordination, slavery, is also noted in its traditional forms such as 'Mediaeval villeinage . . . Russian serfdom . . . the Spanish enslavement of Peruvians & Mexicans . . . American slave-trade' (entry 629), as well as in its most recent manifestation, according to the bitter analysis of Victor Hugo: 'It is said that slavery has disappeared from European civilization. This is a mistake. . . . It weighs now only upon woman, & is called prostitution' (entry A245).

In addition to observations on social inequalities and injustices, there are also many entries from writers with revolutionary social views, positivist, socialist, radical, and utopian, such as Balzac, Baudelaire, Hugo, Charles Kingsley, Leopardi, William Morris, Alfred de Musset, Jean Paul Richter, Zola, and a great number of positivist writers.[38] The amount of quoted material strongly suggests that Hardy sympathized with, perhaps accepted, their views to a great extent. It is to be noted, however, that he studied the problems through the medium of literature and not in first-hand social or political sources. It seems significant, for instance, that the entries Hardy made from the one article on contemporary political movements that he copied anything from at all — 'The European Terror' by Emile de Laveleye, entries 1294–6 — are of a kind suggesting that he was not even familiar with the various socialist movements. He takes down, for example, in the manner of an uninitiated student, elementary information about the varieties of socialism on the Continent and outlines the arguments of Radical Socialism on hereditary succession, the distribution of property, and the nationalization of land.[39]

At first sight it may seem difficult to draw any definite conclusion about Hardy's attitude towards social issues, be it socialism or even democracy itself, on the basis of the notebooks. On the one hand there is reflected in his quotations the insight into, and the implied sympathy for, democratic rule. This is the case, for the instance, with De Tocqueville's observation that 'the common people is more uncivilized in aristocratic countries than in any others' (entry 1135). The debasement of the poor people in England compared to that of France Hardy had also noted from another source: 'Taine in "Notes on England" speaks of the degradation in the poor wearing the old clothes of the rich — the clothes being passed on stage by stage to the bottom — in England. "Among us, a peasant, a workman, is a different man, not an inferior person: his blouse belongs to him as my coat belongs to me — it has suited no one but him. This employment of ragged clothes is more than a peculiarity; the poor resign themselves here to be the footstool of others"' (entry 1026). Hardy was later to use Taine's observation in 'The Dorsetshire Labourer' (Orel, 176; see entry 1026n).

On the other hand, there are unmistakable indications of a basic distrust in the nature of the masses and in the desirability of democracy. From Mahaffy Hardy quoted that 'A free constitution is absurd if the opinion of the majority is incompetent. Until men are educated they

want a strong hand over them. . . . Even yet very few nations in the
world are fit for diffused political privileges' (entry 542). Although
Hardy is likely to have included England among the 'few nations',
several other entries suggest that his view of the common people was not
particularly 'democratic'. Hardy showed interest, for instance, in the fact
that a 'republicanism of intellect' was discernible even in the French
Revolution. From Louis Blanc he learnt that 'The Girondins got to
represent in the Revolution that portion of the citizen-class in whom the
passion for equality did not exclude a certain degree of disdain for the
people, & is at bottom only the natural revolt of talent against factitious
superiorities' (entry 1032). Whether or not Hardy agreed with 'the
natural revolt of talent', he nevertheless quoted several observations with
a similar attitude towards the masses: Plato's 'The madness of the
multitude' (entry 1322), Disraeli's 'the life of the majority must ever be
imitation' (entry 1120), Arnold's argument that since 'the majority are
bad' (entry 1323) one should pay tribute to Plato's 'indestructible
conviction that States are saved by their righteous remnant' (entry 1324).
Such condescending notions towards the common people are not
traditionally associated with Hardy, and it might be tempting to
interpret such entries as depositories of opinions that Hardy rejected, if it
were not for the fact that similar notions are expressed both in the *Life*
and in his novels.[40]

With this view of the masses it is not surprising to find Hardy copying
Arnold's uneasiness about democracy and its effects: '*Democracy, the
difficulty for*, is how to find & keep high ideals. The individuals who
compose it are, the bulk of them, persons who need to follow an ideal,
not to set one; & one ideal of greatness, high feeling, & fine culture
which an aristocracy once [in 18th cent.] supplied to them they lose by
the very fact of ceasing to be a lower order, & becoming a democracy. . . . Our country is probably destined to become much more
democratic; who or what will give a high tone to the nation then?'
Hardy expresses the same apprehension in 1891 after he has witnessed
what he considered the vulgar and insensitive behaviour of the crowds in
front of the art objects in the British Museum: 'Democratic government
may be justice to man, but will probably merge in proletarian, and when
these people are our masters it will lead to more of this contempt, and
possibly be the utter ruin of art and literature' (*Life*, 236; cf. also 185–6,
213).

Hardy had found a basically anti-democratic attitude also in Comte, one of the main sources of his historical or evolutionary view on the development of society.[41] Comte offered, for instance, a fundamentally favourable interpretation of the Middle Ages, of a society, that is, far from democratic. Despite his criticism of mediaeval thought, Comte did not share the common nineteenth-century view of the 'dark' Middle Ages. On the contrary, he pointed out how it formed a necessary transitional period, how its Catholicism 'pointed to the conception of Humanity without realizing it' (entry 688), and how mediaeval feudalism in fact stood out 'as the first type of the right organisation of man's practical forces' (entry 687).

Of at least equal importance to Hardy's historical perspective on society was his reading about antiquity, especially ancient Greece. Hardy noted several inadequacies in Greek society (see entries 502, 507, 510, 533) but the overall impression of Greek life reflected in his notebooks is one of cheerfulness and happiness – an impression which becomes very significant in relation to his fiction, where he depicts modern life, despite its gradual growth of democracy and equality, as far less emotionally satisfying than undemocratic, pagan life. Of course, Hardy does not attribute the sadness of modern life to the growth of democracy but neither does he point to the latter as a source of hope. Again, this suggests in my opinion that political issues have a low priority in the set of values in Hardy's fiction. It would, however, be inadvisable to make too much of the influence of either Comte or 'Hellenism' on Hardy's attitude towards democracy. Nevertheless, it may be assumed that they supported the scepticism Hardy had come across in Arnold and thus meant additional counterbalance to the democratic and egalitarian ideas which he was also familiar with.

If Hardy was ambiguous about democracy, the evidence in the 'Literary Notes' indicates that he was still more hesitant about socialism. In fact, he seems to have accepted the hostile approach taken by Herbert Spencer in an article entitled 'The Coming Slavery'. From it Hardy noted first of all Spencer's argument that misconceptions supporting socialism arise when 'the miseries of the poor are depicted [and when] they are thought of as the miseries of the deserving poor, instead of being thought of, as in large measure they should be, as the miseries of the undeserving poor' (entry 1328). Then he also copied Spencer's striking conclusion: 'All socialism involves slavery. . . . The degree of his [man's] slavery varies according to the ratio between that which he is forced to yield up, & that which he is allowed to retain; & it matters not whether his master is a single person or a society. . . . Towards such an enslavement many recent measures, & still more the measures advocated, are carrying us' (entry 1329).[42] If such entries reflect Hardy's own ideas – and there is no evidence to the contrary – we have yet another reason to de-emphasize revolutionary or progressive politico-economic issues in Hardy's fiction – socialism being, after all, the main politico-economic question at the time.

The material discussed above suggests that whereas Hardy was far from being insensitive to economic and political inequalities and injustices, he was not particularly 'democratic' and certainly not socialistic. It seems desirable to point this out for the purpose of emphasizing the danger of reading more progressive social engagement into his novels than is immediately noticeable.

The picture of Hardy as a social thinker that emerges from the 'Literary Notes' is not the one often given of him as the spokesman of the common man, the crusader for the agricultural labourer – much as he may have felt concerned about them. It is rather that of a man who does not feel strongly about the leading social issues of the day, democracy and socialism, of one who is more concerned about emotional, intellectual and spiritual social problems, of a man whose social criticism approaches to a considerable extent, in fact, the humanistic idealism characteristic of so much of Matthew Arnold's criticism of nineteenth-century society.[43]

There are two quotations from Matthew Arnold in the 'Literary Notes' which perhaps more than any others help to define the main direction of Hardy's social criticism, at the same time as they gave a preliminary idea of how this aspect of Hardy's fiction may owe something not only to Arnold's criticism of society but also to his literary criticism. The first quotation develops Arnold's view of the modern spirit:

> Modern times find themselves with an immense system of institutions, established facts, accredited dogmas, customs, rules which have come to them from times not modern. In this system their life has to be carried forward; yet they have a sense that this system is not of their own creation, that it by no means corresponds exactly with the wants of their actual life, that, for them it is customary, not rational. The awakening of this sense is the awakening of

the modern spirit. The modern spirit is now awake almost
everywhere; the sense of want of correspondence between the
forms of modern Europe & its spirit, between the new wine of the
eighteenth & nineteenth centuries, & the old bottles of the eleventh
& twelfth centuries or even of the sixteenth & seventeenth centuries,
almost everyone now perceives; it is no longer dangerous to affirm
that this want of correspondence exists; people are even beginning
to be shy of denying it. To remove this want of correspondence is
beginning to be the settled endeavour of most persons of good sense.
Dissolvents of the old European system of dominant ideas & facts
we must all be, all of us who have any power of working; what we
have to study is that we may not be acrid dissolvents of it (entry
1017; Hardy's underlining indicated by italics).

It is this kind of social criticism, it seems to me, that we find also in
Hardy's novels: not a concern with political or economic issues, but a
general preoccupation, rooted in humanistic idealism, with the spiritual,
emotional, and intellectual problems of modern society. That Arnold
was more specifically socio-political occasionally, or that, as De Laura
persuasively maintains, Hardy was more impressed by the 'ache' of
modernism than with the promises held out by Arnold in the 1860s, is not
of immediate relevance here.[44] Our concern is with the general tendency
of the material that Hardy singled out for particular study. It may be
difficult to define exactly the significance to be attributed to the passage
quoted above or the essay as a whole – although specific issues raised in it
will be considered below – but that Hardy found great general stimulus
in it is shown by mere physical evidence alone. In addition to the initial
copying of it in 1876, there is the extensive underlining and marginal
markings (as shown in the transcription) as well as the fact that Hardy re-
copied sections of it in 1880 and again in 1887. It seems reasonable to
assume that Hardy's first reaction to the essay was one of recognition, or
partial recognition, rather than of fresh discovery; that Arnold's
observations helped to name and clarify some of Hardy's own feelings
about the clash between traditional values and modern thought, and at
the same time indicated a sphere of mutual interest and concern.

The second quotation which points to an important element in the
Hardy-Arnold relationship, of relevance here, focuses on an aesthetic
principle, by Lionel Trilling even called Arnold's 'literary point of
view', which is as central to Hardy as it is to Arnold: 'The end & aim of

all literature, if one considers it attentively is, in truth, *a criticism of life*' (entry 1180; Arnold's and Hardy's italics).[45] How this principle was to be applied the two may not have agreed on, but without a general acceptance of it Hardy is not likely to have bothered about any kind of social criticism in his creative writing. The principle is implicit in Hardy's fiction and is explicity stated in his 'critical' writing. It is prominent, for instance, in 'The Profitable Reading of Fiction' (see Orel, 113 ff.), but it is most conspicuously professed in the 'Apology' (1926), and with a distinct reference to Arnold. Having noted attacks on his philosophy, Hardy asks: 'Should a shaper of such stuff as dreams are made of disregard considerations of what is customary and expected, and apply himself to the real function of poetry, the application of ideas to life (in Matthew Arnold's familiar phrase)?' (Orel, 53–4). The question is rhetorical, and as Hardy goes on to point out, to follow Arnold's advice exacts a painful price, for differences in opinion between reader and writer are likely to arise 'whenever a serious effort is made towards that which the authority I have cited – who would now be called old-fashioned, possibly even parochial – affirmed to be what no good critic could deny as the poet's province, the application of ideas to life. One might shrewdly guess, by the by, that in such recommendation the famous writer may have overlooked the cold-shouldering results upon an enthusiastic disciple that would be pretty certain to follow his putting the high aim in practice . . .' (Orel, 54). The conditional mode of Hardy's reasoning does not conceal the autobiographical substance of the passage, which also testifies to the permanence in Hardy's thought of the concept of 'the application of ideas to life' – the phrase quoted in the 'Apology' some fifty years after it was first entered into the 'Literary Notes'.

The similarities suggested so far on the basis of two quotations are admittedly too vague and inconsequential to merit much attention either in the field of social criticism or aesthetics. But the general impression of affinity and potential influence given by these excerpts is both strengthened and made more specific by several other entries from Arnold in the 'Literary Notes'. This is not to say that Hardy's knowledge of the older writer was limited to the sources quoted from in the extant notebooks.[46] But the available concrete evidence there alone suggests the possibility of substantial influence and stimulus from Arnold on both the general direction of, and individual elements in, Hardy's social thought.

The 'Literary Notes' indicate that Hardy's main reading of Arnold took place in the second half of the 1870s, with the possibility that the earliest Arnold material, from *Literature and Dogma* (entries 101–4), is of a somewhat older origin. Since it was among some old notes which Hardy asked his wife to copy into his notebook in 1876, it may date back to 1873, the year of publication of *Literature and Dogma*.[47] The chronology for the other Arnold entries is as follows: in 1876 Hardy read 'Bishop Butler and the Zeitgeist' (entries 298–300); in 1877, 'Falkland', and the following essays from *Essays in Criticism*, First Series: 'The Literary Influence of Academies' (entry 1015), 'Maurice de Guérin' (entry 1016), 'Heinrich Heine' (entry 1017), 'Pagan and Mediaeval Religious Sentiment' (entry 1018), and 'Joubert' (entries 1019–22). Two years later he copied material from 'Wordsworth' (entries 1102–9) and from *Mixed Essays*: 'Preface' (entries 1131, 1134), 'George Sand' (entry 1132), 'Democracy' (entries 1135–7), 'Equality' (entries 1138–43), and 'A French Critic on Milton' (entries 1144–5). In 1880 Hardy again took a series of excerpts from *Essays in Criticism*: 'The Function of Criticism' (entries 1159–65), 'The Literary Influence of Academies' (entries 1166–7, 1181–2), 'Maurice de Guérin' (entries 1168–72), 'Heinrich Heine' (entries 1173–5), 'Pagan and Mediaeval Religious Sentiment' (entries 1176–8) and 'Joubert' (entries 1179–80). In 1884, Hardy extracted a few observations from 'Numbers' (entries 1322–6) and finally, in 1887, he again made some excerpts from 'Wordsworth', 'Heine', and 'The Literary Influence of Academies' ('Literary Notes I', p. 219). The excerpts are headed 'Condensed from M. Arnold', and may well have been made from the earlier entries in which the material is found (entries 1015, 1017, 1102, and 1104).

For our present consideration it is significant that even in his last notes from Arnold, Hardy should be intrigued by Arnold's views in the two areas introduced by our first two quotations: with Arnold's concern about the spiritual needs of modern society, and with literature's potential for helping these needs by offering a criticism of life. Thus he again quotes Arnold's call for a change of traditional views: '*Dissolvents* of the old European system of dominant ideas we must all be . . . but . . . not acrid dissolvents of it'; and, again, literature's role in the criticism of life is subscribed to: '*Apply ideas* to life [in literature], nobly and profoundly, your *own* ideas' ('Literary Notes I', p. 219; Hardy's italics).

What the new ideas should be they may have differed about, but the theory *per se* must have been stimulating, and the note of individualism struck at the end of Arnold's exhortation points to what both Arnold and Hardy thought of as a prerequisite for new and adequate ideas: the courage to make the individual human conscience the standard for modern ideas and values. As he was in 1876, Hardy is again in 1887 impressed by Arnold's account of how Goethe, 'that grand dissolvent' (entry 1017), proceeded in his task of dissolution of old ideas: '*Goethe* puts the standard *inside* every man instead of outside him. When he is told such a thing must be so – there is immense authority & custom in favour of its being so – it has been held to be so for a thousand years, he answers – "But *is* it so? Is it so to me?"' ('Literary Notes I', p. 219). In a general sense these questions are indirectly asked in most of Hardy's works, with increasing intensity in the late novels. I emphasize the 'general' meaning of the questions, because when they are raised in, for instance, *Tess* and *Jude*, they relate largely to sex and marriage and are not applied in a sense Arnold would have been comfortable with. The importance here, however, is that Hardy found also in Arnold, as regards intellectual and spiritual problems, views comparable with the 'Religion of Humanity' which he encountered among the positivists. There is a possibility, that is, of some debt on theoretical grounds to Arnold for *Tess* being 'saturated with human & anti-theological morality' – although these qualities, as Frederic Harrison preferred to think, are perhaps primarily to be attributed to positivist influence.[48]

Also as regards the modes of thought by which the individual writer is to help dissolve 'the old European system of dominant ideas and facts', there is at least partial agreement between Arnold and Hardy. Thus we find Hardy committing to his study notes in 1877 Arnold's definition in 'Pagan and Mediaeval Religious Sentiment' of the basic thought process of the modern spirit: 'The poetry of later paganism lived by the senses & understanding, the poetry of mediaeval Christianity lived by the heart & imagination. But the main element of the modern spirit's life is neither the senses & understanding, nor the heart & imagination; it is the imaginative reason' (entry 1018). Hardy was sufficiently struck by the concept of the 'imaginative reason' to re-copy it also in 1880, probably before 21 February (see entry 1183n), when he re-read *Essays in Criticism* (see entry 1176n). Early that year Hardy started writing *A Laodicean*, and, as Michael Millgate has perceptively suggested, the basic conception in Arnold's essay of the clash between the modern spirit and

Mediaeval Catholicism 'responds to the whole situation of *A Laodicean*, lays down, indeed, the lines of its central battle'.[49]

To judge from the entries related to social criticism in the 'Literary Notes' Hardy took a keen interest in social and sociological questions, and he was by no means blind to social injustices. The notes do suggest, however, that he was neither particularly concerned about concrete plans to handle social anomalies, nor enthusiastic about the two most prominent socio-political movements of the day, democracy and socialism. It seems in fact no coincidence that his most favourable entry on democracy should be entitled 'Democratic Art': 'Delivered from scholastic trad.[ns] regarding style & . . . subjects . . . deliv.[d] from pedantry & kind reactionary fervour . . . from depend.[ce] upon aristoc.[c] & eccles.[l] authority – sharing the emancip.[n] of the intellect by mod.[n] science . . . new political conceptions . . . the whole of nature, seen for the first time with sane eyes, the whole of human.[ty] liberated from caste & class distinct.[ns] . . .'[50] It may be somewhat unfair to suggest that as a man Hardy had a primarily aesthetic approach to political and economic social issues – not directly concerning himself, that is. That he did keep a deliberate artistic distance from such issues in most of his fiction is clear from his attitude towards 'fiction with a purpose', and what he says about the need for detachment from philosophical schools is applicable also to social issues.[51] In any case, I believe it is legitimate to conclude that the trends in Hardy's reading here outlined point to an idealistic and visionary social criticism, and that this criticism to a large extent is based on Hardy's 'affective' psychology, his view of man. It is, of course, impossible to assess how much these areas of his thought finally owe to his reading. But, although one should not forget Hardy's own statement that 'He has read well who has learnt that there is more to read outside books than in them' (*Life*, 107), a consideration of his fiction in the light of his 'Literary Notes' still shows that Hardy found extensive and substantial help in his reading for his speculations on, and dramatizations of, the emotional and spiritual problems of man in the English society of the nineteenth century.

NOTES

1. William R. Rutland, *Thomas Hardy: A Study of his Writings and Their Background*, Oxford, 1938, ix.
2. Walter F. Wright, *The Shaping of the Dynasts: A Study in Thomas Hardy*, Lincoln, Nebraska, 1967. Among several good studies in the intervening years, see especially H. C. Webster, *On a Darkling Plain*, Chicago, 1947; rpt. 1964; Evelyn Hardy, *Thomas Hardy: A Critical Biography*, 1954; Carl Weber, *Hardy of Wessex*, New York and London, 1965.
3. Two notebooks labelled 'Memoranda I' and 'Memoranda II' were published as *Thomas Hardy's Notebooks*, ed. Evelyn Hardy, 1955.
4. See pp. 228–230.
5. About half the number of entries in the two volumes entitled 'Literary Notes' are published in *The Literary Notes of Thomas Hardy*, vol. I, ed. Lennart A. Björk, Göteborg, 1974. The second half is being prepared for publication. Subsequent references to the 'Literary Notes' will be made parenthetically in the text and will be, wherever possible, to my edition and to the entry numbers rather than to the page numbers. Where quotations are from notes not yet published, references are to the pagination of the manuscript volumes.
6. For a more detailed account of the evidence, see Introduction to the *Literary Notes*.
7. For sound secondary sources on these influences, see particularly Rutland, Webster, and Wright.
8. Webster, 25.
9. For a comprehensive list of secondary material on Hardy and the Bible, see *Literary Notes*, entry 102n.
10. Rutland, 20.
11. See Robert Gittings, *Young Thomas Hardy*, 1975, 39 ff.
12. Jerome Hamilton Buckley, *The Triumph of Time*, Cambridge, Mass., 1966, 20.
13. Walter Bagehot, *Estimates of Some Englishmen and Scotchmen*, 1858, 280.
14. John Ruskin, 'Of Modern Landscape'; quoted in Buckley, 82.
15. J. S. Mill, *On Liberty*, Pelican Classics edition, 1976, 95.
16. The 'Studies, Specimens etc' Notebook is in the private collection of Richard L. Purdy.
17. *On Liberty*, 95. For a recent discussion of Hardy and Shelley, see F. B. Pinion, *Thomas Hardy: Art and Thought*, 1977, 148–57.
18. See Introduction, *Literary Notes*, xii ff.
19. For a photoreproduction of the Fourier material and a fuller discussion of it, see *Literary Notes*, entry 1 and 1n.

20. Auguste Comte, *System of Positive Polity*, transl. E. S. Beesly *et al.*, 1876, II, 17. Subsequent references to Comte's works are made parenthetically in the text.

21. For a professional account of the roles of biology and sociology in Comte's psychology, see Fay Berger Karpf, *American Social Psychology*, New York and London, 1932, 18 ff. Cf. also Hardy's excerpt from Leslie Stephen: 'Darwinism is as fruitful in its bearing upon sociology as in its bearing upon natural history' (entry 1193).

22. See B. Holländer, *Comte's Analysis of the Human Faculties*, 1892.

23. *Far from the Madding Crowd*, 407. Subsequent references to the novels are made parenthetically in the text and refer to the Wessex edition.

24. Cf. Bernard J. Paris's observation that 'positivist psychology taught that man is innately social and sympathetic', in 'George Eliot's Religion of Humanity,' *ELH*, 29, 424.

25. *Thomas Hardy's Personal Writings*, ed. Harold Orel, 1966, 1967, 146. Subsequent references to Orel's edition are made parenthetically in the text.

26. Leszek Kolakowski, *Positivist Philosophy* (orig. publ. in Polish, 1966; transl. 1968; Pelican Books, 1972), 65.

27. For an analysis of Mill's individualistically oriented psychology, see, for instance, *Brett's History of Psychology*, ed. R. S. Peters, 1953; rev. 1962, 666.

28. Donald Drew Egbert, *Social Radicalism and the Arts*, Princeton, N.J., 1967, 145 ff.

29. Kolakowski, 81.

30. For another possible reflection of Comte's psychological law of development in *Tess*, see *Literary Notes*, entry 751n.

31. Harrison to Hardy, 29 Dec. 1891. DCM.

32. J. B. Bury, *The Idea of Progress*, 1932, rpt. New York, 1960, 335, 345.

33. Kolakowski, 87.

34. Basil Willey, *Nineteenth-Century Studies*, 1959; Penguin Books, 1964, 206–7.

35. *Brett's History*, 498.

36. For a development of this idea see my '"Visible Essences" as Thematic Framework in Hardy's *The Return of the Native*', *English Studies*, 53, 1972, 52–63. Hardy's 'Hellenism' is discussed in my forthcoming 'Psychological Vision and Social Criticism in the Novels of Thomas Hardy'.

37. 'Literary Notes I' p. 221.

38. For the avant-garde social views of these writers, see Egbert, *Socialism and the Arts*.

39. The inequality due to hereditary succession is also noted in entries 1138–40 from Arnold's 'Equality'.

40. Cf. also J. I. M. Stewart's observation that like 'another great writer of peasant origin, Carlyle, he [Hardy] has a fancy for great men. Common people

have the same roles in *The Dynasts* as in Shakespeare's history plays; they huzza,
or they misbehave themselves, or they are quaintly or robustly humorous',
Thomas Hardy: A Critical Biography, 1971, 217. What Stewart says about the
common people in *The Dynasts* is applicable also to the background characters
in Hardy's fiction. For Hardy's use of potentially degrading imagery in relation
to them, see *Literary Notes*, entry 1137n. There are also, as Millgate points out,
notebook entries in especially the first half of the *Life* which 'reveal a
profoundly conservative strain' (p. 178). Millgate also rightly emphasizes
Hardy's 'political eclecticism' and refusal to 'make any political commitment
of a public kind' (pp. 181, 180).

41. For Comte's reactionary tendencies, see also Basil Willey, 197, 208–13.

42. Cf. also entry 1330: '"*Socialism* in its least defensible form – . . . imposing a
tax on the more provident & industrious members of the community to save the
residuum from the alternative of immigration or the workhouse." Hon. Geo.
C. Brodrick. 19th Cent. Apl. 1884.'

43. See Lionel Trilling, *Matthew Arnold*, 1931, rpt. 1963, esp. chs. 7–9, and
Harold Robbins, *The Ethical Idealism of Matthew Arnold: A Study of the Nature and
Sources of His Moral and Religious Ideas*, 1959.

44. David J. DeLaura, '"The Ache of Modernism" in Hardy's later Novels',
ELH, 34, 1967, 380–1.

45. Trilling, 192. Cf. also entries 1102, 1104, 1105, and 'Literary Notes I', p. 219.
For a brief discussion of Hardy's aesthetic principles, see Introduction to *Literary
Notes*.

46. Hardy owned the Macmillan editions of Arnold's *Poetic Works* (1890) and
of *Selected Poems* (1893). Some of Hardy's markings in these volumes are
described by Wright, 22.

47. See Introduction, *Literary Notes*, xxxiii–xxxv.

48. Harrison to Hardy, 29 Dec. 1891. DCM. Related to the general emphasis on
individualism is, of course, the concept of the artist's integrity and right to an
'idiosyncratic mode of regard' (*Life*, 225) – a concept Hardy found supported in
Arnold, see entries 1017, 1104.

49. Millgate, 175.

50. 'Literary Notes II', p. 54.

51. For Hardy's attitude towards 'fiction with a purpose', see Introduction,
Literary Notes, xxiii. In July 1899 he wrote to the Rationalist Press Association:
'Though I am interested in the Society I feel it to be one which would naturally
compose itself rather of writers on philosophy, science, and history, than of
writers of imaginative works, whose effects depend largely on detachment. By
belonging to a philosophic association imaginative writers place themselves in
this difficulty, that they are misread as propagandists when they mean to be
simply artistic and delineative' (*Life*, 304).

5: Hardy and Darwin

ROGER ROBINSON

THOMAS HARDY'S LAST LINES OF VERSE, dictated on his death bed, made a vigorous testimony to his adherence to Charles Darwin. A short and bitter squib, the 'Epitaph for G. K. Chesterton' (published for the first time in the 1976 *Complete Poems*) abuses the 'literary contortionist' Chesterton for twisting the truth, specifically the truth of Darwin's theories:

> *Here lies nipped in this narrow cyst*
> *The literary contortionist*
> *Who prove and never turn a hair*
> *That Darwin's theories were a snare . . .*[1]

The Life of Thomas Hardy says that 'as a young man he had been among the earliest acclaimers of *The Origin of Species*' (p. 153), and this early enthusiasm did not diminish. In 1911 and again in 1924, at the age of 84, Hardy drew up lists of the greatest influences on his thought, and each time cited Darwin and the other evolutionists first: 'Darwin, Huxley, Spencer, Comte, Hume, Mill, and others.'[2] The envelope that contained the last two scraps of verse has confirmed for us that he maintained that priority of commitment to the end of his life.

In sustaining this conviction without abatement or modification, Hardy stands apart from other writers of the post-Darwinian age. He eschewed, contemptuously that last poem suggests, the palliative 'contortions' and compromises with conventional Victorian religion or conventional Victorian progressivism, and lived through the age of moral evolution, of evolutionary meliorism, of creative evolution, of social Darwinism, of post-war progressive universalism, without ever losing his deep initial belief in the absolute truthfulness and the fundamental hopelessness of Darwin's ideas.

Hardy also stands apart in another and more fundamental way, for an imaginative artist. What matters in his work is not any particular formulation or articulation of neo-Darwinian theory. He has to be taken literally in his warnings that he was not attempting any such schematized philosophy, that the 'view of life' ascribed to him was 'really a series of fugitive impressions which I have never tried to co-ordinate' ('Apology' to *Late Lyrics and Earlier, Complete Poems*, 1976, 558). Other creative writers, such as Meredith and Butler, made themselves much more proficient as students of evolutionary literature and proponents of particular variants of evolutionary theory. But whereas they, to put it over-simply, were working on the Darwinian phenomenon, Hardy let it work – and allowed us to watch it work – on him. While they offered versions of evolution, Hardy offers a response to it. Evolutionary science had inflicted perhaps the most severe and sudden shock in history to humanity's conception of itself, expanding man's world not geographically but chronologically, from a span of less than six thousand years to many millions. The last such profound readjustment had come with the new science and astronomy of the late Renaissance, when John Donne recorded the impact in one of the great poems of the human condition:

> *So short is life, that every peasant strives,*
> *In a torne house, or field, to have three lives.*
> *And as in lasting, so in length is man*
> *Contracted to an inch, who was a spanne . . .*
> *And new Philosophy calls all in doubt,*
> *The Element of fire is quite put out;*
> *The Sun is lost, and th' earth, and no mans wit*
> *Can well direct him where to looke for it . . .*
> *Tis all in peeces, all cohaerence gone;*
> *All just supply, and all Relation . . .*
> ('The first Anniversary', 133–6, 205 ff.)

Loss, instability, disorientation, incoherence and, above all, the reduction of man's significance in his own sight: these are the experiences which Hardy also renders through poetry and fiction. He was, I believe, the most honest and sensitive recorder of the shock-wave from the evolutionary discoveries. His response is essential to his own achievement and to the age he lived through.

Two caveats are necessary. The total situation to which Hardy was responding involved, of course, other things than Darwinian science, particularly the local problem of a stable and vital agricultural society turning into an exhausted and nomadic one. From the gentle regret for things passing of *Under the Greenwood Tree* to the frenetic railway-ridden restlessness of *Jude the Obscure*, Hardy records these changes with a perceptiveness that points directly to Forster and Lawrence, with their equal insight into 'this nomadic civilization which is altering human nature so profoundly' (*Howards End*, ch. 31). Clearly, too, Hardy was temperamentally predisposed to respond sympathetically to depressive revelations such as Darwin's. His earliest known piece of verse shows him already reflecting on the timescale of life as a serious teenager who had almost certainly not yet read *The Origin of Species:*

> *A stunted thorn*
> *Stands here and there, indeed; and from a pit*
> *An oak uprises, springing from a seed*
> *Dropped by some bird a hundred years ago.*
> ('Domicilium'. Poem 1. Written 1857–60)

Yet a Darwinian consciousness clearly and often explicitly impelled the many images in which the mature Hardy presented man's diminished place in this timescale. In the ironic 'Drinking Song' in *Winter Words* the poet toasts in turn each of the great advances in human knowledge, from Copernicus and Galileo to Einstein, and celebrates each with the mocking refrain,

> *Fill full your cups: feel no distress;*
> *'Tis only one great thought the less!*

Each scientific discovery has destroyed one of the 'great thoughts' by which humanity has enhanced its own image in bridging the gaps in factual knowledge:

> *Next this strange message Darwin brings,*
> *(Though saying his say*
> *In a quiet way);*

> *We all are one with creeping things;*
>   *And apes and men*
>   *Blood-brethren,*
> *And likewise reptile forms with stings.*
>   Chorus
> *Fill full your cups: feel no distress;*
> *'Tis only one great thought the less!*   (Poem 896)

Here the tone is ironic. Elsewhere, Hardy projects in a series of beautifully-rendered visual images this new awareness of man's reduced significance. The boy Jude scaring birds on a ploughed hillside whose 'brown surface . . . went right up towards the sky all round, where it was lost by degrees in the mist' (Pt. I, ch. 2); Tess and Marian at Flintcomb-Ash, between the brown face of the earth and the white face of the sky, 'crawling over the surface of the former like flies' (ch. 43); the night scene in *Far from the Madding Crowd*, where the narrator takes the reader in imagination to the top of the hill to watch the 'panoramic glide of the stars' and the 'roll of the earth eastward', and then interposes the distant notes of Gabriel Oak's flute coming muffled from the 'small dark object' which is his home (ch. 2); or, as a metaphor for humanity, Mrs. Yeobright watching a colony of ants, 'like observing a city street from the top of a tower' (Bk. IV, ch. 6); the creation of a sense of scale against which human action is set and diminished is the strategy of many of Hardy's most memorable passages. In *Two on a Tower* the central imaginative pivot of that strangely enthralling novel is the constant interplay between the foreground figures of the ingenuous astronomer and his ageing lover and the 'stupendous background of the stellar universe' which his telescope also draws into the tower where their affair is developed.

More obviously Darwinian in its connections, and even more diminishing than the physical setting, is the large-scale chronological background against which Hardy increasingly made his figures move. Wessex is a soil into which, as he says in *The Mayor of Casterbridge*, you can't stick a spade at random without knocking against ancient coins or bones. Its tumuli, Roman rings, medieval ruins, provide him with settings which effect an instant ironic reduction to human shows like the rendezvous between Henchard and Susan at Maumbury Ring or of Farfrae and Elizabeth-Jane by the huge prehistoric ramparts of Mai-Dun

Castle; to Henry Knight waiting for death, eyeball to eyeball with a fossilized Trilobite; or to Tess, also waiting, on a sacrificial stone 'older than the centuries'. At many moments the historic perspective becomes a prehistoric, geological one. In the poem 'At Castle Boterel' his return to the scene of an early love affair takes him among

> *Primaeval rocks [on] the road's steep border,*
> *And much have they faced there, first and last,*
> *Of the transitory in Earth's long order . . .*
>
> (Poem 292)

Against the scale of those newly-discovered 'immense lapses of time' which 'had known nothing of the dignity of man' (*A Pair of Blue Eyes*, ch. 22) the grandest of human enterprises must seem trivial. In the dramatic closing effect to *The Dynasts* Hardy makes his lens recede suddenly outwards through time and space until the great men and affairs of the Napoleonic Wars appear

> *in the elemental age's chart*
> *Like meanest insects on obscurest leaves.*

Human history becomes a scene 'of scantest size' from a viewpoint beyond 'earth-invisible suns'. The other writer with the imaginative leap to turn the new perspectives of modern science into such powerful metaphors of the human condition was H. G. Wells, in the different forms of the scientific romance and the short story. 'Under the Knife' anticipated by ten years Hardy's cinematic concept in the 'After Word' of a vision expanding infinitely as its viewpoint recedes 'into ghastly gulfs of sky'.

The tragic dimension in all this comes from humanity's sense of loss ('one great thought the less') at our diminished significance, from our capacity to suffer emotionally through such knowledge. Lionel Stevenson's seminal essay on Hardy and Darwin in *Darwin Among the Poets* has made famous the passages in Hardy's Notebooks where he argues that man has evolved too far for the imperfect environment in which he is placed. Human emotions, the capacity to feel and therefore to suffer, are 'a blunder of overdoing' in the evolutionary process, 'the nerves being evolved to an activity abnormal in such an environment'.

Stevenson cites several poems which resentfully treat the evolutionary process in these terms, such as 'Before Life and After':

> *A time there was — as one may guess*
> *And as, indeed, earth's testimonies tell —*
> *Before the birth of consciousness,*
> *When all went well . . .*
>
> *But the disease of feeling germed,*
> *And primal rightness took the tint of wrong . . .*
>
> (Poem 230)

This, clearly, is the tint of Tess's 'stealthy . . . movement' and 'rising colour' as she suckles her child, unable to share her mother's acceptance of its birth as 'Nater, arter all' and despite the authorial voice's insistence that she had broken 'no law known to the environment in which she fancied herself such an anomaly' (ch. 14). The same 'disease of feeling' cripples both Clym and Eustacia in *The Return of the Native*. In Egdon Heath, Hardy created his most memorable archetype of the natural environment — immeasurably aged, probably indeed past its best, grudgingly rendering sustenance for a harsh and imperfect human existence. Incapable of the mindless accord with it which contents the unreflecting Thomasin, Clym's more developed consciousness pushes him to aspiration, perplexity and pain, while Eustacia is driven with an increasing frenzy to seek escape into various forms of illusory glamour, most vividly typified in the mumming episode and her association with fire and ritual celebration. F. R. Southerington has very well shown that the notion of the evolved and still-evolving consciousness is the basis of this novel,[3] which constantly evokes the Promethean myth of human aspiration in order to revoke it as something no longer possible to believe in, and which leaves us with a final image of aspiration modified by experience and resigned to its own limitations: Clym the modestly hopeful preacher and blind man, leading others towards a patchy, long-term and uncertain amelioration.

In trying to dramatize the 'disease of feeling' for the popular market for the first time, Hardy fills *The Return of the Native* with scenes so vivid, colourful and even lurid that they remain memorable without ever really eliciting a sensitive engagement with the sensitivities of the characters. In *Jude the Obscure*, with the experience of *The Woodlanders* and *Tess of the d'Urbervilles* behind him, Hardy wrote a much more moving novel of the inner consciousness. Arabella here fulfils the function which has been performed by the choric rustics of the earlier novels, with her unreflecting acceptance of life and her own place in it: 'Pigs must be killed' and 'poor folks must live' (I, 10). Living entirely for the present, mating, separating, bearing and discarding offspring, re-mating, all without compunction, Arabella accepts the reality of the struggle for survival with matter-of-fact self-interest. In Jude and Sue, however, Hardy takes one stage further his concept of the over-evolution of sensitivity. The especial pathos of their situation is that they not only suffer themselves, but suffer with others' sufferings. Jude's agonized sympathy with the pig is heightened by Arabella's indifference equally to the pig's feelings and to Jude's. The scene where Jude and Sue are both kept awake by their sufferings on behalf of the trapped rabbit indicates that this is an important part of the bond between them. When Arabella reappears and appeals to Jude at Aldbrickham, Sue recognizes that his compulsive sensitivity is helpless against Arabella's self-interest: 'An inconvenient sympathy seemed to be rising in Jude's breast at the appeal' (V, 2).

Hardy then makes it quite explicit, through Arabella's mockery of Jude as a 'tender fool. . . . Just as he used to be about birds and things', and in the couple's own dialogue about their abortive attempts to get married, just after they have been joined by Little Father Time: ' "We are horribly sensitive; that's really what's the matter with us, Sue!" he declared.' Sue's reply makes clear Hardy's intention to present their sensitivity as part of a still-continuing evolution towards yet greater pain:

'Everybody is getting to feel as we do. We are a little beforehand, that's all. In fifty, a hundred, years the descendants of these two [children] will act and feel worse than we. They will see weltering humanity still more vividly than we do now . . .' (V, 4)

The sensitivity which torments and finally destroys Jude and Sue is evolved to an activity even more abnormal in Little Father Time. It is perhaps because he exists in the novel so obviously to embody this extreme of evolutionary pessimism that he fails so badly as a fictional creation. For once, Hardy has imposed a schematized idea on to a character, instead of following the method which gives such integrity and richness to almost all his fiction – allowing the ideas to emerge, as 'fugitive impressions', from the author's changing responses to the characters. (I shall return to this idea.)

And so, in a world in which human actions and beliefs have just been trivialized by the discovery of the true immensity of their context of time and space, when faith in man's divine origins and immortal prospects has been undermined, a tragic sensitivity to suffering continues to evolve to the point at which the next generation represents 'the beginning of the coming universal wish not to live' (*Jude*, VI, 2). Insisting on such truths and giving such powerful imaginative shape to them, in defiance of an age 'breezily' confident of progress, Hardy is indeed fulfilling his own demand that 'if way to the Better there be, it exacts a full look at the Worst' ('In Tenebris II', Poem 137).

He had still one more painful twist to give to man's newly-fitted tail. Perhaps the most disturbing of all the implications to be drawn from Darwin's work is the deterministic notion that the characteristics of both the individual and the race are preconditioned by mechanical forces outside humanity's control. Very often, of course, Hardy personifies these forces variously as the Immanent Will, First Cause, Spinner of the Years, unweeting Mind, Nature, Crass Casualty or simply as an unbenevolent and somewhat incompetent God. (On one occasion, in 'A Philosophical Fantasy', he speculates on the possibility of this Deity being female.) Reading *The Origin of Species* probably helped to confirm the young Hardy's rejection of the Christian God. Evolutionary science certainly instilled into him that sense of 'passionless impersonality' (in Thomas Huxley's phrase) which underlies all his versions of a Life Force. It is a mistake, however, to cite any one version as Hardy's ultimate theological conclusion, as so many interpreters have jostled to do, although – or rather, because – each version is so imaginatively appropriate to the mood of its context. Hardy seems to me to have operated always at a personal rather than philosophical level, inventing such variations of the Life Force as he needed them, to explain humanity's plight, to blame for it, or to make it bearable.

These unattractively maladroit deities are in any case only metaphors for the forces that condition and constrain human life. Hardy also rendered the quite literal operation of those forces – environment and heredity – with an unequalled vividness and power.

Writing for the largely urban serial-reading public of the 1870s and 80s Hardy established a reputation as a pithy chronicler of the rural environment. He played the role quite consciously in describing the different breeds of sheep in *Far from the Madding Crowd*, the procedure of a timber auction in *The Woodlanders* or the problem of garlic flavouring the butter in *Tess*. His observation is fine and impeccable. He tells how to find your way through farmland at night by the different sounds made by rain falling on pasture, on the leaves of root crops and on 'naked arable' (*Desperate Remedies*, ch. 17); how to follow others through woodland by the clashing flight of pigeons and the imprint of boots on mud (*The Woodlanders*, ch. 7); and how to know where a cow has lain for the night by the dry compression in the dewy grass (*Tess*, ch. 20). In doing these backgrounds 'from the real', Hardy also communicates a real sense of how they shaped the lives of the characters he puts into them. This is evident as early as the simple seasonal divisions of *Under the Greenwood Tree* and develops into the works-of-the-month pattern of *Far from the Madding Crowd* (with Troy so often an incongruous intrusion), the actual colouring of people by the environment in *The Return of the Native* and the more complex patterns and problems of labour that shape *The Woodlanders*. John Holloway, in one of the most illuminating essays yet written about Hardy,[4] was the first to show how the stories of Henchard and Tess are charted quite consciously in terms of the Darwinian struggle for survival: Henchard a superseded species fighting with the wrong weapons against forces he cannot understand, Tess's every state of existence conditioned by the environments she moves among. She survives with a begrudged adequacy on her home soil of Blackmoor, thrives in the fertile and vitalizing valley of the Froom, barely subsists on the starveacre barrenness of Flintcomb-Ash, and finally becomes extinct (as an independent organism) in the exotic and artificial setting of a seaside resort. This causal consonance between Tess's environment and her condition is sustained even more carefully than Holloway suggested. After conducting the deserted Tess to a Talbothays gray, mean and muddy with winter, Hardy completely cuts the next spring and summer from the narrative action, so as to drive her in mid-winter again to the 'bleak upland' of Flintcomb-Ash; the wheat-threshing is in March; in spring, instead of a new beginning, the family is forced to move and Tess is trapped again. Thus when she rejoins Angel it is May, 'the weather was serenely bright', and it is as if life reverts to the point before the crisis: 'The gloomy intervening time seemed to sink into chaos, over which the present and prior times closed as it never had been' (ch. 58). Hardy thus creates an environment which both physically conditions Tess and metaphorically figures her, which is both an unflinching testimony to Darwinian science and a poetic device of great richness and flexibility.

Environment was always a preoccupation of Hardy's; heredity became so only towards the end of his novel-writing career. At the time of beginning work on the book which became *Tess of the d'Urbervilles* he was busy with jottings about the declined fortunes of his own family. *Jude the Obscure* started with his investigation of a family scandal of two generations earlier, then took on Hardy's growing personal sense of being himself a prisoner of inherited tendencies.[5] This negation of the will is most despondently described in the poems 'Heredity' and 'The Pedigree', with its self-vision of utter helplessness and abasement as the poet realizes that every response he makes has been preconditioned by his ancestors:

> *Said I then, sunk in tone,*
> *'I am the merest mimicker and counterfeit! –*
> *Though thinking, I am I,*
> And what I do I do myself alone'.   (Poem 390)

Hardy took trouble to work this depressing awareness into *Tess of the d'Urbervilles*. As he developed a romantic potboiler called *Too Late Beloved* into the deeply serious and immaculately written finished novel, one of his major changes was a drastic heightening of the emphasis on the heroine's ancestry, to which there are only three references in the first state of the manuscript.[6] In the final version the theme is kept prominently in front of the reader's attention, in the changed title itself, and from the opening scene – Parson Tringham's revelation of John Durbeyfield's pedigree, which introduces the theme dramatically and implies that this is the starting point of Tess's troubles – to the novel's last words on Tess herself: 'And the d'Urberville knights and dames slept on in their tombs unknowing.' The heroine's visit to the family tomb at

Kingsbere was moved from being a passing incident in Rose-Mary's journey to the Vale of the Great Dairies and made into the ironic nadir of the family's fortune and the cause of Tess's own final entrapment by Alec. The spurious 'kinship' between heroine and villain was a late thought, as was her first brief visit to 'claim kin' from a seducer originally called Hawnferne. Another major addition was the unforgettable description of the d'Urberville portraits at Wellbridge Manor. Hardy included the passages emphasizing their ugliness, arrogance and cruelty as late as the First Edition, after the novel had appeared in its bowdlerized weekly-serial form in *The Graphic*.

The effect of this calculated emphasis on Tess's place at the exhausted ending of a long family line is to put her in a tragic situation from which there can be no escape, a captivity made the more harrowing because her every response to it may be seen as having been conditioned by that very heredity. Her fatal supineness under the assaults of Alec and her failure to claim her own rights from Angel, her tendency to 'drift into acquiescence' and her habit even of dropping asleep at critical moments – all this is presented as the passivity of spent family energies. Angel makes the connection openly: 'I cannot help associating your decline as a family with this other fact – of your want of firmness. Decrepit families imply decrepit wills, decrepit conduct' (ch. 35).

There is, of course, another and contrasting aspect of Tess's behaviour under harsh treatment – her sudden brief outbursts of retaliation. When she is riding behind Alec through the Chase and he slides his arm round her, 'with one of those sudden impulses of reprisal to which she was liable she gave him a little push from her' (ch. 11). This was another late alteration, replacing a gauche piece of melodrama in which Rose-Mary sends Hawnferne tumbling completely off the gig on which they are riding. By the careful wording of Tess's 'little push' – insufficiently sustained, as always, to deter Alec completely – and the generalized comment about 'sudden impulses of reprisal', Hardy prepares us for similar but more critical impulses later – when she slaps Alec with the leather threshing glove, slams the window on to his hand and, finally, when she kills him. The 'impulse' is the hereditary concomitant of her passivity, an inbred d'Urberville response. When she swings the gauntlet into Alec's face, the narrative voice observes: 'Fancy might have regarded the act as the recrudescence of a trick in which her armed progenitors were not unpractised' (ch. 47). I shall return to the comment. For the moment, all that can be said seems to be that Tess is simply trapped, like the innumerable trapped birds and small beasts which suffer in both the action and the imagery of the novel, like the 'entrapped flies and butterflies' in the gauzy skirts of the milkmaids going to church, trapped like the workers on the juddering threshing machine, even (I am tempted to undermine my argument by saying) trapped like Jack Dollop in the milkchurn, mechanically pounded into submission – trapped by her heredity and her conditioning.

For some readers this has been the whole of Tess's tragedy. Few critics have been as gloomily well-informed about evolutionary scientific literature as Peter R. Morton, whose important 'Neo-Darwinian Reading of *Tess of the d'Urbervilles*'[7] argues that for the hubris of classical tragedy, for Fortune's wheel, 'Hardy substituted hereditarian determinism'. Hardy's hard-line Darwinism was confirmed, Morton argues, by reading the German neo-Darwinian August Weismann's postulation of 'the complete immutability of the conveyor of heredity, the germ plasm, which creates and passes through the bodies of generation after generation as a parasite passes from host to host'. It's an expertly-marshalled argument. But as a response to the novel, as a guide to Hardy's own response to Darwin, I shall try to show, it is not enough.

For this was Hardy's most complete, complex and deeply-felt rendering of the whole Darwinian matter. He brings together here those two other major aspects of his response to Darwin – reductive environment and excessive consciousness. Tess's wanderings are set against a large geographical background – the two vales spread out on either side of the chalk ridge along which she makes her marathon walk to Emminster – and a vast chronological one. The thousand-year scale marked by the medieval and d'Urberville references, the Cistercian Abbey and the enigmatic monolith of the Cross-in-Hand, is itself diminished by the scene at Stonehenge and the many passages which convey the primeval antiquity of the natural landscape:

> The harts that had been hunted here, the witches that had been pricked and ducked, the green-spangled fairies that 'whickered' at you as you passed; – the place teemed with beliefs in them still, and they formed an impish multitude now. (Ch. 50)

And Tess, as I have shown, suffers like Clym and Jude from the burden of over-evolved sensitivity. Her sense of guilt and her susceptibility to others' miseries initiate each downward turn in her own sad drama of alienation.

Yet even at her moment of most total abnegation, this is not the whole of the response which Hardly presents through Tess. When Angel rejects her after her confession on the wedding-night, she protests: 'I have not told of anything that interferes with or belies my love for you. . . . It is in your own mind what you are angry at, Angel; it is not in me. O, it is not in me' (ch. 35). Angel's charge that her 'want of firmness' is the decrepitude of a decayed family stock makes every reader indignant, not only because of the sexual double standard, but because of the callousness with which it rigidly categorizes an episode as blurred in outline and as complex in interpretation as Hardy deliberately made Tess's loss of virginity in the Chase. This is only the last and most degrading of Angel's many attempts to classify Tess. Hardy tells us in an important earlier passage that Angel had learned the inadequacy of his old preconception of all rustics as just 'Hodge': 'as they became intimately known to Clare, [they] began to differentiate themselves as in a chemical process . . . men every one of whom walked in his own individual way the road to dusty death' (ch. 18). But Tess has still appeared to Angel as 'a visionary essence', an ideal rather than an individual woman, and the wedding-night crisis merely changes her label: 'Here was I thinking you a new-sprung child of nature; there were you, the belated seedling of an effete aristocracy!' (ch. 35). The reader is affronted by this charge because it so heartlessly ignores the central fact of Tess's existence – her individuality, her special oneness, the 'throbbingly alive' quality of her mental responses. When Angel seeks to idealize and typify her, she in the most simple and direct terms asserts her selfhood:

> She was no longer the milkmaid, but a visionary essence of woman – a whole sex condensed into one typical form. He called her Artemis, Demeter, and other fanciful names half teasingly. . . .
>   'Call me Tess', she would say askance; and he did. (Ch. 20)

The final title is thus a careful summary of the novel's most basic concerns. The main title brings together the two forces which Hardy places in such powerful tension: She is 'of the d'Urbervilles', subject to the reductions, pressures and preconditioning which I discussed in the first part of this essay; yet she is still, simply and defiantly, 'Tess'. And where Angel has tried to refashion her as 'a visionary essence' of purity, Hardy defiantly asserts her existence as 'a pure woman', with the emphasis fully capable of falling on the last word.

Through Tess Hardy makes an assertion that has been repeated by many twentieth-century novelists – that the individual must fight for this individuality of existence with every breath. 'Tess was trying to lead a repressed life, but she little divined the strength of her own vitality' (ch. 19). Therefore she rejects learning which will merely tell her that she is a germ plasm or an insect trapped in gauze:

> Because what's the use of learning that I am one of a long row only – finding out that there is set down in some old book somebody just like me, and to know that I shall only act her part; making me sad, that's all. The best is not to remember that your nature and your past doings have been just like thousands' and thousands', and that your coming life and doings'll be like thousands' and thousands'. (Ch. 19)

This protest strikingly echoes that even earlier cry of existentialist defiance hurled by Dostoevsky through the narrator of *Notes from Underground* (1864):

> 'Good Lord, what do I care about the laws of nature and arithmetic, if for some reason I don't like those laws and this two times two makes four. Of course, I won't ram through such a wall with my head if I really don't have the strength to ram through it, but I will not submit just because I have a stone wall before me and I don't have enough strength'.[8]

Laws, whether of arithmetic or of natural selection and heredity, cannot finally explain or contain the individual human existence, and in Dostoevsky's thesis the 'intensified consciousness' is the resource and salvation as well as the painful burden of the 'normal' human spirit. Man's often harmful or stupid desires will guarantee for him that he is a man and not a piano key, says Dostoevsky's narrator (I, 8), just as Hardy insists that each of his country girls 'had a private little sun for her soul to bask in; some dream, some affection, some hobby, at least some remote and distant hope which, though perhaps starving to nothing, still lived on, as hopes will' (ch. 1); just as he asserts later that the rustic denizens of Crick's dairy are in reality 'beings infinite in difference', a phrase reminiscent of Hamlet's meditation on man's capacities.

The similarity of Hardy's position to that of twentieth-century existentialists like Camus and Sartre has been finely observed in an essay by Jean R. Brooks.[9] But there is no need to advance into the twentieth century for confirmation of the nature of Hardy's attitude. His cry and Dostoevsky's are fully part of the structure of their own age, uttered in response to the new power of scientific law which by its very novelty seemed capable of being the whole truth of life. Hardy insists on the truth of that law; but he also insists on defying it, the more remarkably because his cry is one of pity rather than rage.

Therefore we suffer most deeply when Tess seems most helplessly the victim of mechanical forces or most submissive to deadening categorizations, when she suffers on the threshing machine or in the abbot's coffin or overhearing the picture drawn of herself by Angel's brothers on Emminster Hill. Her relationship with Alec is a long struggle between her individuality and his efforts to degrade her into a stereotype. At times – when she remains for 'some few weeks' after her first seduction or rape at The Slopes, when she cries 'Once victim, always victim – that's the law!' at Flintcomb-Ash, and again at Sandbourne – she acquiesces and conforms. Yet Alec, himself ironically rendered by Hardy as a stagey stereotype, is perpetually surprised by Tess's unpredictable refusals to fit the role: '"You are mighty sensitive for a cottage girl" said the young man' (ch. 8). Tess is strongest, seeming to gain ground in the real struggle for survival, when she asserts her individual existence most defiantly; not mindlessly, like Arabella, but still sensitively, and the more powerfully because her selfhood is so deeply felt. Thus when she repudiates the Vicar's certain reasons' and 'strict notions' and challenges him to speak 'as a man', she gains real consolation for herself, if not in the official eyes of the Church, for Sorrow's death (ch. 14).

Her passionate letters to Angel are her most deeply-felt acts of self-assertion, the first appealing, the other protesting, neither decadent gestures of submission nor Norman impulses of reprisal, but the most wholly personal and even egotistic statements that she ever makes. She insists that she is a feeling creature and that therefore her feelings matter:

'Think – think how it do hurt my heart not to see you ever – ever!

Ah, if I could only make your dear heart ache one little minute of
each day as mine does every day and all day long, it might lead you
to show pity to your poor lonely one. . . . Come to me – come to
me, and save me. . . .' (Ch. 48)

'O why have you treated me so monstrously, Angel! I do not
deserve it. . . . You know that I did not intend to wrong you – why
have you so wronged me? . . . I will try to forget you. It is all
injustice I have received at your hands!' (Ch. 51)

Her final attack on Alec is made in the same wholly personal terms, in
that remarkable ballad-like lament and protest which precedes the blow:

'And my sin will kill him and not kill me!. . . O, you have torn my
life all to pieces . . . made me be what I prayed you in pity not to
make me be again! . . . O God – I can't bear this! – I cannot!' (Ch.
56)

Again, the first person is dominant. Together these self-affirming protests
do gain for her a new life, brief but rich, in the phase of 'Fulfilment' with
Angel.

Finally Angel comes indeed to acknowledge and respect her special
individuality. He now rejects his mother's attempt to classify Tess as 'a
mere child of the soil' (ch. 53) and pleads to Tess herself 'I did not see you
as you were!' (ch. 55). Angel is left with his faults, still capable of
conventional snobbish pleasure at her d'Urberville connection, but in
the last phase 'Tenderness was absolutely dominant in Clare at last' (ch.
57). We may see here what Hardy meant elsewhere by 'loving-
kindness': a tender respect for the individuality of others. When Swithin
St. Cleeve finally reaches that way of feeling towards Viviette, in the
cruder anticipation of Angel's development in *Two on a Tower*, Hardy
comments that loving-kindness is 'a sentiment perhaps in the long-run
more to be prized than lover's love' (ch. 41). Through all the negating
pressures of the post-Darwinian world Hardy still asserts the value of
individual life to the individual who possesses it and the responsibility of
others to respect it – that is the one 'great thought' he is determined to
hold on to:

Tess was no insignificant creature to toy with and dismiss; but a woman living her precious life – a life which, to herself who endured or enjoyed it, possessed as great a dimension as the life of the mightiest to himself. (Ch. 25)

It was not a new thought to Hardy. As early as *Desperate Remedies* Cytherea's plight elicits from Mr. Raunham the clergyman the same recognition as Clare reaches here of the woman's priceless individuality, expressed in the same straightforwardly assertive language: 'She had but one life . . .' (ch. 18. 2). Cytherea herself is given moments of self-assertion which engage the reader's response more deeply than anything else in the book:

> '[People] will pause just for an instant, and give a sigh to me, and think, "Poor girl!" believing they do great justice to my memory by this. But they will never, never realize that it was my single opportunity of existence as well as of doing my duty, which they are regarding; they will not feel that what to them is but a thought, easily held in those two words of pity, "Poor girl!" was a whole life to me. . . .' (Ch. 13. 4)

In this novel and later in *A Pair of Blue Eyes* and *Two on a Tower* Hardy imposes a quirky kind of ironic double-focus. For the most part these books were written with a self-consciously stylized adherence to the conventions of tone, language and action of popular fiction, a stylization that at times becomes actually mocking towards his own characters. Yet he also provides moments of sympathetic insight or assertion which convince us that they nevertheless matter, as individual and emotionally conscious people. It is as if he were fulfilling the obligations of popular literary conventions almost cynically, but then turning them into what is effectively another metaphor for constraint and compulsion upon the individual. Thus Viviette Constantine has to break through the prejudices and restrictions of the literary form in which she has her being as well as the social world in which she has been placed. When she does so, eliciting our loving-kindness as well as Swithin's, the effect is remarkable indeed.

But these are isolated moments of breakthrough in books where credible human response remains largely buried under the machinery of romance and sensationalism. The novel in which individualism is the foundation of the whole action and thought is, of course, *The Mayor of Casterbridge*. Even Holloway, showing how Henchard's career is presented through Darwinian images of conflict for territory, hunting and trapping, confrontation, expulsion and extinction, did not do justice to the enormous resilience of the individual self which survives all these assaults. It survives even Henchard's actual defeat and death to live on as the dominant imaginative effect of the book. The subtitle testifies to it: 'A Story of a Man of Character'. So does Henchard's will on the penultimate page: demanding to be ignored and forgotten in death, it makes even that annihilation into a positive claim of the individual's right to choose. It ends with the climactic thump of self-assertion, 'To this I put my name. MICHAEL HENCHARD'.

Hardy is saying more through all this than that the poor beetle which we tread upon in corporal sufferance feels a pang as great as when a giant dies. He builds into *Tess*, especially, and other works, the concept, even closer to twentieth-century existentialism, that the world is actually created by the individual vision. He makes an early reference to the idea when Swithin and Viviette disagree about the strength of the wind and she quotes Hamlet: 'There is nothing either good or bad, but thinking makes it so' (ch. 16). In *Tess* it is central to his conception of her life and experiences and the loving-kindness he demands for her:

> Upon her sensations the whole world depended to Tess; through her existence all her fellow-creatures existed, to her. The universe itself only came into being for Tess on the particular day in the particular year in which she was born. (Ch. 25)

Elsewhere, as she glides in harmony with the hills and dales she lives among, 'her whimsical fancy would intensify natural processes around her till they seemed a part of her own story. Rather they became a part of it; for the world is only a psychological phenomenon, and what they seemed they were' (ch. 13).

Sometimes, Hardy touches on the question of multiplicity of vision which is raised by such extreme psychological individualism. When Giles and Grace in *The Woodlanders* drive together from Sherton, 'the fact at present was merely this, that where he was seeing John-apples and farm-buildings she was beholding a much contrasting scene' (ch. 6). The poem 'Alike and Unlike' tersely records the severance that follows from such a moment of disparate response:

> *We watched the selfsame scene on that long drive,*
> *. . . But our eye-records, like in hue and line,*
> *Had superimposed on them, that very day,*
> *Gravings on your side deep, but slight on mine! —*
> *Tending to sever us thenceforth alway;*
> *Mine commonplace; yours tragic, gruesome, gray.*
>
> (Poem 672)

Much of the conflict of *The Return of the Native* arises from the incompatibility of Clym's and Eustacia's separate perceptions of the same experiences.

But for the most part the tension in Hardy's works is not between rival individualities but between individuality and everything in the post-Darwinian world that threatens to crush it. The tension is real, for defiance is imaginatively as powerful as science. My reference earlier to the poem 'At Castle Boterel' was incomplete:

> *Primaeval rocks form the road's steep border,*
> *And much have they faced there, first and last,*
> *Of the transitory in Earth's long order;*
> *But what they record in colour and cast*
> *Is — that we two passed.*
>
> (Poem 292)

The rocks are ageless and do indeed reduce to insignificance all the transitory incidents enacted among them. Yet at the same time they are his rocks and the only thing they mean is what they mean to him. Similarly, in 'The Roman Grave Mounds' the man furtively digging there sees the mounds as significant not for their archeological fame but simply as the secluded grave of the pet cat whose death matters to him much more.

There is paradox and inconsistency as well as pathos in all this, of course. Yet the inconsistency is, I think, creative, the source of much of the extraordinary tension and imaginative power in Hardy's vision of man, which has never been adequately identified. Tess, at a moment of self-absorption, 'was conscious of neither time nor space'. The novelist makes the reader aware of them in all the ways I have shown, but the awareness somehow enhances rather than destroys her value. Similarly

'The Darkling Thrush' plays a vibrant counterpoint between the poet's gloomy knowledge of the bleakness of time and place, and the bird's ecstatic and defiant expression of a living 'joy illimited' (Poem 119). The word itself is a cry of defiance in so limiting a setting. This is the dimension missing from Morton's account when he says 'Tess's sparrow sings because its hormones make it, because a billion years of selective evolution deny even the possibility of its doing anything else' (p. 48). Caged birds may be the most obviously recurrent of Hardy's images, but joyfully self-fulfilling creatures are just as potent – carolling thrush or dancing widow or zestful rustic bellringer.

If a hard-line Darwinism were Hardy's last word, then the ending of *Tess of the d'Urbervilles*, with its prospect of union between Angel and 'Liza-Lu, would satisfy us more than it does. In Morton's reading, it is a heartless last word, securing the germ-plasm and fulfilling Tess's own wish: 'if she were to become yours it would almost seem as if death had not divided us' (ch. 58). But 'would almost seem' is not 'is' and the prevailing sense of tragic personal loss makes the novel's last sentence a far from heartless conception. Tess might wish, like Henchard or her namesake in the poem 'Tess's Lament', to 'unbe' (Poem 141), but 'the strength of her own vitality' is imaginatively far too powerful for the reader to acquiesce. In spite of everything, Tess continues to exist in the reader's mind as something far more special than a 'visionary essence' or a 'cottage girl' or a 'moment of a maid' or a belated d'Urberville or a germ plasm. These are crude texts painted in capital letters on stiles. Hardy provides other capital letters of at least equal impact: 'Call me Tess' or 'Come to me' or 'MICHAEL HENCHARD'.

The final answer is that there is no final answer, that Hardy can no more say the last word on Tess than he can explain the origins of the Cross-in-Hand, and it is a mistake to read him as if he tries to do so. A single novel in his hands is 'simply an endeavour to give shape and coherence to a series of seemings, or personal impressions, the question of their consistency or their discordance, of their permanence or their transitoriness, being regarded as not of the first moment'. Here, in the 1895 Preface to *Jude*, he speaks of a novel in exactly the same way as he does of a miscellaneous collection of poems in the 'Apology' to *Late Lyrics and Earlier*. It gives illuminating guidance as to how his novels should be read.

Thus when Hardy speculates about the impulses behind Tess's striking

Alec with the threshing glove, he does so in language which is qualified, circumlocutory and ponderously academic: 'Fancy might have regarded the act as the recrudescence of a trick in which her armed progenitors were not unpractised' (ch. 47). The comment is obtrusive, its interpretation hedged. The abiding impression is that she does it. The blow itself is rendered in language which is stunningly direct and specific: 'she passionately swung the glove by the gauntlet directly in his face'. How a fanciful historian might regard the act adds a possible meaning, a 'seeming', an 'impression', but is no more a final and authoritative summing up than when the ignorant Tess tells Abraham that we live on a blighted star (ch. 4), or when Hardy himself responds to the agony of her final tragedy by inventing a malignant deity to take the blame until the worst of grief is past. In one of his earliest surviving poems, 'Hap', Hardy had stated the psychological need for a deity, even a hostile one, to make life's sufferings bearable:

> If but some vengeful god would call to me
> From up the sky, and laugh: 'Thou suffering thing,
> Know that thy sorrow is my ecstasy,
> That thy love's loss is my hate's profiting!'

> Then would I bear it, clench myself, and die,
> Steeled by the sense of ire unmerited;
> Half-eased in that a Powerfuller than I
> Had willed and meted me the tears I shed.   (Poem 4)

And so he steels himself and his reader to bear the sorrow of one of the most moving tragedies in literature: '"Justice" was done, and the President of the Immortals, in Aeschylean phrase, had ended his sport with Tess.'

It is pointless to object that the novel's view has not been Aeschylean. Of course it hasn't. But the novelist's recourse to such an explanation, illogically and inconsistently, at the moment of deepest grief and pity, adds a further level of response to his work. We are as moved by Hardy's pity, by his need to invent a malicious god, as by Tess's plight. If such a reading is true to his intentions, Hardy has written in effect a novel which is to be read as a poem. Instead of the consistent and all-embracing authorial vision of Tom Jones, Emma, Middlemarch or The Ambassadors we watch in Hardy's richest novels a kind of double drama – the experiences of Tess and the experiences of Hardy contemplating Tess. He responds to her situations with all the sensitivity and inconsistency with which we must all interpret to ourselves the pain of others. And finally he puts her out of her misery with as much brutal tenderness as she does the wounded pheasants, 'her tears running down as she killed the birds tenderly' (ch. 41).

Such a way of reading only takes Hardy at his word, in the Preface to *Jude* and elsewhere, that 'impressions' were more his affair than consistency. It is justified by the 'unadjusted impressions', often (as he says in the 'Apology') contradictory, that make up the body of his poetry. It was his habit, moreover, to extract separate 'impressions' from his novels and turn them into short poems like 'Tess's Lament' or 'The Recalcitrants', always to be taken as one of his many varied responses to the action of the novels, never as the final word or key. My reading is justified, too, by the very failure of novels which do achieve consistency, such as *The Pursuit of the Well-Beloved*, almost exactly contemporary with *Tess*, a carefully-wrought dramatization of a single Darwinian theory – consistent, coherent and comprehensively dull.

Consistency is a scientific virtue but not necessarily an artistic one. What makes Hardy the greatest artist of the Darwinian crisis and *Tess of the d'Urbervilles* its greatest work is that he provides not a version of Darwinism but a work made up of deeply-felt responses to it. While insisting on the truth of Darwin, sparing no pains to put in imaginative form the effects on the human condition of heredity, environment and the evolution of consciousness, he still asserts, as movingly and honestly as another contemporary poet, that

> *This Jack, joke, poor potsherd, patch, matchwood,*
> *immortal diamond*
> *Is immortal diamond.*

The works Hardy wrote in response to Darwin are in the fullest sense the tragic epic poems in prose of that troubled generation.

NOTES

1. *The Complete Poems of Thomas Hardy*, ed. James Gibson, 1976, Poem 946. All poem numbers cited hereafter refer to this edition.

2. I am indebted here to an article discussed more fully later: Peter R. Morton, '*Tess of the D'Urbervilles*: A Neo-Darwinian Reading', *Southern Review* (Adelaide), VII, 1974, 38–50.

3. '*The Return of the Native*: Thomas Hardy and the Evolution of Consciousness', in *Thomas Hardy and the Modern World*, ed. F. B. Pinion, Dorchester, 1974, 37–47.

4. 'Hardy's Major Fiction', in *The Charted Mirror*, 1960, 94–107.

5. See J. O. Bailey, 'Ancestral Voices in *Jude the Obscure*', in *The Classic British Novel*, ed. Howard M. Harper and Charles Edge, University of Georgia, 1972, 143–65.

6. See J. T. Laird's indispensable *The Shaping of 'Tess of the D'Urbervilles'*, Oxford, 1975.

7. See Note 2. Here, esp. pp. 42–3.

8. Ed. Robert G. Durgy, trans. Serge Shishkoff, New York, 1969, 13.

9. '*Tess of the D'Urbervilles*: The Move towards Existentialism', in *Thomas Hardy and the Modern World*, 48–59.

6: Hardy and the English Language

NORMAN PAGE

RIGHT FROM THE START, and almost unremittingly thereafter, Hardy's style seems to have exposed itself as an easy target for critical sniping. Nearly all those who reviewed his books as they appeared had something to say on the subject, and nearly all of what they said was unfavourable, or, at best, was praise of a very qualified kind. In noticing *Desperate Remedies*, his first published novel, the *Athenaeum* detected 'a few faults of style and grammar', and the *Saturday Review* deplored 'a little too much of laboured epigram';[1] and as Hardy continued to produce fiction over the next quarter of a century, the reproaches and reproofs, mild or strong, faithfully reappeared. 'Cumbrous words . . . where simpler ones would have served the purpose'; 'monstrous periphrases . . . specimens of the worst "penny-a-liner's" language'; 'mannerism and affectation'; 'forced allusions and images'; 'far-fetched' similes and metaphors; rustic dialogue which is 'neither one thing nor the other'; diction which 'continually mak[es] one grind one's teeth'; 'an excess of pedantic phraseology'; 'errors of style which belong to journalese and recall Marie Corelli'; – this miniature collage of one aspect of nineteenth-century Hardy criticism is derived from reviews of novels from *A Pair of Blue Eyes* to *Jude the Obscure* more than twenty years later;[2] so that what is in question is the reaction not simply to the imperfections of a young writer learning his craft but to a permanent set of attributes of Hardy's prose. 'His old faults, chiefly of style, are as prominent as ever' was the slightly fatigued observation of a reviewer of *The Mayor of Casterbridge*,[3] a novel of Hardy's maturity which has often been voted his best. Nor, when it appeared, did the poetry fare much better: 'a needlessly inflated diction'; 'he crowds syllables together inharmoniously'; a style 'harsh and rough, uncouth and uncanny'; even Lytton Strachey, in a perceptive review of

Satires of Circumstance, referred to 'ugly and cumbrous expressions . . . and flat, prosaic turns of speech'.[4]

If such charges had been confined to Victorian and Edwardian reviewers, we might have been tempted to dismiss them as proceeding from the prejudices and limitations of the critically benighted. But later critics from Harold Child and Edmund Blunden to David Lodge and Irving Howe have found Hardy guilty of an unhappy mixture of clumsiness and pretentiousness in his use of language.[5] Soon after Hardy's death, T. S. Eliot delivered the magisterial verdict that 'he was indifferent even to the prescripts of good writing: he wrote sometimes overpoweringly well, but always very carelessly; at times his style touches sublimity without ever having passed through the stage of being good' (*After Strange Gods*, 1934, 54–5). And exactly one hundred years after the reviews of his first novel which I have referred to, a 'Christminster' critic wrote of *Jude the Obscure* that 'those who amuse themselves with the oddities of Hardy's prose style have a happy hunting ground in this final novel' (J. I. M. Stewart, *Thomas Hardy*, 1971, 191). Evidently there are elements in Hardy's style capable of provoking these responses, and calling for explanation if not justification. Since the prose and verse raise different (though not wholly different) issues, I shall deal with them for the most part separately.

As one reads through the early criticism of the novels, two stylistic grievances recur with striking regularity. One is Hardy's failure, or refusal, to conform to accepted canons of 'good', 'correct' or 'pure' English, and his propensity for awkwardness, pedantry, affectation and verbosity. The other is the tendency of his rustic dialogue towards idealization, shunning a Wordsworthian 'language really used by men' in favour of highly conventional and literary forms of uneducated and regional speech. Since both of these objections raise important issues, I shall say something about each of them in turn. But it ought first to be said that relevant to both of them are the peculiar personal circumstances, constraints and sensitivities of the young man from the provinces who began to write fiction when he was living in London in the late eighteen-sixties. When F. A. Hedgcock published a book on Hardy (*Thomas Hardy: penseur et artiste*) in 1911, he permitted himself some unauthorized biographical speculations which annoyed his subject intensely. Hardy's copy of the book is now in the Dorset County Museum, and his caustic annotations of Hedgcock's text are notably frequent in the pages dealing with his childhood; on page 6, against the statement that he spoke dialect as a child, he wrote: 'he knew the dialect, but did not speak it – it was not spoken in his mother's house, but only when necessary to the cottagers, and by his father to his workmen . . .'. Whether or not this is strictly true matters little: it seems clear that Hardy, like Tess Durbeyfield, grew up between the two worlds of dialect and standard speech, and must quite early have developed a highly self-conscious attitude towards language. 'His mother's house' is a revealing phrase: Jemima Hardy was a woman of some literary culture who gave her small son copies of Dryden's Virgil and Johnson's *Rasselas* (*Life*, 16) – books that would hardly have been found in every Dorset village home. Revealing, too, is the social self-consciousness of 'cottagers' and 'workmen'. But Thomas Hardy senior, who employed labour but also worked with his hands, was necessarily closer to the dialect-speaking villagers, though his contracts also involved him in negotiations with the educated and the well-to-do. With such a background, combined with an education largely self-conducted and derived from books, it would have been surprising if Hardy's attitude to language had been altogether free from an anxious calculation of its effects, a degree of uncertainty as to the appropriateness of its different forms to different occasions, and a caution in the face of its possible betrayals.

As his literary ambitions developed, so far from expressing himself with the natural ease born of social assurance, he seems to have been driven to conduct a deliberate and painful search for a style. There is, in the Dorset County Museum, a group of letters written to Hardy by his friend Horace Moule, who was both friend and mentor. As a clergyman's son and a Cambridge man, a classical scholar and a London reviewer, Moule had access to areas of society to which Hardy had only aspirations, and he must have been regarded as a reliable source of counsel. Hardy's side of their correspondence seems to have disappeared, but it is not difficult to sense from Moule's replies the nature of the help he was seeking. In one of them, Moule writes: 'I would not advise you to read [any writer] *for his style*. Acquaint yourself with his *thoughts*. That is the first step. Doubtless you will catch from him some felicitous methods or phrases which may turn out useful in the treatment of collateral subject matter. But you must in the end write *your own* style, unless you would be a mere imitator. . .'. What is revealing here is the implication that Hardy, instead of getting on with his writing, was anxiously seeking models: spending his time weight-lifting instead of joining the race. He was obviously chary of taking risks, for the style that came most naturally to the boy from Little Bockhampton might (painful thought!) excite the scorn of metropolitan and middle-class critics and readers. Hardy's anxiety extends to minor matters of usage, for we later find Moule instructing him in the use of the subjunctive in English. After Moule's suicide, Hardy was left to his own devices; and as late as 1875 he notes in his diary: 'Read again Addison, Macaulay, Newman, Sterne, Defoe, Lamb, Gibbon, Burke, *Times* leaders, etc., in a study of style' (*Life*, 105). One imagines him culling samples: he is unlikely to have read Macaulay or Gibbon, perhaps, *in toto*; but it looks as though he was still in patient quest of models, and one would like to know what common elements he discovered in such a very mixed bag of authors. It should be remembered that by this time he was no youth taking his first uncertain steps on the road to authorship, but a professional novelist in his mid-thirties whose *Far from the Madding Crowd* had enjoyed a considerable success. It is impossible to imagine Dickens or Henry James at a comparable stage of their careers exhibiting such a lack of linguistic self-confidence; and this tentativeness of Hardy's – which can also be viewed, more positively, as an openness to influences – goes far towards explaining the unevenness and inconsistencies of his style.

The other man who played a vital role in Hardy's search for a style was much older than Moule (considerably older, indeed, than Hardy's father). William Barnes, Dorset clergyman, schoolmaster, poet and philologist, had started publishing his work a generation before Hardy's birth. They met when Hardy was sixteen and were friends for thirty years; the only review Hardy ever wrote was of Barnes's poems, and he commemorated his death in a fine poem ('The Last Signal') and a touching prose obituary. Barnes's influence on Hardy's poetry was an important one, and I shall turn to it later. For the moment, it will be enough to draw attention to the resemblance between a quality Hardy finds in Barnes's verse, and a principle he articulates as fundamental to his own prose style. In his preface to the *Selected Poems of William Barnes* (1908), he notes Barnes's use of 'sudden irregularities' as a deliberate corrective to the tendency to become the slave of form. He is speaking of Barnes's highly original experiments with metre, but in his own hands 'sudden irregularity' becomes a stylistic principle of broader application.

As he writes more fully elsewhere: 'the whole secret of a living style and the difference between it and a dead style, lies in not having too much style – being, in fact, a little careless, or rather seeming to be, here and there. It brings wonderful life into the writing. . . . It is, of course, simply a carrying into prose the knowledge I have acquired in poetry – that inexact rhymes and rhythms now and then are far more pleasing than correct ones' (*Life*, 105). As we shall see, this deliberate rupturing of an otherwise smooth verbal surface, this carefully applied roughness of texture, is a prominent feature of Hardy's own verse. It is, of course, a two-edged instrument, easily mistaken for lack of skill or polish; whether it can be invoked to explain and even excuse some of the apparent defects of Hardy's prose is worth considering.

The other major legacy of Barnes was his lifelong campaigning on behalf of the Dorset dialect. On one occasion, in order to demonstrate that homely local speech was in no way inferior to the standard or literary language as a vehicle for the expression of lofty sentiments, he performed the experiment of rendering into the Dorset dialect Queen Victoria's speech on the opening of Parliament in 1863:

> 'T have a-been a happiness to Her Majesty to zee the law-heedèn mind, that happily do show itself all drough Her dominions, and that is so needvul a thing in the well-beën and well-doen ov steätes . . .

As this example suggests, some of Barnes's endeavours verged on the eccentric, and Hardy firmly declined to take up his mantle as a fully committed dialect poet: though he uses dialect words in moderation, almost none of Hardy's own poems is dialect verse in a Barnesian sense. As his metaphor 'the screen of dialect' (used in the preface to his selection from Barnes) implies, he was concerned that his own writings should reach a much wider audience than would be prepared to tolerate the limitations and difficulties of an uncompromisingly regional literature. But there is no doubt of his sympathy with Barnes's general aims and principles. He endorsed his regret that the court moved to London and thus rendered another dialect the basis of Standard English, and he has been quoted as saying that if history had taken a different turn, and Winchester had remained the political and cultural capital, 'we might have preserved in our literary language a larger proportion of the racy

Saxon of the West Country'.[7] His lifetime saw the steady disappearance
of the Dorset dialect as a living form of speech, and in the preface from
which I have already quoted he writes: 'Since Barnes' death, education
in the west of England as elsewhere has gone on with its silent and
inevitable effacements, reducing the speech of this country to
uniformity, and obliterating every year many a fine old local word.'
(Compare the slighting reference in the third chapter of *Tess* to the
National School's 'London-trained mistress'.) Any reader of the Wessex
Novels will recall passages exemplifying precisely the same kind of
regret at the destruction of the dialect of the region — not only for
historical, antiquarian and sentimental reasons, or through local pride,
but because a loss of words means a loss of expressiveness, variety and
vitality.

I have been trying to suggest something of the importance of Hardy's
relationship with Moule and Barnes as keys to an understanding of the
two opposing directions in which he was pulled in his search for a style:
towards a standard or metropolitan literary language, and towards a
vigorous but threatened local speech. It will be useful now to adduce
some samples of his prose — a task that can hardly avoid exacting a look at
the Worst, but should not overlook the Better that also abundantly
exists. Reading or re-reading the early novels, one is struck by the
nagging intrusions of the moralizing and generalizing narrator, who has
apparently come under the joint influence of George Eliot and *The Times*
leader-writers. For example:

> Had not Ethelberta's affection for Christopher partaken less of
> lover's passion than of old-established tutelary tenderness, she might
> have been reminded by this reflection of the transcendent fidelity he
> had shown under that trial — as severe a trial, considering the
> abnormal, almost morbid, development of the passion for position
> in present-day society, as can be prepared for men who move in the
> ordinary, unheroic channels of life. (*The Hand of Ethelberta*, ch. 25)

The syntax here is unprofitably convoluted, the diction excessively
abstract, and the alliteration ('passion for position in present-day. . .') far
from apt; moreover, the reflective posture seems to render Hardy deaf to
the sound of words, or he could never have written such a phrase as
'passion for position'. Yet in the same novel he can write with admirable

concreteness and directness, as in a description of a London sunrise (ch. 30). Even as early as *Desperate Remedies*, he can show a vigorous precision when he portrays the cider-maker 'packing the pomace into horse-hair bags with a rammer', while his man is 'occupied in shovelling up more from a tub at his side. The shovel shone like silver from the action of the juice'; 'some little boys, with straws in their mouths, [were] endeavouring, whenever the men's backs were turned, to get a sip of the sweet juice issuing from the vat' (Ch. 8). Another kind of precision is to be found in the description in *Under the Greenwood Tree* of the effect of sunlight on an indoor scene:

> the sun shone obliquely upon the patch of grass in front, which reflected the brightness through the open doorway and up the staircase opposite, lighting up each riser with a shiny green radiance and leaving the top of each step in shade. (II. 6)

Evoking sounds rather than visual effects, Hardy can write crisply in *The Return of the Native* of the wind which 'rasped and scraped at the corners of the house, and filliped the eavesdroppings like peas against the panes' (V. 8); and in *A Pair of Blue Eyes*, in language which matches in its cool precision the delicately exact quality of the observation: 'it was so early that the shaded places still smelt like night time, and the sunny spots had hardly felt the sun' (ch. 11). In these examples, Hardy has his senses finely tuned in relation to the object and resists the seductions of the generalizing impulse. As the cider-making passage shows, he is, like Kipling, fascinated by specialized skills and tools, by the processes and the jargon of the practitioner whose ease is born of long experience – by what Hopkins calls 'all trades, their gear and tackle and trim'; unlike Kipling, though, he is interested less by machines and modern technology than by traditional rural occupations and the necessary discrimination of differences which might be overlooked by the townsman, whether breeds of sheep, varieties of rose or potato, or types of cart are in question. This taste for a loving exactness and authenticity is the happy antithesis of that other urge towards self-conscious formality that has already been noted. Sometimes the two impulses in Hardy, generating two distinct 'voices', are found within a single sentence, as in this memorable instance from *The Woodlanders*:

Owls that had been catching mice in the outhouses, rabbits that had been eating the winter-greens in the gardens, and stoats that had been sucking the blood of the rabbits, discerning that their human neighbours were on the move, discreetly withdrew from publicity, and were seen and heard no more until nightfall. (Ch. 4)

This begins with the fine specificity of *outhouses* and *winter-greens*, but with the literary word *discerning* there is a sudden onset of self-consciousness, and the sentence ends with the arch detachment of 'human neighbours' and 'discreetly withdrew from publicity'.

Hardy's stylistic troubles arise partly from a failure to judge tone correctly and to maintain it consistently; but Eliot's verdict that he wrote 'always very carelessly' seems irresponsible, for Hardy is careful to a fault, and even his awkwardness is generally the result of a misconceived scrupulosity. As one goes through the novels chronologically one finds him bringing the regrettable epigrammatic tendency under control and fixing his acutely observant eye more consistently on the object, the physical situation or the process: Susan Nunsuch slowly melting the wax image of Eustacia over the turf fire; Giles Winterbourne and Marty South planting young trees; Jude and Arabella killing the pig – the writing in such scenes as these could hardly be bettered. Some of Hardy's best prose is to be found in *Tess of the d'Urbervilles*, as in this account of Tess and Angel engaged in cheese-making:

They were breaking up the masses of curd before putting them into the vats. The operation resembled the act of crumbling bread on a large scale; and amid the immaculate whiteness of the curds Tess Durbeyfield's hands showed themselves of the pinkness of the rose. Angel, who was filling the vats with his handfuls, suddenly ceased, and laid his hands flat upon hers. Her sleeves were rolled far above the elbow, and bending lower he kissed the inside vein of her soft arm.

Although the early September weather was sultry, her arm, from her dabbling in the curds, was as cold and damp to his mouth as a new-gathered mushroom, and tasted of the whey. . . . (Ch. 28)

This is prose which combines simplicity and directness with a sensuousness and poetic suggestiveness hard to match in the 1890s: indeed, we have to go to *Sons and Lovers* twenty years later to find fictional prose evoking the physicality of the quotidian world so triumphantly. Hardy transforms the circumstances of a routine and rather messy chore into the basis of a highly particularized erotic experience, playing off the homely local detail of *curds*, *bread*, *mushroom*, against the Keatsian image of the 'inside vein of her soft arm' (part of a pattern of recurring red-and-white symbolism throughout the novel). A little earlier (ch. 20), there is an equally fine description of the morning mists as Tess and Angel go out into the fields to milk the cows: 'At these non-human hours. . .'.

Interestingly enough, it was *Tess of the d'Urbervilles* that was singled out by 'Vernon Lee' for analysis in her early book of practical criticism, *The Handling of Words* (1923), with results far from flattering to Hardy. Her section of *Tess* (pp. 222–41) represents probably the first attempt to subject his prose to close and systematic scrutiny, and she concludes that it is repetitive, unfocused, conceived in slackness of attention and demanding no energetic involvement or concentration on the part of the reader. Her parting remark that 'he belongs to a universe transcending such trifles as Writers and Readers and their little logical ways' is hardly calculated to press down the scale in Hardy's favour. It is significant, though, that her analysis is based on a single 500-word passage, the prose of which is partly narrative and descriptive but also to a large extent reflective. A different choice of passage might have produced quite different conclusions, and her counting of different types of word has no general validity: with Hardy, even more than with most authors, judgements made on the basis of small samples are of little value. It is only fair to add, too, that several lines of defence of Hardy's alleged verbal clumsiness or pedantry have been proposed. Least convincingly, to my mind, his awkwardness has been seen as some kind of a guarantee of integrity, as if there were something morally suspect in stylistic refinement. More persuasively, it has been argued by C. H. Salter that the ink-horn terms Hardy often favours, like his frequent allusions to books and pictures (which sometimes seem no more than an irritating or embarrassing name-dropping), help to define the larger world beyond Wessex and to reinforce that contrast between the greater and smaller worlds which is so central to his work. I would suggest, too, that what appears to be a pedantic or affected fondness for the unusual word is often a concern for precision, a legitimate desire to call things by their proper names; and that Hardy may consciously have undertaken a genuine and worthwhile expansion of the range of language susceptible of being utilized in a work of fiction.

Furthermore, by way of explanation if not extenuation of his lapses, it is relevant to remind ourselves that Hardy's fiction, like that of some other Victorian novelists, suffered the constraints of contemporary publishing conventions: the dominance of the multi-volumed novel, the highly specific requirements of magazine fiction, the Procrustean bed of serialization, and the far-reaching demands and prohibitions of editors and publishers. When a novelist contracted to supply a work of a given length or in a given number of instalments, he laid himself open to the temptations of digressiveness and prolixity; when he undertook to satisfy not only a heterogeneous public but also the commercial purveyors of literature, he incurred the hazards of verbal and other kinds of compromise. Hardy's fatal Cleopatra is the habit not simply of taut-ology, as Vernon Lee suggests, but of risking dissipation of the fictional mood by a just-relevant but incongruous reference from a domain alien to the fictional world. Richard Le Gallienne acutely diagnosed this defect as arising from 'sudden moments of self-consciousness in the midst of his creative flow'.[8] *The Return of the Native* offers a convenient example: Eustacia, in a prototypical Hardyan attitude, stands in the dark watching three figures with silent but eager curiosity:

> She strained her eyes to see them, but was unable. Such was her intentness, however, that it seemed as if her ears were performing the functions of seeing as well as hearing. This extension of power can almost be believed in at such moments. The deaf Dr. Kitto was probably under the influence of a parallel fancy when he described his body as having become, by long endeavour, so sensitive to vibrations that he had gained the power of perceiving by it as by ears. (II. 3)

The tension of the dramatic scene abruptly slackens as Hardy turns from his imaginative construction of it as occurring in a particular place at a particular moment to a scientific digression. We know from his notebooks that he had encountered 'the deaf Dr. Kitto' in Herbert Spencer's *Principles of Biology*: but what is Herbert Spencer doing on Egdon Heath? Many Victorian reviewers detected the influence of George Eliot working for the worse at such moments; but with George

Eliot one feels, as one often does not with Hardy, that the reading has become thoroughly absorbed in the experience of life and in sustained reflection on human nature and human conduct. Hardy has difficulty in resisting the allure of the superfluous gloss on an already vivid and sufficient statement. In *The Mayor of Casterbridge*, for instance, when a rustic girl exclaims to her lover, who is departing for another district, "'I shall never see 'ee again!'", the narrator feels impelled to add: 'it was, indeed, a hopeless length of traction for Dan Cupid's magnet'; Mixen Lane is described as 'a back slum of the town, the *pis aller* of Casterbridge domiciliation' (the embryonic Joycean joke of *piss alley* is surely far from Hardy's mind at this moment); as harvest-time approaches, we are told that 'the weather changed . . . the temperament of the welkin passed from the phlegmatic to the sanguine'. At such moments, Hardy's language moves, almost perversely and to the point of self-parody, from plainness towards solidifying polysyllabic abstractions. It has been argued that these intrusive parades of information and superfluous paraphrases into a mandarin style take their origin in the autodidact's enthusiasm to display his hard-won knowledge; but I believe that the nineteenth-century custom of buying its fiction by weight, so to speak, as well as the struggle of the novel to become an intellectually as well as a morally respectable form of literature, must share some of the blame. Of *Far from the Madding Crowd*, published as a *Cornhill* serial in twelve instalments, Henry James wrote:

> Mr. Hardy's novel is very long, but his subject is very short and simple, and the work has been distended to its rather formidable dimensions by the infusion of a large amount of conversational and descriptive padding and the use of an ingeniously verbose and redundant style.[9]

There are passages in that novel which justify these strictures, though there are also episodes which one would certainly not wish to see abridged. It is surely significant that *Under the Greenwood Tree*, which was not written for serialization, is written with an economy rare for Hardy. Also blameworthy in some degree is the influence of Mrs. Grundy, which fell so inauspiciously on the later novels in particular. When he had sent *Jude the Obscure* to the publishers for volume-publication, after he had restored the text mangled to suit the requirements of *Harper's Magazine*, Hardy confessed to his diary that 'on account of the labour of altering [it] to suit the magazine, and then having to alter it back, I have lost energy for revising and improving the original as I meant to do' (*Life*, 269); and although there are some powerful and haunting scenes, it is true that his last novel represents a falling off from the high stylistic achievement of *Tess*.

The vicissitudes of those late novels remind us that one of the most fruitful directions for Hardy scholarship in the next few years would seem to be in the area of the systematic study of his manuscripts and of the development of his text through serial and later versions. Some useful work in this area has already been done by Dale Kramer, J. T. Laird, John Paterson and Robert Slack, but more remains to be done, and the findings of such research are likely to force us to reconsider some longstanding assumptions concerning Hardy's style. Kramer has shown that it was normally Hardy's habit to revise scrupulously, overlooking 'neither the smallest word nor the largest passage'; and Laird's recent exhaustive study of the textual history of *Tess* from manuscript to definitive edition shows unmistakably a serious and sustained concern on Hardy's part with questions of language, tone and texture.[10] My own examination of his prose manuscripts suggests that this kind of intensive attention to style was not confined to the major novels: even the short stories, so often dismissed as pot-boilers, were scrupulously worked over. On a single page of the manuscript of 'An Imaginative Woman', for example, I have counted nearly fifty revisions, many of them stylistic. Hardy's habit of revising his prose writings minutely and sometimes long after original publication hardly bears out the view of him as indifferent to the quality of his fiction. In the face of the evidence, Eliot's statement that he wrote 'always very carelessly' is without foundation. Indeed, as some of my examples have already suggested, Hardy's lapses are less likely to be the result of carelessness than of trying too hard or of not knowing when he has said enough. And if there are frequent lapses, ranging from the infelicitous to the ludicrous, there are also many passages which show a masterly control of language; and no account of his style will be adequate which does not take acount of this wide range of performance. Against the passages quoted a little earlier from *The Mayor of Casterbridge* may be set others of irreproachable quality from the same novel – for instance, these two epitaphs, in very different modes, on Susan Henchard:

'Well, poor soul; she's helpless to hinder that or anything now,' answered Mother Cuxsom. 'And all her shining keys will be took from her, and her cupboards opened; and little things a' didn't wish seen, anybody will see; and her wishes and ways will all be as nothing!' (Ch. 18)

and, a dozen pages later, describing her burial in a Roman cemetery:

Mrs. Henchard's dust mingled with the dust of women who lay ornamented with glass hair-pins and amber necklaces, and men who held in their mouths coins of Hadrian, Posthumus, and the Constantines. (Ch. 20)

A similar range of quality is to be found in the specific area of dialogue writing. In Somerset Maugham's *Cakes and Ale*, it is said of the imaginary novelist who bears a strong resemblance to Hardy that 'his dialogue was such as could never have issued from the mouth of a human being'; and without going so far as Maugham, it must be conceded that Hardy's presentation of the discourse of educated people often shows an extraordinary failure of judgement. Edmund Gosse observed that Sue and Jude 'talk a sort of University Extension jargon that breaks the heart'; but some of their predecessors, especially in the bourgeois world of the minor novels, are guilty of even more extravagant lapses from plausibility. On another level there is the rustic dialogue which I have already cited as having been singled out for criticism by so many of Hardy's contemporaries. A few samples from different novels will convey the essential flavour:

'You'll be like chips in porridge, Leaf – neither good nor hurt.' (*Under the Greenwood Tree*, II. 4)

'. . . for a wet of the better class, that brought you no nearer to the horned man than you were afore you begun, there was none like those in Farmer Everdene's kitchen.' (*Far from the Madding Crowd*, ch. 8)

'Not encouraging, I own,' said Fairway. '"Get out of my sight, you slack-twisted, slim-looking maphrotight fool," is rather a hard way of saying No. But even that might be overcome by time and patience, so as to let a few grey hairs show themselves in the hussy's head.' (*The Return of the Native*, I. 3)

' . . . I don't see noo harm in it. To respect the dead is sound
doxology; and I wouldn't sell skellintons – leastwise respectable
skellintons – to be varnished for 'natomies, except I were out of
work. But money is scarce, and throats get dry. Why *should* death
rob life o' fourpence? I say there was no treason in it.' (*The Mayor of
Casterbridge*, ch. 18)

It is clear that Hardy has devised an idiom which reproduces some of
the observable features of peasant speech but which also sets itself standards of concentration and fluency, sense of rhythm and resolute
picturesqueness, that real speech rarely and then only momentarily
attains. Concrete and formulaic, allusive and alliterative, delightfully
mangling standard forms and yet venturing unabashed on the linguistic
preserves of their social betters while proferring dialect words like bright
treasures, the speech of Hardy's rustics owes as much to Shakespeare as to
Wessex: among the ancestors of Thomas Leaf and Joseph Poorgrass are
Falstaff's 'sufficient men' and Peter Quince's 'company', and the two
constables who appear briefly in connection with the skimmity-ride in
The Mayor of Casterbridge (ch. 39) strongly recall Dogberry and Verges.
Victorian critics were troubled by Hardy's readiness to effect a
compromise between dialogue presented in Standard English and a
scrupulous rendering of dialect forms – a compromise which, it seems,
satisfied neither those who were looking for regional realism, nor those
for whom the prime virtue of dialogue was intelligibility. Thus the
Athenaeum complained that the rustic characters of *Under the Greenwood
Tree* 'speak too much like educated people', while the *Spectator* said in
1879 that Hardy's rural characters are 'neither rustic nor critic, but
something halfway between the two', and the same journal remarked a
couple of years later that Hardy's 'thorough knowledge of the dialectical
peculiarities of certain districts has tempted him to write whole
conversations which are, to the ordinary reader, nothing but a series of
linguistic puzzles'.[11] Since what is in question, however, is a humorously
choric commentary by a group of minor characters, there seems no
reason why Hardy should not exploit the well-established conventions
of fictional dialect. When we are required to take a rustic character more
seriously, as with Marty South or Joan Durbeyfield, the literary features
of rustic speech, at least in their more extravagant manifestations, tend to
disappear. And Hardy was, after all, better qualified than many novelists

who have resorted to dialect to reproduce its characteristic idioms and rhythms. Personal experience apart, he had a genuine interest in the subject which was human as well as scholarly, as his letters and diaries often attest. On a visit to Lyme Regis in 1882, he met an old man who had had an operation for cataract on one eye, the other remaining blind; he quotes the man's account of the operation, conducted without anaesthetic, and it concludes with the canny observation:

> 'So he didn't do the other. And I'm glad 'a didn't. I've saved half-crowns and half-crowns out of number in only wanting one glass to my spectacles. T'other eye would never have paid the expenses of keeping en going.' (*Life*, 154)

If this has not been too artfully retouched in the process of transcription, it suggests that life could provide parallels to art. And on occasion Hardy could capture quite brilliantly the flavour of uneducated speech, as in Bathsheba's interview with her employees on the farm:

> '. . . Temperance Miller – ah, here's another, Soberness – both women, I suppose?'
> 'Yes'm. Here we be, 'a b'lieve,' was echoed in shrill unison.
> 'What have you been doing?'
> 'Tending thrashing-machine, and wimbling haybonds, and saying "Hoosh!" to the cocks and hens when they go upon your seeds, and planting Early Flourballs and Thompson's Wonderfuls with a dibble.'
> 'Yes – I see. Are they satisfactory women?' she inquired softly of Henery Fray.
> 'O mem – don't ask me! Yielding women – as scarlet a pair as ever was!' groaned Henery under his breath. (Ch. 10)

Temperance and Soberness strike just the right note of preoccupation with the specific to be found in working-class speech.

The question of dialect brings us back again to William Barnes, and reminds us that a natural link exists here between Hardy's prose and his verse. His debt to Barnes's metrical experiments has been widely recognized. What I should like to emphasize here is the influence on his diction of Barnes's linguistic principles and ideals. When Samuel Hynes claimed nearly twenty years ago that 'the direction of [Barnes's] influence [on Hardy] is the direction taken by English poetry in the transitional period between High Victorianism and the twentieth century', in its 'movement away from conventional, circumscribed poetic diction',[12] I do not think he was claiming too much; which makes it seem odd that no reference to Barnes is to be found in Donald Davie's *Thomas Hardy and British Poetry* (1972). The bizarre and extremist side of Barnes's views on language ought not to blind us to the fact that he represents an important break with the dominant post-Romantic poetic style. It is no coincidence that Hopkins too was an admirer of Barnes.

Barnes both advocated and practised a strictly purist doctrine that sought to purge the English language of non-native elements, and to uphold what he called in the 'Fore-Say' to his *Outline of English Speech-Craft* (1878) 'our own strong old Anglo-Saxon speech'. To this end he wrote grammars utilizing a new terminology: in the work just mentioned, for example, which W. D. Jacobs has described as 'a climax in purism' (*William Barnes, Linguist*, Albuquerque, 1952, 41), he proposed *word-stock* for *vocabulary*, *word-sameness* for *synonym*, *fair-speaking* for *euphemism*, *breath-sounds* for *vowels*, and so forth; sometimes he is driven to circumlocutions of equal ingenuity and awkwardness, as in suggesting *lip breath-penning* for *labial*, *clue to matters handled* for *index*, and *under-sundrinesses of time-takings* for adverbs! Elsewhere, he claimed that native equivalents could be used or devised in place of words of Latin origin for the general word-stock: *fairhood* for *beauty*, *upshot* for *conclusion*, *inwit* and *forewit* for *conscience* and *prudence*. Everyday objects received similar treatment: he wanted a perambulator to be called a *pushwainling*, and Hardy himself tells the anecdote of Barnes who, on his deathbed, 'became quite indignant at the word "bicycle". "Why didn't they call it 'wheel-saddle'?" he exclaimed.'

In Hardy's own poems, Barnes's influence can be seen at work in several ways. Although Hardy is not a dialect poet, he does not hesitate to enlist dialect words when there is a case for doing so — a practice of which he gives due warning in the preface to his first collection of verse, *Wessex Poems*:

> Whenever an ancient and legitimate word of the district, for which there was no equivalent in received English, suggested itself as the most natural, nearest, and often only expression of a thought, it has been made use of, on what seemed good grounds.

Linhay, drongs, mammet, ho, coll, lewth, vamp, and *dumbledores* are a few
examples of such words: all of these particular examples are duly listed in
Barnes's *Glossary of the Dorset Dialect* (1886). More generally, Hardy
often goes out of his way to use words of Saxon origin, even if it involves
reviving an obsolete word or coining a fresh combination: some
examples are *cark, clam, dorp, dree, fulth, irk, weet, wonning; craft-wit, house-
gear, lipwords, mind-strife, heart-wrings, foredames*. Nor, when it suits him,
does Hardy shirk a Barnesian circumlocution in preference to a
Latinism: he will say *fellow-yearsmen* rather than *contemporaries*, *life-doings*
rather than *experiences*, and *foot-folk* rather than *pedestrians*. In reviewing
Barnes's poems, he drew attention to the effectiveness of the 'compound
epithets', praising them as 'singularly precise, and often beautiful,
definitions of the thing signified'; and he himself, in both prose and
verse, shows a marked fondness for such formations: *amber-yellow, cinder-
gray, rusty-red, blast-beruffled, heath-hemmed, kine-cropt, wind-thridded*, etc.
Some of Hardy's unexpected word-choices were no doubt influenced by
the exigencies of rhyme and by his enthusiasm for alliteration; but it
seems certain that he would not always have written thus if he had not
known and admired Barnes and his work.

There is a whole category of words with the negative prefix *un-* (*unbe,
unbegun, unbloom, uncare, undoubt, unforetold, unheed, unhope, unknow,
unshame, unsight*, etc.) which Hardy, indifferent to accusations of
eccentricity, seems to favour on account of their peculiarly blunt, bleak,
uncompromising quality; many of them are not recorded in *OED*, or are
recorded as rare or obsolete (the most recent example cited for *unhope* is
dated 1477, and apart from Hardy's own use of *unsight* the only instance
recorded is *c.* 1412). The trouble with such listings, however, is that they
tend to exaggerate the oddity of Hardy's poetic diction: it needs to be
remembered that they are drawn from a large body of work (947 poems
in the most recent edition) and that Hardy is far from being narrowly
exclusive or doctrinaire on questions of diction. If he had learned from
Barnes to go for Saxon plainness and energy rather than a Tennysonian
or Swinburnian fluidity and musicality, and to favour such phrases as
'thwartly smitten' ('The Moth-Signal') and 'wedlock's aftergrinds'
('Honeymoon Time at an Inn') – and who but Hardy would have titled
a poem 'Mismet'? – he is also prepared to call on virtually any word, in
or out of the dictionary, standard or dialect, homely or specialized,

familiar or neologistic. He can surprise the reader with a sudden Latinism
which would have caused Barnes a pang:

> *Waking but now, when leaves like corpses fall,*
> *And saps all* retrocede.   ('The Last Chrysanthemum')

and he can begin a poem with the word 'Reticulations', and use
elsewhere such ostentatiously classical words as *cerule*, *necrologic* and
fenestration. But he can also descend into the calculatedly prosaic in a
manner of which Barnes would have thoroughly approved:

> *The candle slanting sooty-wick'd,*
> *The thuds upon the thatch,*
> *The eaves-drops on the window flicked,*
> *The clacking garden-hatch . . .*
>
>   ('She Hears the Storm')

And if he can at times write like a late Romantic, he can also remind us of
Hopkins, making subtle music out of sound-changes or exploiting the
consonantal strength of the English language:[13]

> *. . . slow-born tears that brinily trundled*
>   *Over the wrecked*
> *Cheeks that were fair in their flush-time, ash now with anguish,*
>   *Harrowed by wiles.*
>
>   ('In Front of the Landscape')

or, in single phrases, 'kennels dribble dankness' ('Exeunt Omnes'),
'icicles grieving me gray' ('The Tree and the Lady'). Hardy can use a
familiar word unexpectedly, so that it delivers a tiny shock of surprised
pleasure: 'the salt fog *mops* me' ('The Sailor's Mother'); the 'lazy *flounce*'
of the sea ('A Conversation at Dawn'); 'the *spry* white scuts of conies'
('The Revisitation'); 'the night's *pinch*' ('The Pedestrian'); and he can
anticipate later poets in a bold use of a commonplace but highly
expressive word: his line 'Saw morning *harden* upon the wall' ('The
Going') is echoed in Louis MacNeice's 'The sunlight on the garden /
Hardens. . . .' As many of my examples have already shown, some of
Hardy's most telling effects are obtained by the use of monosyllables:

> *And the flap of the flame,*
> *And the throb of the clock.*
>
> ('A New Year's Eve in War Time')

> *And a cab-hack's wheeze, and the clap of its feet,*
> *In its breathless pace on the smooth wet street, ...*
>
> ('In a London Flat')

the blink of a dip	('One We Knew')
the cold sneer of dawn	('A Daughter Returns')
the sea's slap	('She Would Welcome Old Tribulations')
I gad the globe	('The Seven Times')
she pomped along the street	('The Old Gown')
[a car] whangs along	('Nobody Comes')

But the careful placing of a polysyllabic word is responsible for some of the most poignant moments in all Hardy's poetry: *equanimity* makes its presence powerfully felt among the curt monosyllables of 'I Look into my Glass', and in 'Last Words to a Dumb Friend' the word *insignificance* has a resonance comparable with that of Macbeth's 'Signifying nothing'.

When further work has been done on Hardy's poetic manuscripts, it will be possible to judge the stylistic directions of the repeated revising process to which he was so addicted. As a tentative and provisional statement, I would suggest that these revisions often involved replacing a familiar word by an uncommon one, or a word in current or standard usage by an archaism or dialect word; there is also a marked tendency to increase the incidence of alliteration and compound epithets. Thus, to take some random examples, *thwart* (a favourite word) is substituted for *sick*, *bruit* for *spread* (verb), *wanzing* for *growing*, *full-fugued* for *general*, *lank limbs* for *bare stems*, *quizzings* for *notice*, *raw rolls* for *brown lines*, *wind-warped* for *nibbled*. It will be evident, too, that detailed study of Hardy's language would be greatly aided by the existence of a concordance to the *Complete Poems*, as well as variorum editions of the verse and the fiction. Paul Zietlow has recently shown that the revisions to 'The Casterbridge Captains' propel the language of that poem towards a 'cruder, tougher diction and syntax'. So far from being the accidental products of gaucheness or ill-judgement, these qualities in Hardy's poetry are carefully contrived to give, in Zietlow's phrase, 'a bite of strangeness'.[14]

As a novelist, Hardy devised a prose style which, for all its frequent imperfections, was versatile enough to accommodate a wide range of varieties or registers: didactic and descriptive, allusive and direct, narrative and dialogue of distinct kinds. This openness to the full resources of language carried over into his poetry, and may be one interpretation of Ezra Pound's gnomic comment on the verse: 'there *is* the harvest of having written 20 novels first'. Pound cannot count, and as Richard Taylor points out elsewhere in this volume he oversimplifies a complex matter, for Hardy was a poet before and during the time he was a novelist as well as after; but he rightly stresses the continuity of Hardy's work. Hardy would, I think, have readily subscribed to the Wordsworthian dictum that 'there neither is, nor can be, any *essential* difference between the language of prose and metrical composition'; but this does not prevent the verse from being more original and experimental, stylistically speaking, than the prose, or from having a greater capacity to surprise by an excess that is often fine (though now and again, it is true, the gamble does not come off). His poetic language keeps open house to all sorts and conditions of words, whereas his fiction does no more than leave the door slightly ajar. As a result, perhaps, his stylistic influence as a novelist has been minimal, whereas in reading his poems we seem to hear from time to time the voices not only of those whom he had absorbed (notably Wordsworth, Barnes, and Browning), but also of some who followed him: Edward Thomas, W. H. Auden, John Betjeman, Philip Larkin. Hardy believed, and often asserted, that poetry derives its power from a greater concentration than prose usually achieved (though it is not easy to think of anything, anywhere in his writings, more concentrated than certain passages in *Tess*). In a letter written to Arthur Symons on 8 September 1904 he confessed:

> I have . . . of late years lapsed so deeply into my early weakness for verse, and have found the condensed expression that it affords so much more consonant to my natural way of thinking and feeling – that I have almost forgotten the prose effusions for the time.

(It was characteristic of Hardy's modesty to refer to a quarter of a century's continuous labours as 'the prose effusions'!) And on another occasion he wrote:

I still feel that I have in many cases concentrated into a page or two of verse what in the novels filled scores of pages.[15]

That special capacity of verse to foster 'condensed expression' is fully exploited in his best poems; the *strenuousness* that Donald Davie has recognized in such a typical phrase as 'purples prinked the main'[16] is the positive aspect of what might at first glance appear to be a capricious or wilful unevenness of language and tone. Because Hardy himself is liable to make sudden and rapid transitions from one kind of language to another within a poem, or even within a single line, he demands an alertness and agility on the part of his reader to maintain a flexible response to a use of language whose unpredictability makes for extraordinary vitality.[17]

NOTES

1. Cox, 2, 7.
2. *Ibid.*, 15, 19, 39, 47, 51, 134, 178, 194, 298.
3. *Ibid.*, 133.
4. *Ibid.*, 325, 331, 332, 436.
5. A useful list of references is given by C. H. Salter, 'Hardy's Pedantry', *Nineteenth Century Fiction*, XXVIII, 1973, 145–6.
6. William Barnes, *A Grammar and Glossary of the Dorset Dialect*, Berlin, 1863, 10.
7. R. T. Hopkins, *Thomas Hardy's Dorset*, 1922, 156–7.
8. Cox, 178.
9. *Ibid.*, 28.
10. Dale Kramer, 'Revisions and Vision: Thomas Hardy's *The Woodlanders*', *Bulletin of the New York Public Library*, LXXV, 1971, 229; J. T. Laird, *The Shaping of 'Tess of the d'Urbervilles'*. Oxford, 1975.
11. Cox, 10, 56; *Spectator*, LIV, 1881, 1277. Hardy replied to the latter charge in the following week's issue (1308).
12. Samuel Hynes, 'Hardy and Barnes: Notes on Literary Influence', *South Atlantic Quarterly*, LVIII, 1959, 53.
13. Max Beerbohm neatly and not unfairly hits off this quality of muscularity in his parody of Hardy's poetic style, 'A Luncheon': '. . . the farmers are casting rueful looks / At tilth's and pasture's dearth of spryness'.
14. Paul Zietlow, *Moments of Vision: the Poetry of Thomas Hardy*, Cambridge, Mass., 1974, 30–1.

15. Both letters are in the Dorset County Museum; the second is undated.

16. Donald Davie, 'Hardy's Virgilian Purples', *Agenda*, X, 1972, 138.

17. A useful short article by Dennis Taylor ('Victorian Philology and Victorian Poetry', *Victorian Newsletter*, LIII (1978), 13–16) came to hand after this essay was written. Taylor notes that the 1860s, the decade in which Hardy 'came to poetic consciousness', was a period of intense philological activity in England; he also makes the suggestion — worth pondering in conjunction with Roger Robinson's essay in the present volume — that 'Hardy's anomalous vocabulary reflects his sense that current language is a compound of many kinds of language at many stages of evolution'.

Quotations from unpublished material appear by kind permission of the Trustees of the estate of the late Miss E. A. Dugdale.

7: *The Hardy Tradition in Modern English Poetry*

SAMUEL HYNES

I

WRITING ABOUT TRADITION in modern poetry, one has to begin not with Hardy but with Eliot. 'Tradition and the Individual Talent' set a modern meaning for the term that critics of my generation accepted as doctrinal: one would no more have questioned Eliot's formulation than one would have doubted that a dissociation of sensibility occurred in the seventeenth century, or that emotions have objective correlatives. But modernism was younger then; now that it has aged and become history, we may, indeed we must look at Eliot's ideas historically, as part of the past to be understood, rather than as a body of doctrine to be believed.

Eliot's essay begins with one of those characteristically Eliotian statements: 'In English writing we seldom speak of tradition, though we occasionally apply its name to deploring its absence.' Perhaps in 1919, when the essay was written, 'we' (whoever Eliot included in that pronoun) didn't talk much about tradition; but once Eliot had said so, we did. When *Selected Essays* appeared in 1932, 'Tradition and the Individual Talent' was placed first, so that *tradition* was the first word to catch the reader's eye, and through all the years that followed, when Eliot's essays were being read as a manual of how to be modern, tradition was accepted as a central concept.

Not that Eliot ever defined exactly what the word meant for him – he was essentially a coiner of critical terminology, not a definer. Still, one could get a sense of his meaning from the essay, and particularly from this crucial paragraph:

Yet if the only form of tradition, of handing down, consisted in following the ways of the immediate generation before us in a blind or timid adherence to its successes, 'tradition' should positively be discouraged. We have seen many such simple currents soon lost in the sand; and novelty is better than repetition. Tradition is a matter of much wider significance. It cannot be inherited, and if you want it you must obtain it by great labour. It involves, in the first place, the historical sense, which we may call nearly indispensable to anyone who would continue to be a poet beyond his twenty-fifth year; and the historical sense involves a perception, not only of the pastness of the past, but of its presence; the historical sense compels a man to write not merely with his own generation in his bones, but with a feeling that the whole of the literature of Europe from Homer and within it the whole of the literature of his own country has a simultaneous existence and composes a simultaneous order. This historical sense, which is a sense of the timeless as well as of the temporal and of the timeless and the temporal together, is what makes a writer traditional.[1]

No critical argument of Eliot's is easy to abstract: there is always a certain defensive opacity in his pronouncements, a smoke-screen of illogic hanging over the text. But what he seems to be doing here is dismissing the customary meanings of *tradition*, in order to substitute his own. The customary meanings are, first of all, tradition as a 'handing down' – the literal meaning of the Latin word; and second, tradition as an inheritance – the thing transmitted. In both cases, the word carries a sense of a natural, involuntary process: tradition, in this sense of the term, is a genetic sequence, something that will appear naturally, like a dominant gene, in generation after generation.

But Eliot would not have it so. Tradition, he said, must be consciously sought after, the poet must work at it. What exactly he must work at is not at all particularized in the essay: the poet does not apparently seek out this tradition or that one, but simply *tradition*. The fact that Eliot places no article before the noun suggests that he is not thinking of genetic models, but of a concept far more oceanic and abstract, a concept like History or Time, containing all of the past. His definition has, in fact, only one limitation: his *tradition* contains only literature; apparently no other aspect of the past was relevant to poetry.

For Eliot, then, a traditional writer was one who consciously laboured to discover and to assimilate the literary past. The appropriate metaphor for this activity would surely be one from archaeology. Eliot disdained this connection in his essay,[2] but it is nevertheless the right analogy for the process he describes: tradition is the past that you laboriously dig up. This notion was clearly a necessary one for Eliot at the beginning of his poetic career, and for the modernist movement at the end of the First World War. It expressed the modernist sense of the past as the sum of European culture, now fragmented, ruined, lost; and it established a modernist relation to that past – as individual, volitional, and effortful. It was a theory in terms of which a poet might make a new tradition from a heap of broken images.

Eliot's archaeological idea of tradition has its place in literary history: it helps to explain the construction of poems like *The Waste Land* and *The Cantos*, those international assemblages of symbolic bits that have so dominated modern poetry, and critical thinking about modern poetry, during the last half-century. But it is of no use at all in explaining the *other* kind of poetry that went on being written, and that was traditional, one might say, in a more traditional way. This kind of poetry was not international, it was not symbolic, it was not fragmented; it was, rather, explicitly English, descriptive, lyrical, and formally regular and whole. It did not seem to be arrived at by great labour (except in the sense that all good poetry demands creative energy), but simply to be there – the natural way for an English poet to do it, because other, earlier English poets had done it that way. The poems I mean constitute a tradition in a sense different from Eliot's, a tradition that is a living line of inheritances, and must be thought of in genetic rather than in archaeological terms.

If I call this line 'The Hardy Tradition', I do so because I am interested in English poetry of the past hundred years, and Hardy was the principal progenitor of the tradition in this century; but I recognize that in a literary tradition, as in a genetic strain, there is no First Parent, and that Hardy too had his ancestors, and that indeed the line runs unbroken from the present back to the beginnings of English lyric verse. Still, it is useful to begin with Hardy, to establish the nature of the tradition of which he was such a great exemplar, and to note the line of continuity stretching from his work into the present. For to do so is to argue a view of modern poetry that is not often considered by critics, though it is obviously true: that much modern poetry is traditional and continuous with the past, and that the apocalyptic uniqueness of modern experience has been exaggerated.[3]

Perhaps the best way to make clear exactly what I mean by 'The Hardy Tradition' is to quote what seems to me a typical example from Hardy, and then to comment on it. I choose a minor poem, not so far as I am aware much anthologized or commented on – a characteristic rather than a superlative case.

She Hears the Storm

There was a time in former years –
While my roof-tree was his –
When I should have been distressed by fears
At such a night as this!

I should have murmured anxiously,
'The pricking rain strikes cold;
His road is bare of hedge or tree,
And he is getting old.'

But now the fitful chimney-roar,
The drone of Thorncombe trees,
The Froom in flood upon the moor,
The mud of Mellstock Leaze,

The candle slanting sooty-wick'd,
The thuds upon the thatch,
The eaves-drops on the window flicked,
The clacking garden-hatch,

And what they mean to wayfarers,
I scarcely heed or mind;
He has won that storm-tight roof of hers
Which Earth grants all her kind.[4]

The first thing to say about this poem is that it is not sharply individual: it contains none of the eccentricities of diction and syntax that we think of as 'Hardyesque', and it is certainly not markedly 'modern'. It is a poem, one might say, written as much by the tradition as by the poet. (One sign of this collective mode is in the last stanza, where the figure that completes the poem is one that Hardy shares with Wordsworth and Housman.) 'All we can do', Hardy told the young Robert Graves, 'is write on the old themes in the old styles, but try to do a little better than those who went before us,'[5] and that apparently is what he was doing in this instance. This is the traditional view put in the simplest possible terms, and it describes the nature of Hardy's achievement in many poems. Hardy was traditional in this sense more often than we perhaps realize, for being moderns we look for what is unique, and so overlook poems in the common style; no doubt that is why every rereading of Hardy uncovers unobtrusively fine small poems, like wild flowers under a hedge, that one had not noticed before.

The verse form of 'She Hears the Storm' is Common Metre, the metre of hymns and ballads, and this make another point – that the Hardy tradition is entirely English in its genetic line, and is rooted in traditional English popular culture. Both hymns and ballads imply a sharing community, and a fairly confined one: not Europe or the world, but a country, or a county, or a congregation – some homogeneous group with a body of common experience. Hardy was extraordinarily inventive in his use of 'the old styles', and rarely repeated a stanza form exactly, but his inventions are mainly variations on familiar verse forms, which confirm and conserve the life of the tradition by extending it.

The world of the poem is as familiar and English as the metre – though *world* is obviously the wrong term for so circumscribed a setting, and *parish* would be more exact. Virtually everything that is excellent in Hardy's work is localized, and taken together poems and novels amount to a kind of imagined parish history. Hardy was willing to call such writing provincial, but he did not see this as a limitation. 'Arnold is wrong about provincialism', he wrote in his journal in the early '80s, 'if he means anything more than a provincialism of style and manner in exposition. A certain provincialism of feeling is invaluable.'[6] It is more than invaluable: it is essential to the continuance of the tradition to which Hardy belongs. One cannot love the whole earth, or write its poetry; indeed, one cannot even be an all-of-England poet. Every important writer in the tradition has his spot, his Grasmere or his Mellstock, his microcosm of the world that we all inhabit. That particularity of location is a definitive aspect of the tradition.

The temporal aspect of particularity of location is expressed in the relation between past and present, and the ways in which the poem draws upon and uses the resources of memory. One might say, I suppose, that memory is tradition as it exists privately in individual minds, and communally in parish history; for a provincial poet like Hardy it plays a centrally important role. He did not exactly live in the past, but his present was full of past realities, and more and more so as he grew older. His memories were invoked by familiar places and familiar objects, and these stirred two contrary responses: a melancholy but stoic regret that the passage of time was irrevocable, and a feeling that the past was somehow still alive and real. When Hardy was very old he wrote in his journal: 'Relativity. That things and events always were, are, and will be (e.g. Emma, Mother and Father are living still in the past)';[7] and that sense of the living reality of the past is a constant formative element in his poetry, and in that of the entire tradition. Eliot's notion of the presence of the past seems by comparison abstract, bookish, and cold.

One other aspect of the Hardy tradition – and a crucial one – is evident in the last stanza of 'She Hears the Storm' in the figure that Hardy shares with Wordsworth and Housman – the figure of the dead loved one, roofed and sheltered by the earth. The implications of this figure, in all three poets, are that man and nature participate in a common natural order, and that that order has behind it order-creating powers and principles in the universe. That is, the implications are *religious*. In this sense the English poetic tradition has always been essentially religious, and indeed all poetry has. But the religious impulse is manifested in a different way in nineteenth-century poetry – as an effort to preserve *for* poetry and *through* poetry this fundamental sense that the universe is informed by order and value, and that man belongs to it.[8] In Romanticism, one might say, the religious sense became self-conscious, an effort that had to be made against the resistance of a materialistic world. T. E. Hulme called Romanticism 'spilt religion', but it would be more accurate to say that science had done the spilling, and that poetry was trying to save what had been spilt.

A religious poem, in this sense, is any poem that deals, on however small a scale, with man's relations with the universe, and that must include even the most mundane of 'nature' poems – the plainest poems of Wordsworth or Clare or Christina Rossetti, or for that matter of Edward Thomas or Geoffrey Grigson. In such poems the subject is ordinary physical reality; but that reality includes a sense of immanence, or aura, of the presence of permanence and value in the humblest particulars of the earth. Such poems are not simply celebrations of nature: they are rather about what follows from man's presence in the natural world, and his consciousness of his presence. Poems in the tradition usually raise the questions that religion is all about – the meaning of suffering, of mortality, and of the powers that shape existence – questions that religions don't answer, but that they help man to make his peace with.

In this sense, Hardy was a religious poet, but like many other modern poets in the tradition he was a religious poet without a religion. When the religious impulse exists, but the form doesn't, then religious feelings will attach themselves to lesser phenomena, and what follows will be sometimes a poetry of immanence (like Wordsworth's), and sometimes a poetry of superstition – which is after all only the sense of immanence, shorn of its glory. Hardy wrote a number of explicitly superstitious poems – 'Signs and Tokens' is one of the best – and many others in which a will-to-believe in the paranormal is so strong as to amount to superstition (as for example in 'The Shadow on the Stone' and 'Night-Time in Mid-Fall'). In still other poems the force of irony is so strong, and so manifest, as to function as a kind of malign force, superstitiously believed in (I am thinking of poems like 'The Convergence of the Twain').[9]

What Hardy seems to be doing in such poems is making exceptions, out of feeling and experience, to the general denial of metaphysical reality that his reading of positivist philosophy and science had forced upon him. If there was no God in the universe – and the best modern thought persuaded him that there was not – yet there were phantoms, ghosts, and dreads in his personal world of Wessex, and in the created cosmos of *The Dynasts* there were spirits of Irony and Pity. Hardy's natural world is dense with manifestations of the forces that the imagination feels, but that science cannot describe or credit. Such manifestations are common in the tradition to which Hardy belongs, from the poems of Wordsworth and Coleridge to those of de la Mare and Graves; they provide a way of extending the emotional vocabulary of 'nature poetry', of bootlegging a vaguely religious sense of reality into a world that denies it.

Another way of saying this is to say that the tradition is not concerned with transcendence, or with asserting or creating an alternative reality. Reality, in the Hardy tradition, is the world we experience; but that world is not confined to what is quantifiable and verifiable: it is *more* than the world of science, and that *more* includes feelings that can be felt but not explained, and questions that can be asked but not answered, which is to say that it includes that sense of aura or immanence that I have been talking about. A simple example of what is meant is Hardy's little poem, 'A January Night':

> *The rain smites more and more,*
> *The east wind snarls and sneezes;*
> *Through the joints of the quivering door*
>   *The water wheezes.*
>
> *The tip of each ivy-shoot*
> *Writhes on its neighbour's face;*
> *There is some hid dread afoot*
>   *That we cannot trace.*
>
> *Is it the spirit astray*
> *Of the man at the house below*
> *Whose coffin they took in to-day?*
>   *We do not know.*[10]

The poem begins with the natural world, precisely observed; but by mid-poem that world has expanded to include a dread that is felt, but cannot be explained – a kind of superstitious feeling, which the unanswered question at the end expresses. It is a characteristic rendering of Hardy's reality: it consists of the natural forces and objects that can be observed by the senses, *plus* the feelings that observation and reason cannot explain. These elements, the material and the non-material, exist unstably together, each questioning the reality of the other; is the dread simply a response to natural phenomena? Or is there something else there? And if there is, what is it? But the questions are not answered; it was enough for Hardy to record the feelings that they express.

The natural world in 'A January Night' is rendered with minute particularity, and this is also characteristic of Hardy. He thought of his role in life as 'the man with the watching eye'[11] and what he saw as he watched were often small details, precisely observed – raindrops on a gate, a dead leaf blown into a room, the sounds that the wind makes in trees. Out of such particulars, Hardy created that 'provincialism of feeling' that he so valued, the sense of an actual, circumscribed world. He admired the same quality in other poets in the tradition: in the *Later Years*, for example, he quotes the following from his journal of 1896: 'A novel, good, microscopic touch in Crabbe. . . . He gives surface without outline, describing his church by telling *the colour of the lichens*.'[12] What Hardy is praising here is a use of synecdoche which avoids metaphysical, 'fanciful' language by making a real part stand for the real whole. He does the same thing in his own poems, working by 'microscopic touches', describing by telling, working by actualities rather than by metaphors. Perhaps he felt that metaphors assumed connections in the world too easily, took for granted a universe of ordered and significant relationships, whereas Hardy was only sure of the reality of the physical world that he could see, and of his own feelings and memories. And he kept his poems – the best of them, at least – faithful to his sense of reality, even at the expense of figurative power.

Such poems may sound a trifle flat, at least to ears accustomed to more decorated styles. But there is an honesty in that flatness that makes it a virtue in the Hardy tradition. One of Hardy's poetic descendants, Robert Graves, writing about another of his ancestors, John Clare, observed that 'I don't even mind the so-called dull poems – such as Clare's Nature poems – if they ring true; but at the least touch of rhetoric or insincerity I close the book without marking the page.'[13] He might have said the same of Hardy – that his Nature poems ring true, even when they seem flat or dull, but that what he called 'my fancies, or poems of the imagination'[14] are usually less effective: and indeed the distinction seems to apply to the entire tradition – including Graves.

I have been using the phrase 'Nature poem' to identify the sort of poem that links Hardy to other poets in the tradition like Clare, Crabbe and Graves, but the term requires some glossing. If it meant simply a poem treating of some feature of the natural world, and only that, then it would scarcely do for Hardy: the only nature poems he wrote in that sense are 'The Calf', 'The Yellow-hammer', and 'The Lizard', three little pieces that he contributed to children's books edited by his second wife (and of those, 'The Calf' is not really one). But for Hardy and his tradition, the subject is not simply nature, but the relation between man and nature. *Nature* here means physical, material reality, the context in which man exists, and of which he is conscious. And that consciousness is a part of the poem; so there is always a human factor in Hardy's poems – a figure in the landscape, or an observer of it.

Sometimes that figure will be an agent – a husband or a wife or a lover – but more often, and more characteristically, the human figure is an observer, removed from action, ironic, self-effacing – a man self-consciously alone in reality. He observes the world that he inhabits, and he remembers the past, and these observations and memories compose the ironies of which the poems are made. But he is not introspective in the usual Romantic sense; the poems tell us much about the poetic consciousness, but virtually nothing about the poetic self. The reader is constantly aware of the observing presence, but primarily through what he observes, rather than through his responses, which are reticent and detached. He is also aware of the distance that separates the observer from the natural world that he observes. In the poems, man exists and the world exists, but the space between them, which was once filled by religious perceptions of connection and order, is now empty.

This mode of observation in Hardy's poems has obvious consequences for imagery and for language. The imagery depends on sight, and to a lesser degree on sound – the two distanced senses – and almost never on touch or taste or smell – the intimate senses. It is descriptive and literal, more often than figurative; and it is confined to the physical particulars of Hardy's own 'parish' – there is scarcely an image in the poems that is not a literal part of the Wessex world. The language of the poems is also a language of separateness and of local reality – a substantive language of naming and identifying. Here is an example of what I mean:

Exeunt Omnes

I

> *Everybody else, then, going,*
> *And I still left where the fair was? . . .*
> *Much have I seen of neighbour loungers*
> *Making a lusty showing,*
> *Each now past all knowing.*

II

> *There is an air of blankness*
> *In the street and the littered spaces;*
> *Thoroughfare, steeple, bridge and highway*
> *Wizen themselves to lankness;*
> *Kennels dribble dankness.*

III

> *Folk all fade. And whither,*
> *As I wait alone where the fair was?*
> *Into the clammy and numbing night-fog*
> *Whence they entered hither.*
> *Soon one more goes thither!*[15]

This is a poem made up largely of substantives that name ordinary Wessex reality. There is no figurative language except for the odd verb, 'wizen', of line ten, no vivid imagery, nothing very striking in cadence or diction. The whole poem is, of course, a figurative utterance – life is like a fair, which has ended and left the old Hardy behind – but it is not metaphorical in the customary sense; one might say, rather, that the poem is a *revelation* of the human condition, its transitoriness, its brief excitement, its blank and empty end. Is it a nature poem? Is it, as I have said Hardy's poems are, a *religious* poem? The answer to both questions, I think, is 'Yes, in a way.' Certainly the poem is located in the world of material reality, the natural attributes of which are also its meaning. And certainly it is concerned with what the catechism calls Last Things.

If it is just as certainly not a conventional nature or religious poem, that is perhaps because such poems were not possible for a poet of Hardy's time, with Hardy's convictions. The relation between man and nature, the sense of implicit analogies existing between human experience and the natural world, was an easy and evident subject for Wordsworth, but by Hardy's day it was a good deal more difficult – the aura was dimmer and darker, and the order that it implied more tenuous. But this does not mean that the two poets were not in the same natural religious tradition; Hardy was simply farther along. Perhaps if he had been born earlier he would have written better poems; certainly they would have been different. Still, as Eliot remarked, a poet cannot choose the world into which he is born; he must make his poetry out of the world that he is given. And that is what Hardy did.

II

'Poetry and religion,' Hardy wrote near the end of his life, 'touch each other, or rather modulate into each other; are, indeed, often but different

names for the same thing.'[16] This can only be true if religion is defined as
a feeling rather than as a body of doctrine, and that is the way in which
Hardy defined his own religiousness; he was, he wrote, 'churchy; not in
an intellectual sense, but in so far as instincts and emotions ruled'.[17] It is
from those instincts and emotions that the poems came, and it is those
instincts and emotions that the poems express.

This idea of the essential religiousness of poetry is a Romantic one, but
by the time that Hardy espoused it it was becoming more and more
difficult to defend, as the authority of science and the scientific account of
reality dominated western thought. For to say that poetry and religion
are different names for the same thing is to affirm the reality of the
element that they share – that changeless value in things which art and
religion have traditionally celebrated. But that value is not verifiable,
and is therefore, in the scientific view, not true.

It is ironic that in the scientific attack on the religiousness of poetry,
Hardy should have been claimed as a hero of the scientific view, when he
was in fact a major figure on the other side. That he was is partly his own
fault – he talked like a materialist, though he *felt* like a supernaturalist –
and partly the work of I. A. Richards, whose importance in establishing
modern attitudes towards modern poetry can scarcely be exaggerated.
The crucial document on this point is Richards's *Science and Poetry* (1926),
which told its readers – as Richards was then telling his Cambridge
students – how to think about Eliot, and what to think about Hardy.
Richards's essential argument was that modern science had altered men's
understanding of the world in fundamental ways, and that poetry
would have to change to meet the changes in human consciousness.
'Contemporary poetry,' he wrote,

> . . . must be such as could not have been written in another age than
> our own. It must have sprung in part from the contemporary
> situation. It must correspond to needs, impulses, attitudes, which
> did not arise in the same fashion for poets in the past, and criticism
> also must take notice of the contemporary situation. Our attitudes
> to man, to nature, and to the universe change with every
> generation, and have changed with unusual violence in recent
> years. We cannot leave these changes out of account in judging
> modern poetry. When attitudes are changing neither criticism nor
> poetry can remain stationary.[18]

The unexamined assumption here is that the changes of attitude created by modern science have been absolute, and have rendered past attitudes obsolete and useless, and Richards did in fact argue this position explicitly in his remarks on *The Waste Land*.

'The central dominant change' in the world-picture, Richards argued, was '*the Neutralization of Nature*, the transference from the Magical View of the world to the scientific.' He defined the Magical View as 'roughly, the belief in a world of Spirits and Powers which control events, and which can be evoked and, to some extent, controlled themselves by human practices', and he added that 'the belief in Inspiration and the beliefs underlying Ritual are representative parts of this view',[19] and that perhaps poetry and the other arts arose with it. A less polemical materialist might prefer to call this view *Religious*, and to argue that it is a constant in human consciousness (Hardy would surely have taken that position).

Richards's chief example of this process of transference as manifested in poetry was the work of Hardy: 'not only does his work span the whole period in which what I have called the neutralization of nature was finally effected, but it has throughout definitely reflected that change'. Richards shrewdly found the grounds for his assertion not in Hardy's explicitly philosophical poems, but in

> the tone, the handling and the rhythm of poems which treat other subjects, for example *The Self-Unseeing*, *The Voice*, *A Broken Appointment*, and pre-eminently *After a Journey*. A poem does not necessarily accept the situation because it gives it explicit recognition, but only through the precise mutation of the attitudes of which it is composed.[20]

This last sentence is somewhat obscure, but what Richards was referring to must be the way in which, in these poems, the 'aura' of a past event is acknowledged to be past, the relentlessness with which Hardy records the passage of time and the finality of change and death. Certainly it is true that Hardy poems often record such mutations of attitudes; still, I would not say that this implied a denial of the Magical View exactly, and I think one might make Richards's point differently, and more precisely.

Let us look at Richards's first example, which is also the simplest one – Hardy's 'The Self-Unseeing'.

Here is the ancient floor,
Footworn and hollowed and thin,
Here was the former door
Where the dead feet walked in.

She sat here in her chair,
Smiling into the fire;
He who played stood there,
Bowing it higher and higher.

Childlike, I danced in a dream;
Blessings emblazoned that day;
Everything glowed with a gleam;
Yet we were looking away![21]

What are we to say about the tone, the handling, the rhythm of this little poem? I am struck by two things in it: first, that the tone is celebratory, that the blessings in the third stanza are true blessings; and second, that the remembered event has a kind of present existence (note the firm, present-tense assertion of the first line). Hardy is saying that when the blessed scene occurred, the participants were unaware of its glory, and that only now, when it is past, can the rememberer perceive its gleam. This is a characteristically Hardyan irony, and many of his other poems are constructed in a similar manner: there is a past, filled with happiness and hope, and a present that denies the permanence of that happiness; Time is the great reality, and it is irreversible (a superlative example is 'During Wind and Rain'). This ironic form is perhaps what Richards meant by the 'precise mutations of the attitudes of which it is composed'. But the mutations do not deny experience its aura — the day *did* gleam — nor do they, so far as I can see, neutralize nature, or commit Hardy to a scientific view of the world. In fact, 'The Self-Unseeing' is an expression in verse of the remark from the *Later Years* that I quoted above, 'That things and events always were, are, and will be.'

Two of the other poems that Richards cites treat of the pastness of the past in similar, but more complicated ways. Both 'The Voice' and 'After a Journey' belong to the 'Poems of 1912–13', the sequence of elegies that Hardy wrote after the death of his first wife. They are poems about love and loss, both the loss of love in time, and the ultimate loss in death. In all of these elegies Hardy is scrupulous to acknowledge both kinds of loss, and to accept the finality of loss. Yet in both of these examples, and in many others of the sequence, the dead wife appears as a real, felt presence – as a voice, or as a 'voiceless ghost', summoning the grieving man to re-enter their shared past, and he, addressing her, affirms her reality and is comforted by it, though his rational mind denies it. So 'After a Journey' ends:

> *Soon you will have, Dear, to vanish from me,*
>   *For the stars close their shutters and the dawn whitens hazily.*
> *Trust me, I mind not, though Life lours,*
>   *The bringing me here; nay, bring me here again!*
>   *I am just the same as when*
> *Our days were a joy, and our paths through flowers.* [22]

There are two attitudes here, corresponding to what Richards called the scientific view and the Magical View, and both are expressions of Hardy's divided mind. His wife is dead, yet she can call him to her; their love died, yet it lives; Hardy is old and changed, yet he is just the same. Heart and mind may move on contrary tracks, but neither invalidates the other, both speak truths.

Richards said of Hardy – and it was clearly intended as the highest praise – that 'he is the poet who has most steadily refused to be comforted. The comfort of forgetfulness, the comfort of beliefs, he has put both these away.' And he went on to explain the consequences of this refusal:

> Hence his singular preoccupation with death; because it is in the contemplation of death that the necessity for human attitudes, in the face of an indifferent universe, to become self-supporting is felt most poignantly. [23]

Some of this is true; Hardy did refuse to forget (or at least he went on remembering, and making poems out of memory), and he did reject the consolations of belief in the conventional religious sense. But he was by no means as complete or as cosy in his disbelief as Richards would have him. 'Half my time', he explained in a letter written during the First World War, '– particularly when writing verse – I "believe" (in the modern sense of the word) not only in the things Bergson believes in, but in spectres, mysterious voices, intuitions, omens, dreams, haunted places, etc., etc.'[24] That half-belief keeps his poems from being as comfortless as Richards would wish; the comforts they contain come from Hardy's ability to preserve the Magical View in at least a superstitious, will-to-believe way: the past still gleams in memory, the dead woman calls, the thin ghost beckons, and will beckon again. And so, though the universe may be indifferent (certainly *time* is indifferent), the speaker is not self-supporting; he is supported by realities that neither reason nor science will accept, but that are for Hardy realities nonetheless.

Richards was quite correct in observing that Hardy refused the comforts that belief in a divine principle in the world would give, and he might have cited many better examples to support his point – for instance the final stanza of 'The Going'. But if there is no doctrinal belief expressed in the poems, there is an acknowledged need for such comforts as belief has traditionally afforded. This need is surely as much a source of poetry as it is of religion. Richards failed to recognize it in Hardy, because he was himself insensitive to it; he was simply too cheerful, and too enthusiastic about a universe emptied of Magic, to read an essentially religious poet with a proper sympathy.

The criticism of Richards, like that of Eliot, belongs now to the past, and must be of mainly historical interest. And it is very interesting indeed that in the years after the First War a theory of poetry that denied 'the Magical View' should have been formulated, and received with such respect. It seems to me to tell us a good deal about the post-war mood, but nothing at all useful about poetry. And certainly in the case of Hardy it produced a mis-reading of both his mind and his art that has influenced the criticism of fifty years, and that is still with us.[25] I suggest that we abandon the notion of Hardy as the first poet of a new tradition of neutralized Nature, and see him rather as a great poet in an old and central tradition, a poet conscious of the pressures working against belief, but asserting against those pressures his instinctual and emotional convictions that the universe was informed by value, and that man and nature shared a relation to that value.

III

I have called this essay 'The Hardy Tradition in Modern English Poetry', because I wished to call attention to the continuance of the tradition in the twentieth century, but I have left myself little space to do so at any length. I must therefore content myself with two final offerings: first, a summary definition of what I think the Hardy tradition to be, and second, some names of poets who seem to me to represent the tradition since Hardy.

The tradition has many variations, but its constants seem to me to be these: it is English and primarily concerned with actual nature and with man's relation to it; it is physical, not transcendental, but it is nevertheless religious in the sense that its nature is not 'neutralized'; it is descriptive rather than metaphorical or symbolic; it is rooted in time, but not in history; it is often concerned with the reality of memory, and so is retrospective, sometimes regretful and melancholy, but also ironic and stoic; it observes the world, not the self. Formally, the tradition is conservative, but inventive: Hardy played endless variations on inherited stanza forms, and rarely repeated one, but the base of the variations was traditional. The verse is never free, the syntax is never fragmented, the sense is never in doubt – difficult, yes, but not doubtful.

This tradition has lived on through modern changes of literary fashion; it has survived the era of Pound and Eliot (without really noticing that it had occurred), and it will surely go on surviving as long as English poets find it possible to think of themselves as English, and to feel in the world around them an aura of value. The line after Hardy is a rich and populous one: there has never been a time in this century when excellent poets were not writing in the Hardy tradition. Most of the names are obvious ones, if you think about it: Frost (the only American in the line, I think; but then his formative years were spent in England, among English Georgians, and he seems to me the best of the Georgians rather than the best of New England), Edward Thomas, the early, rhyming D. H. Lawrence, Edmund Blunden, Andrew Young, Cecil Day Lewis, Geoffrey Grigson, Philip Larkin. Not all of these poets have attracted the attention of the weighty modernist critics and anthologists (though Larkin's *Oxford Book of Twentieth-century English Verse* gives the tradition due acknowledgment), but I'm sure they are more often read voluntarily, outside of classrooms, by people who simply enjoy reading poetry, than most of the Major Moderns are.

Theirs is not, on the whole, a poetry of the topical, the contemporary, the current; it does not alter its traditional forms to shape models of the difficulties of being modern. It assumes a continuity of mode which implies a continuity of human experience; the natural world remains, human beings go on living, remembering, suffering, and dying in ways that history does not change very much. This is a conservative view of the human situation – but the very idea of a tradition is conservative, and not in any direct political sense. To deny the validity of such a view is to reject the art of the past as merely historical (as Richards seemed to be doing in *Science and Poetry*). But the experience of reading poetry must persuade us very quickly that this is not the case, that the past lives for us in its verse. And we must trust our experience before we trust our critics.

NOTES

1. 'Tradition and the Individual Talent', *Selected Essays 1917–1932*, 1932, 14.
2. 'Seldom, perhaps, does the word appear except in a phrase of censure. If otherwise, it is vaguely approbative, with the implication, as to the work approved, of some pleasing archaeological reconstruction. You can hardly make the word agreeable to English ears without this comfortable reference to the reassuring science of archaeology.' ('Tradition and the Individual Talent', 13.)
3. Here too Eliot must bear a share of the responsibility; the famous passage in 'The Metaphysical Poets' about modern civilization and the necessity of difficulty is another of those doctrinal statements that have been accepted without sufficient scepticism.
4. 'She Hears the Storm', *The Complete Poems of Thomas Hardy*, ed. James Gibson, 1976, Poem 228. All poem numbers cited hereafter refer to this edition.
5. Graves, *Goodbye to All That*, 1929, 379.
6. *Life*, 146–7. Hardy wrote a more elaborate defence of his provincialism in his 'General Preface' to the Wessex Edition of his works.
7. *Life*, 419.
8. Cf. Alfred North Whitehead, *Science and the Modern World*, New York, 1925, 138: '. . . the nature-poetry of the romantic revival was a protest on behalf of the organic view of nature, and also a protest against the exclusion of value from the essence of matter of fact'.
9. Edward Thomas thought that *The Dynasts* was an extreme example of the same thing: 'Twentieth-century superstition can no further go than in that enormous poem,' he wrote ('Thomas Hardy of Dorchester', *Poetry and Drama*, I, June 1913, 182).
10. Poem 400.

11. *Life*, 431.

12. *Life*, 284.

13. Graves, 'Dame Ocupacyon', *The Crowning Privilege*, 1955, 98.

14. *Life*, 409. The same is true of the novels; see his arrangement of the Wessex Edition into 'Novels of Character and Environment' (all the important novels), 'Romances and Fantasies', and 'Novels of Ingenuity'.

15. Poem 335.

16. *Complete Poems*, 561. The essay first appeared as the introduction to *Late Lyrics and Earlier* (1922).

17. *Life*, 376.

18. I. A. Richards, *Science and Poetry*, 1926, 44.

19. *Ibid.*, 47.

20. *Ibid.*, 68–9.

21. Poem 135.

22. Poem 289.

23. *Science and Poetry*, 70.

24. *Life*, 370.

25. See for example Donald Davie, *Thomas Hardy and British Poetry*, 1972.

8: Hardy and His Readers

JAMES GIBSON

I T IS WELL-KNOWN that Hardy was forced by Victorian morality to censor his own writing in order to have it published. We have been told almost too often how in the serialization of *Tess of the d'Urbervilles* in *The Graphic* in 1891 Tess and her milkmaid friends had to be wheeled across a flooded lane in a wheelbarrow because the Editor thought that his readers would be offended by Hardy's first proposal that Angel Clare should carry them across in his arms. But the extent to which Hardy was influenced by the attitudes of his readers, or by what his editors and publishers thought those attitudes to be, and the nature of the changes forced upon him are still insufficiently understood. For Hardy his quarter of a century of novel writing was a constant duel with Mrs. Grundy, who was then in her Victorian prime. My aim in this essay is to give some idea of the extent to which he was influenced by Grundyism, to illustrate some of the ways in which this influence made itself felt, and to look at the effect of this influence on his achievement as a writer.

The influence was substantial and it was felt from the beginning. His first novel, *The Poor Man and the Lady*, was rejected by Macmillan in 1868. In a courteous letter to Hardy, Alexander Macmillan admitted that the pictures of the upper classes were 'sharp, clear, incisive, and in many respects true', but he thought that readers would 'throw down the volume in disgust', and that it lacked 'the *modesty of nature* of fact'. Was it, he asked,

within the range of likelihood that *any* gentleman would pursue his wife at midnight and *strike* her?[1]

Hardy's second novel was likewise rejected by Macmillan. John Morley, the adviser, said in his report that the novel was ruined by the disgusting and absurd outrage which is the key to its mystery. The violation of a young lady at an evening party, and the subsequent birth of a child, is too abominable to be tolerated as a central incident from which the action of the story is to move.[2]

The publisher, Tinsley, had fewer scruples than Macmillan, and in 1871 *Desperate Remedies* became Hardy's first published novel. The reviewer in *The Athenaeum* found it 'unpleasant', and, after considering the possibility that it might have been written by a lady, referred to expressions which it contained which were

so remarkably coarse as to render it almost impossible that it should have come from the pen of an English lady.[3]

The Spectator found in it

no display of passion except of a brute kind, no pictures of Christian virtue . . .[4]

Hardy was, like most writers, extremely sensitive to reviews, and in *The Life of Thomas Hardy* he describes how

He remembered, for long years after, how he had read this review as he sat on a stile leading to the eweleaze he had to cross on his way home to Bockhampton. The bitterness of that moment was never forgotten; at the time he wished that he were dead. (p. 84)

Although the reviews were not wholly as bad as these extracts suggest, the effect on Hardy, coming on top of his exchanges with Macmillan, must have been considerable. His first encounters with Mrs. Grundy had taken place and he was wounded.

Yet, interestingly enough, there were sexual aspects of *Desperate Remedies* which were in some ways as overt as anything he was to write later, and which show that Hardy already had a remarkable ability to explore imaginatively subconscious levels of human feeling. There is the obviously physical attraction felt by Miss Aldclyffe for Cytherea. At their first meeting Miss Aldclyffe muses upon Cytherea as a 'creature who could glide round my luxurious indolent body'. Subsequently, she engages Cytherea as her personal maid, and the description of Cytherea's undressing of her employer after the state dinner is full of suppressed sexuality. After removing her mistress's dress, Cytherea finds Miss Aldclyffe in her nightdress, and sees in the looking-glass

> the fair white surface, and the inimitable combination of curves between throat and bosom,

while

> In the midst of her breast, like an island in a sea of pearl, reclined an exquisite little gold locket. (Ch. 5)

When Hardy, in 1912, revised *Desperate Remedies* for the Wessex Edition, 'breast' was changed to 'chest', and it is difficult not to conclude that he was trying to tone down the sexual implications of what he had written forty years earlier.

Back in her own room, Cytherea looks in her own glass at the reflection of 'her own magnificent resources in face and bosom', and Hardy makes it clear that their attractiveness is, in his own word, 'unadorned'. Shortly afterwards, there is a remarkable scene in which Miss Aldclyffe comes in to Cytherea's bed, beseeches her to kiss her, and then shows an impassioned jealousy because Cytherea has already been kissed by a man:

> I thought I had at last found an artless woman who had not been sullied by a man's lips . . . Find a girl, if you can, whose mouth and ears have not been made a regular highway of by some man or another! Leave the admittedly notorious spots – the drawing-rooms of society – and look in the villages – leave the villages and search in the schools – and you can hardly find a girl whose heart has not been *had* – is not an old thing half worn out by some He or another. (Ch. 6)

Hardy knew his Shakespeare well and was almost certainly aware that 'highway' and its synonyms had strong sexual connotations in the Elizabethan drama.[5] It is also noticeable that the word 'had' has been underlined. At this moment Miss Aldclyffe's feelings for Cytherea seem to be a not impossible mixture of maternal and sexual love, and the sexuality of such phrases as 'I have been sipping at your mouth as if it were honey' and Hardy's comment that 'Miss Aldclyffe was as jealous as any man could have been' cannot be missed.

There are also strong sensual elements in the chapters in which the reader is kept in suspense as to whether Edward will be able to find Cytherea on her wedding-night before the villain she has married, bigamously as it is now believed, takes her to bed. Even when Hardy has to describe a minor character like Anne Seaway, we are told that

> Her form was full and round, its voluptuous maturity standing out in strong contrast to the memory of Cytherea's lissom girlishness.

When we remember that Cytherea had 'magnificent resources' in that area herself, we may perhaps wonder where Hardy's creative imagination was leading him!

I have spent some time on the sensual element in *Desperate Remedies* partly because it is interesting what went unnoticed, or ignored, in 1871, but more because I want to establish that this element does exist in Hardy's writing from the beginning, and that there was something here which was bound to lead to difficulties with his Victorian readers.

Nothing in Hardy's career is more astonishing than his rapid growth to full maturity as a novelist. *Far from the Madding Crowd*, the next novel I want to look at, was published only three years after *Desperate Remedies*, but it is one of his greatest novels. Leslie Stephen, the Editor of the *Cornhill Magazine*, in commissioning it as a serial, asked Hardy to provide a little more incident than there had been in *Under the Greenwood Tree*, but hastened to add that he didn't want a murder in every number. In writing his serial Hardy had much to contend with. Stephen wrote to him in January 1874,

> I have ventured to leave out a line or two in the last batch of proofs from an excessive prudery of which I am ashamed; but one is forced to be absurdly particular. May I suggest that Troy's seduction of the young woman will require to be treated in a gingerly fashion, when, as I suppose must be the case, he comes to be exposed to his wife? I mean that the thing must be stated but that the words must be careful − excuse this wretched shred of concession to popular stupidity; but I am a slave.[6]

He added that three respectable ladies had written to object to an improper passage which had already been published. Later, when the novel came out in book form, *The Times'* reviewer quoted with commendation that very passage, and that enables us to identify it. Impressed by Hardy's ability to portray and use his rustic chorus, the reviewer quotes some of the chat about the fickle Mr. Everdene who found it difficult to be both married and happy until he hit upon the idea of making his wife take off her wedding-ring when they made love:

> 'And so as soon as he could thoroughly fancy he was doing wrong and committing the seventh, a' got to like her as well as ever, and they lived on a perfect example of mutel love.' (Ch. 6)

We have a good example here of the gap between the Editor of the *Cornhill* and the reviewer of *The Times*, and of the complexities of the situation with which Hardy was having to cope. Hardy has described the end of this incident with Stephen:

> As soon as I met him, I said, 'You see what the *Times* says about that paragraph; and you cannot say that the *Times* is not respectable.' He was smoking, and replied tardily: 'No; I can't say that the *Times* is not respectable.' I then urged that if he had omitted the sentences, as he had wished he had done, I should never have taken the trouble to restore them in the reprint, and the *Times* could not have quoted them with approbation. I suppose my manner was slightly triumphant; at any rate, he said, 'I spoke as editor, not as man. You have no more consciousness of these things than a child.'[7]

Robert Gittings, in his biography, *Young Thomas Hardy*, suggests that Leslie Stephen's evangelical upbringing led to a puritanical obsession about sex, and I wonder to what extent Stephen's own fears are behind his anxiety to alert Hardy to the protests of the three respectable ladies.

But the important thing for Hardy was that these attitudes existed. He was a young writer with a small income and about to be married. He desperately wanted to succeed as a novelist and writer of serials, and more than anything else he wanted to write about the subject which fascinated him – love between man and woman. This was to be his dominating theme throughout all his writing, and his character was such that he had to find a way of writing about it as frankly and as honestly as was possible. This involved coming to terms with his own sensuality, and contending with respectable Mrs. Grundys and with puritanical or fearful editors. In *Far from the Madding Crowd* he gives us a novel about a young girl who is seduced by a handsome soldier, and about her mistress who also succumbs to the soldier's flattery and physical appeal. His problem was to present this without causing offence. It is part of the greatness of *Far from the Madding Crowd* that he does so, and in doing so makes a virtue out of necessity. He does so by a consummate piece of craftsmanship, the use of highly suggestive description and imagery. At their very first meeting, in darkness, the softness of Bathsheba's skirt is caught by the sharpness of Troy's spur, and she feels the physical presence of Troy in his 'warm clothes and buttons'. Their relationship develops rapidly in the hay-field, and then in hiving the bees where Bathsheba is embarrassed to be caught by Troy at the top of a ladder. It is, of course, June, and when they next meet in the hollow amid the ferns Hardy's writing is at its most sensuous and suggestive. It is eight o'clock on a midsummer evening and the sun is a 'bristling ball of gold in the west'. The tall thickets of fern are plump and diaphanous and caress Bathsheba with their soft feathery arms up to her shoulders. Troy is like a peacock putting on a mating display. His sword is described as being like a living thing, and, as if to emphasize the sexual implications, Hardy makes him compare his sword strokes to 'sowing' and 'threshing', words long associated in the folk-songs Hardy knew so well with the physical act of love-making. It is typical of Hardy's richness as a writer that, at the same time as these words are used as sexual symbols, they are full of irony because of the contrast between the creative act of farming and the destructive nature of soldiering. There follows another powerful piece of writing in which we see Bathsheba, even though she is frightened that he may hurt her, mesmerized by the brilliance of the sword-play as he measures 'her breadth and outline', and a climax is reached in which his lips are 'tightly closed in sustained effort'. It is not surprising that 'she felt powerless to withstand or deny him' and that Troy takes his first kiss. Hardy had more consciousness of these things than Stephen gave him credit for.

So far I have been looking at the sensuality which was necessarily present in some of the early novels, and suggesting one way in which Hardy portrayed this successfully even in the Grundian society he had to write for. Before moving on to consider other aspects of my subject, I wish to emphasize that this sensuality is to be found throughout Hardy's writing. It is present very strongly indeed in passages of *The Return of the Native* and of *The Woodlanders*. It is central to *Tess of the d'Urbervilles* and *Jude the Obscure*. It is even present in such short stories as 'An Imaginative Woman', in which there is a notable passage in which the romantic and love-starved Mrs. Marchmill, bored by a prosaic husband and passionately in love with a poet she has never met, retires to bed with the poet's portrait, murmurs that the poet is 'more intimate with the real me' than her husband, and is described by Hardy as 'sleeping on a poet's lips, immersed in the very essence of him, permeated by his spirit as by an ether'. The nature of the writing makes it clear that a symbolic mating is taking place and provides another example of Hardy's use of erotic imagery.

By such means he had found one method of dealing with the susceptibilities of his readers. In the novels that followed *Far from the Madding Crowd* he was increasingly to use a second method: the provision of alternative versions of each novel. In fact, it is not easy to accept his statement to Leslie Stephen that he would not have restored that passage about Mr. Everdene, because this was to become an essential part of his literary activity. In the *Life* we read of Hardy's

> artistic inability to rest content with anything that he wrote until he had brought the expression as near to his thought as language would allow. (p. 451)

Textually this makes his novels a rich field for study, and it is regrettable that we still lack variorum editions with all that they would reveal of Hardy's craftsmanship and his painstaking revision, a revision which occurred at manuscript stage, serial, first edition in two or three volumes, first one-volume edition, in the Osgood, McIlvaine·Edition of 1895–6, and in the first and subsequent printings of the Wessex Edition. Many of these verbal alterations are stylistic, but not a few are what I shall call Grundy revisions. (The term will be used in this essay to cover both revisions prompted by the need to avoid giving offence and revisions in the direction of a greater frankness: in both cases the variants in the text have their origin in a reaction to editorial or public sensitivity). Some I have already mentioned. In so far as it is possible to generalize, without having variorum editions available, the movement is from a bowdlerized serial to a less bowdlerized first edition and an even less bowdlerized and more explicit Osgood, McIlvaine Edition. It is worthy of mention that the comparatively few alterations in the Wessex Edition seem to show Hardy, now in his seventies, having second thoughts about some of his earlier revisions, and indulging in some rebowdlerization. The scale of revision shows a marked increase during the twenty-one years from *Far from the Madding Crowd* to *Jude the Obscure*.

Grundy revisions occur even in a novel as early as *Far from the Madding Crowd*, but they are on a comparatively small scale. 'Loose songs' in the serial was later to become 'ba'dy songs'. Bathsheba in the edition we read today is described as having depth enough for 'alarming exploits of sex', but in the serial this read 'alarming potentialities of exploit'. Cain Ball's grandfather in all editions until 1912 used to 'bide about in a public-house', but in the Wessex Edition this was altered to 'bide about in a public-house wi' a 'ooman'.

Textual revisions of a more serious kind were necessary in *The Return of the Native*. Hardy first offered this as a serial to the *Cornhill*, but Leslie Stephen refused to accept it until he could see the complete manuscript because he feared that relations between Eustacia and Wildeve might develop into something too 'dangerous' for a family magazine. Frank Pinion has shown that Hardy had previously offered it to Wm. Blackwood, but their Editor, too, had worries about it. Finally, it was published in the *Belgravia*, and John Paterson in his book *The Making of 'The Return of the Native'* indicates the extent to which changes were forced on Hardy. Eustacia suffers most, and Hardy's problem is to write a novel about a deeply sensual woman without mentioning her sensuality too obviously. He again uses the device of suggestive imagery. From her first appearance Eustacia is associated with fire and heat. She stands by a bonfire which lights the darkness of Egdon Heath. The fire is a signal for her lover, Wildeve, who describes himself as suffering from the 'curse of inflammability' and refers to her 'hot little bosom'. Again and again she is described in terms that suggest the passion that is on fire within her. If we could have seen the colour of her soul, it would have been 'flame-like'. Indignation spreads through her like 'subterranean heat', and 'scalding tears' trickle from her eyes. And at the end of Book 5, as Eustacia's warmth and passion are to be extinguished for ever in the cold waters of Shadwater Weir, Hardy introduces into her final soliloquy, in an 1895 revision, these words about Wildeve:

'He's not *great* enough for me to give myself to – he does not suffice for my desire!' (V. 7)

Hardy may have been building up here the evidence that Eustacia's death was no accident, but of that we cannot be certain. What is certain is that by means of a Grundy revision in the 1895 Edition, Hardy leaves no doubt as to what the relationship of Eustacia to Wildeve had been. In all previous editions she says to Wildeve when they meet by the bonfire, 'but I won't encourage you any more'. In 1895 this becomes 'but I won't give myself to you any more'. It is also significant that in early editions Eustacia describes the heath as her 'cross, misery and death', but in 1895 this becomes her 'cross, shame and death'.

The Trumpet-Major deserves brief consideration because, although in this story there was no risk of conflict with the moral Establishment, it provides an excellent example of the skill with which Hardy can now write. *The Trumpet-Major* first appeared as a serial in *Good Words* in 1880. *Good Words* was a monthly magazine, edited by Dr. Macleod, one of Her Majesty's Chaplains for Scotland, and printed, appropriately enough, by a firm with the name of Virtue & Co., Ltd. Some idea of the character of this publication can be obtained from a letter written by Hardy in 1925 in which he said:

I met Dr. Macleod whenever he came to London and discussed small literary points with him, all of which I have forgotten except two: that he asked me to make a lover's meeting, which I had fixed for a Sunday afternoon, take place on a Saturday, and that swear-words should be avoided – in both which requests I readily acquiesced, as I restored my own readings when the novel came out as a book.[8]

The major revision, or restoration, occurs, however, at the end of the novel. In the serial we read:

The candle held by his father shed its waving light upon John's face and uniform as he turned with a farewell smile on the doorstone, backed by the black night; and in another moment he had plunged into the darkness, the ring of his smart step dying away upon the bridge as he joined his waiting companions-in-arms, and went off to blow his trumpet over the bloody battlefields of Spain.[9]

The First Edition is similar until, right at the very end, we read that John 'went off to blow his trumpet till silenced for ever upon one of the bloody battle-fields of Spain.' Hardy is seen here coping with the Victorian convention of the happy ending in his serial version. It was enough that Anne should have married what many readers would have regarded as the wrong brother. To kill off the right brother as well was intolerable, particularly in a journal called *Good Words*! To the sensitive reader, however, the suggestions of death are already there in the serial. John is 'backed by the black night': he plunges 'into the darkness': the ring of his smart step is heard 'dying away upon the bridge'. The technique is similar to that we have seen him using in *Far from the Madding Crowd*. By craftsmanship of this kind Hardy turned the difficulties under which he had to write to his advantage. By such means he developed that skill in the use of language which in later years was to be the foundation of his greatness as a poet, and which gives the lie to those who have described him as a 'provincial manufacturer of gauche and heavy fictions',[10] or as being 'indifferent even to the prescripts of good writing'.[11]

The *Mayor of Casterbridge*, which first appeared as a serial in *The Graphic* in 1886, shows Hardy entering a new phase of his duel with Grundyism. So far he has been able to meet the restrictions which were placed on him by evoking rather than stating, and by the use of what I have called Grundy revisions. Most of these revisions have so far been comparatively small verbal changes. But with *The Mayor* there emerges a new situation which is to become highly important in *Tess* and *Jude*. As Hardy finds himself wanting to write about more serious and adult areas of human experience, and to write about them more critically, it becomes necessary for him to make substantial changes in the stories themselves in the different editions. Thus, in the serial version of *The Mayor*, Henchard marries Lucetta in the belief that his first wife is dead. When she returns, he hides his second marriage from her. However, in the book version Lucetta is not his wife but his mistress, an arrangement that Hardy knew would not be acceptable to the Editor of *The Graphic*. This change, which was made more complex by the fact that in the serial the wedding had taken place only a fortnight before the first wife, Susan, returned, and by the fact that the bigamous wife was just about to turn up in Casterbridge, involved Hardy in far more re-writing between serial and First Edition than had been customary in earlier novels, and it must have added greatly to the strain on him, even though he was becoming adept at revision and did it with exceptional competence and facility.

A typical example of the changes required can be found in Chapter 18, where Lucetta writes to Henchard after Susan has returned. In the serial the letter reads:

> I quite forgive you for landing me in such a dilemma, remembering that you concealed nothing before our ill-advised marriage, hasty as it was; and that you really did set before me the fact of there being a certain risk in marrying you, slight as it seemed to be after eighteen years of silence on your wife's part.[12]

In the First Edition Hardy has altered 'ill-advised marriage' to 'ill-advised acquaintance' and 'the fact of there being a certain risk in marrying you' becomes 'the fact of there being a certain risk in loving you'. By 1895 this has become 'the fact of there being a certain risk in intimacy with you', and Hardy must have been aware that 'intimacy' is a well-known euphemism for sexual intercourse, and had been since the seventeenth century. And when later in the story Henchard, jealous of Farfrae, attempts to force Lucetta to marry him, he threatens in the serial to 'disclose all' if she marries Farfrae, whereas in the First Edition this has been changed to 'reveal our intimacy'.

But in addition to the sizeable structural changes to be found in the book versions of *The Mayor*, there are other small but important verbal changes which throw light on Hardy's hardening attitudes. In the first chapter, where, in versions before 1895, Henchard and Susan are seen walking along the road and we are told that they must be man and wife because

> No other than such relationship would have accounted for the distinctive atmosphere of domesticity which the trio carried along with them . . .[13]

we find a change in 1895 to an 'atmosphere of stale familiarity'. Here we have a harshening of the attitude towards marriage, possibly a reflection of a deterioration in Hardy's own marriage between 1886 and 1895.

Marriage plays a large part in *The Woodlanders*, as it was to do in *Tess* and *Jude*, but Hardy is not involved on this occasion in any massive re-writing of his story. In his excellent essay, *Revisions and Vision: Thomas Hardy's 'The Woodlanders'*, Dale Kramer has examined the textual changes in eight different versions of the novel, and has shown how revisions and additions are designed to bring out the innate sensuality of Grace and to emphasize Fitzpiers's amorous nature to such an extent that there seems little hope of happiness for Grace in her marriage with him.

Hardy's task in *The Woodlanders* was to tell his story for its serial appearance in *Macmillan's Magazine* in 1886–7 in such a way that one of the main themes, that the divorce laws at that time were such that a woman could find no escape from a promiscuous husband, could be put across without giving offence. If the marriage-divorce theme were to be developed fully, then Fitzpiers had to be shown as a philanderer, but not too obviously so. Thus, when Grace sees Suke Damson leaving Fitzpiers's house in the early hours of the morning, the serial tells the reader that she was wearing a 'long loose garment'. It was not until 1896 that Hardy felt able to add words which would have been unacceptable ten years previously. Suke Damson's long loose garment, he writes, was 'like a nightdress'.

The process of revision to make more explicit can be seen even more strikingly in an earlier chapter, where the affair between Suke and Fitzpiers begins on Midsummer's night in the woods. Mowbray Morris, the Editor of *Macmillan's Magazine*, saw the dangers inherent in Suke as soon as she appeared on the scene, and he wrote to Hardy as follows:

> You will, I am sure, not mind my giving you a gentle hint on one small matter – the affair between Miss Damson and the Doctor. I am not afraid (as you may imagine) for my own morals: but we have, I fancy, rather a queer public: pious Scottish souls who take offence wondrously easily. . . . Of course, it is very annoying to have to reckon for such asses: still, I can't help it; an editor must be commercial as well as literary; and the magazine has scarcely so abundant a sale that I can afford to disregard any section of its readers. So, I think, if you can contrive not to bring the fair Miss Suke to too open shame, it would be as well. Let the human frailty be construed mild.[14]

Hardy was used to this kind of thing now and knew how to deal with it. In the serial Fitzpiers and Suke behave on Midsummer's night in a reasonably decorous manner. Fitzpiers chases her over the fields, sinks down panting on to the 'next hay-cock', and gives her a single kiss. For those who have ears to hear, Hardy's comment that 'while they remained silent the coarse whirr of the eternal night-jar burst sarcastically from the top of a tree' may have significance. In the First Edition Fitzpiers is more amorous. He kisses her again, and there is an added sentence at the end of the chapter:

> It was daybreak before Fitzpiers and Suke Damson re-entered Little Hintock.

For some reason, too, the night-jar has become a night-hawk, possibly because a secondary meaning of night-hawk is one who seeks his prey by night. In 1896 there are further changes in this passage. Fitzpiers now sinks down on the same hay-cock, not only kisses her again but presses her close to him, and the couple don't just remain silent but they remain silent 'on the hay'.

Here we see an increasing sexual frankness, version by version. We see it again in the way in which the incident in the hay-field which began the Fitzpiers-Damson affair is just 'the incident in the wood' in all early editions, but becomes in 1896 'the intimacy established in the hayfield'. Again, when Mrs. Charmond tells Grace of her relationship with Fitzpiers, the early editions have

> 'Oh, my great heaven!' she exclaimed, thunderstruck at a revelation transcending her utmost suspicion. 'Can it be – can it be!'

But Grace's words are significantly different in 1896:

> 'O, my great God!' she exclaimed, thunderstruck at a revelation transcending her utmost suspicion. 'He's had you! Can it be – can it be!'

Noticeable here is not just the increased frankness, but also the change of 'heaven' to 'God', something which will remind us that even in his use of exclamations Hardy had to bear in mind the sensibilities of his readers.

In our examination of Hardy's continual struggle to say what he wanted to say, *The Woodlanders* is of considerable textual interest. After his study of the texts, Dale Kramer came to the conclusion that despite the limitations on Hardy's spontaneity in writing he is always adjusting, modifying, strengthening and altering. This is my conclusion, too, and I see the greatness of these later novels as the result of an organic process of which we have been looking at one vital aspect.

John Laird in his scholarly and illuminating textual study, *The Shaping of 'Tess of the d'Urbervilles'*, comes to the same conclusion. He writes of *Tess* that

> Even the enforced changes were usually handled by Hardy with genuine creative artistry: the stimulus may have been external and censorious but most of the author's ultimate alterations were imaginative and vivifying.[15]

In his examination of the highly complex textual situation he shows that it is wrong to think of *Tess* as simply a novel with a bowdlerized serial version. In fact, the manuscript reveals that the novel went through many stages, and that, in John Laird's words, 'the evolutionary process turns out to have been one of amelioration'. Again, then, we find that Hardy has made a virtue out of necessity.

For many reasons *Tess of the d'Urbervilles* is for me Hardy's greatest novel. The one I am concerned with here is that in *Tess* the powers which have been developing in the earlier novels are at their finest. Here we have one of Hardy's frankest statements about the sexual side of the man-woman relationship. He tells a story of seduction and pregnancy and an illegitimate birth, of a woman deserted by a man who believes that there should be one standard of morality for men and another for women, of a murder and a hanging. Such tales have been told before, but Hardy's special achievement was to bring to his story unique qualities of thought and feeling and craftsmanship, and in a novel which is a remarkable blend of realism and symbolism, of deeply felt compassion and loving-kindness, to question the whole basis of the morality of the day. 'Who was the moral man? Still more pertinently, who was the moral woman?' The challenge to him was to show the circumstances of Tess's seduction by Alec and her rejection by Angel sufficiently fully and vividly to gain his readers' sympathy without offending their taste. It may not be easy for us in these post-Lady Chatterley days, when no sexual holds are barred, to appreciate how difficult Hardy's task was.

We find him again using all three of the techniques we have seen evolving during the previous twenty years: suggestive imagery, Grundy revisions, and different versions of the story. Finding that he could not get his story published as a serial without mutilating it, he did just that. In the serial Tess is not seduced and does not have a baby. She is tricked into a mock marriage by Alec, discovers that she has been hoaxed, and returns home. As a result of this change, the powerful scene in which Tess baptizes her baby has to go. Other changes which become necessary if the readers of *The Graphic* are not to be offended include the omission of Tess's meeting with the painter of texts and of Angel's invitation to Izz to accompany him to Brazil, and the concealment of the fact that, when Angel finds Tess at Sandbourne, she is living there as Alec's mistress. It will be obvious that by these changes Hardy has damaged his serial far more seriously than has happened with any previous novel, but, fortunately, the serial is not the final version, and the damage is but temporary. The version we read today is the end-product of a remarkable evolutionary process.

The verbal alterations to placate Mrs. Grundy are particularly interesting, and we are again indebted to John Laird's study of the manuscript for the knowledge that, as he had at one time conceived his story, Hardy had intended the reader to know that Tess had been Alec's mistress for a month after her seduction. The most quoted sentence in the novel,

> 'Justice' was done, and the President of the Immortals, in Aeschylean phrase, had ended his sport with Tess.

had first appeared in *The Graphic* in the much less challenging form of,

> 'Justice' was done, and Time, the Arch-satirist, had had his joke out with Tess.[16]

Other changes indicate a like tendency to write more freely. In the serial, for example, Tess on her journey to Flintcomb-Ash is described as reaching

> the irregular chalk table-land or plateau, pimpled with prehistoric tumuli, which stretched between the valley of her birth and the valley of her love.[17]

In the First Edition of 1891 the plateau is no longer 'pimpled with prehistoric tumuli' but 'bosomed with semi-globular tumuli', and by 1892 the plateau and its tumuli are being compared to Cybele the Many-breasted lying supinely. As we have already to some extent seen, Hardy is fascinated by bosoms. In *Tess* Car Darch is described as having 'faultless rotundities'. In *Jude* Arabella, we are told, has a 'round and prominent bosom', 'a capacious bosom', and 'an inflated bosom'. Even at the age of eighty Hardy was still thinking of Arabella's bosoms. I recently discovered in his copy of *Jude* in the Dorset County Museum an amendment to that last phrase which was made in the 1920s and has never been published. For 'inflated bosom' he wished to substitute 'breast's superb abundance'.[18] Obviously he remained young at heart!

In the chapter following that in which he described the tumuli, Hardy brings in yet another sexual image in his later editions. The loose white flints which were described in the serial as being of 'bulbous, cusped and nondescript animal shapes' become in the First Edition of 'bulbous, cusped, and phallic shapes', and to make sure that the reader doesn't miss this, he adds to the 1895 Osgood, McIlvaine Edition the information that Marian, who had been drinking,

> primed to a humorous mood, would discover the queer-shaped flints aforesaid, and shriek with laughter, Tess remaining severely obtuse. (Ch. 43)

Here Hardy is emphasizing the coarseness of the ethos in which Tess moved, and, by this means, drawing attention to the purity of Tess, who remains undefiled in the midst of it. And yet Tess is no anaemic figure, and, as Desmond Hawkins points out in his *Thomas Hardy: Novelist and Poet*,

> Hardy evidently intends Tess to arouse desire in a more than ordinary degree by the suggestion of a sensual responsiveness which, though veiled and inarticulate, is vivid enough to infatuate first Alec and then Angel. To do this he makes an extraordinary and obsessive use of the mouth as an erotic symbol.[19]

Desmond Hawkins then quotes a whole series of references to the attraction of Tess's mouth – 'her mobile peony mouth', 'the pouted-up

deep red mouth', 'that too tempting mouth' and Alec's pressing a
strawberry into her mouth against her will; an incident that ends with
the words ' "Nonsense!" he insisted; and in a slight distress she parted her
lips and took it in.'

When Mowbray Morris rejected *Tess* as being unsuitable for
publication in *Macmillan's Magazine*, he gave as one of his reasons that
Tess's capacity for stirring sensuous admiration was too much
emphasized, and he went on:

> You use the word *succulent* more than once to describe the general
> appearance and condition of the Frome Valley. Perhaps I might say
> that the general impression left on me by reading your story — so far
> as it has gone — is one of rather too much succulence.[20]

Morris was referring to one aspect of what has become a most admired
feature of the novel — Hardy's ability to provide emotional significance
through the quality of his description. I know of no richer or more
sensuous description of spring and summer than that in the chapters
telling of Tess's arrival at Talbothays, her meeting with Angel Clare,
and their falling in love. These chapters have the sensuous and sensual
qualities of the Song of Solomon and they are a masterpiece of our prose.
They are the culmination of a skill which in part grew out of his need to
use imagery to suggest what could not be said directly. Even then, nearly
twenty years after he had begun to develop that skill in *Far from the
Madding Crowd*, it was impossible, perhaps undesirable, to describe fully
the deep physical passion Tess and Angel feel for each other. But no
sensitive reader of these pages can fail to be aware of the erotic
atmosphere built up to suggest the compulsive power of Nature. Tess
sets out 'on a thyme-scented, bird-hatching morning in May'; she arrives
at the dairy where the milk from the cows 'oozed forth and fell in drops
to the ground'; she stands in the garden which 'was now damp and rank
with juicy grass which sent up mists of pollen at a touch', and she listens
to the notes of Angel's harp which have a 'stark quality like that of
nudity'. The season develops and matures, and

> Rays from the sunrise drew forth the buds and stretched them into
> long stalks, lifted up sap in noiseless streams, opened petals, and
> sucked out scents in invisible jets and breathings. . . . Amid the

oozing fatness and warm ferments of the Var Vale, at a season when
the rush of juices could almost be heard below the hiss of
fertilization, it was impossible that the most fanciful love should not
grow passionate. The ready bosoms ['hearts' in the serial] existing
there were impregnated by their surroundings. (Chs. 20, 24)

It is a superb pattern of imaginative and suggestive writing, and it is all
done with a delicacy and skill which today make us aware of the
clumsiness and vulgarity of so much contemporary writing about sexual
matters.

One of the most valuable features of Robert Gittings's recent
biography was his revelation of how humble were Hardy's origins and
how rough his background. There is no doubt of the drunkenness and
sexual freedom of many of the country people among whom he lived.
Hardy himself was conceived out of wedlock. In the *Life* we read in an
entry dated April 1893 a conversation Hardy has recorded between a
young man turned street-preacher and a girl:

He: Do you read your Bible for your spiritual good?
She: Ho-ho! Get along wi' thee!
He: But do you, my dear young woman?
She: Haw-haw! Not this morning!
He: Do you read your Bible, I implore?
She: (tongue out) No, nor you neither. Come, you can't act in that
show, Natty! You haven't the guts to carry it off! (p. 253)

And Hardy tells us that they then went off into the woods together. On
page 59 of Timothy O'Sullivan's delightful illustrated biography of
Hardy there is an illustration of one of the music-books belonging to the
Stinsford church-choir. Above the signature of Hardy's grandfather
there is an eight-line poem full of sexual double-meanings which
provides a fascinating example of the blending of the sacred and the
profane! It is against this background that Hardy writes. In describing
the dance at Chaseborough in *Tess*, Hardy subtly paints a scene of
drunkenness and lechery, and again he uses erotic imagery. In addition to
the orgiastic suggestions implied in the description of the

floating, fusty *debris* of peat and hay, mixed with the perspirations
and warmth of the dancers, and forming together a sort of vegeto-
human pollen. . . .

we have a subtle use of allusion to convey to those who know their Classical mythology the physical purpose of the dancing:

> Of the rushing couples there could barely be discerned more than the high lights – the indistinctness shaping them to satyrs clasping nymphs – a multiplicity of Pans whirling a multiplicity of Syrinxes; Lotis attempting to elude Priapus, and always failing. (Ch. 10)

And we know that, although in the myth Lotis did escape from Priapus, Tess is not to escape from Alec who waits in the background, cigar in his mouth, for his moment to come. Meanwhile the dance continues, the movement grows 'more passionate', couples fall over each other, and on the floor there is discernible 'a twitching entanglement of arms and legs'. It is no wonder that Hardy claimed to have overlooked these pages in his earlier revisions and they did not get published until 1912. They provide a further example of Hardy's powers of suggestion at the height of his career.

The incident of the girl and the street-preacher is echoed in Arabella's temptation of Jude in *Jude the Obscure*, the last novel Hardy was to write. For me *Jude* is a brave failure, a work of genius but flawed in a number of ways. *Jude the Obscure* is the culmination of Hardy's exploration of the man-woman relationship, and particularly of that relationship seen in the institution of marriage. As he says in his Preface to the novel, it is his attempt to

> deal unaffectedly with the fret and fever, derision and disaster, that may press in the wake of the strongest passion known to humanity; to tell, without a mincing of words, of a deadly war waged between flesh and spirit.

It is his opinion that

> a marriage should be dissolvable as soon as it becomes a cruelty to either of the parties – being then essentially and morally no marriage.

The candour with which Hardy wanted to write, and the nature of his material, meant that the serial version, which appeared in *Harper's*

Magazine in 1894–5, is even more damaged than the serial edition of *Tess*. Jude cannot be seduced by Arabella, so instead of tricking him into marriage by implying that she is pregnant, she gets him to marry her by the weak ruse of making him believe that he has a pressing rival for her hand. This leads, of course, to a major falsification – Hardy is mincing his words and he is no longer dealing with the strongest passion known to humanity. Arabella does not throw at Jude 'the characteristic part of a barrow-pig' but a 'portion of a recently killed pig'; she is not described by Hardy as 'a complete and substantial female animal' but as 'a complete and substantial female human'; Jude does not gaze 'from her eyes to her mouth, thence to her bosom' but 'thence to her shoulders'. Arabella does not speak in a 'hungry tone of latent sensuousness' but in a 'fierce tone of latent passionateness'.

Hardy had assured the Editor of *Harper's Magazine* that he would provide a story that 'could not offend the most fastidious maiden', and, to quote Michael Millgate, he

> seems persistently to have entertained an obscure hope, perhaps never consciously formulated, that *this* time he would break through the editorial barriers which sealed him off from the magazine audience.[21]

Before long the Editor was complaining. His objections, he insists,

> are based on a purism (not mine, but our readers'), which is undoubtedly more rigid here [that is, in America] than in England. Our rule is that the Magazine must contain nothing which could not be read aloud in any family circle. To this we are pledged. You will see for yourself our difficulty, and we fully appreciate the annoyance you must feel at being called upon to modify work conscientiously done, and which is best as it left your hands, from an artist's point of view. (Purdy, 90)

Editors of nineteenth-century magazines, you will observe, run true to type on both sides of the Atlantic. When we look at the pig-killing scene which had caused the Editor concern, we can see how Hardy has been forced to censor his work. The serial reads:

'You must not!' she cried. 'The meat must be well bled. We shall lose from fifteen shillings to a pound on the carcass if the meat is red and bloody. Just touch him, that's all. I was brought up to it, and I know.'[22]

In the First Edition this becomes,

'You must not!' she cried. 'The meat must be well bled, and to do that he must die slow. We shall lose a shilling a score if the meat is red and bloody! Just touch the vein, that's all. I was brought up to it, and I know. Every good butcher keeps un bleeding long. He ought to be eight or ten minutes dying, at least.' (I. 10)

Editorial influence of this kind is designed to protect readers from the brutal truth, and just as the death of the pig is made less harsh in the serial, so likewise is the death of Jude himself.

As we can see here, and in many other places, Hardy was able in his 1896 First Edition to get closer to what he really wanted to say, and his frankness and courage are remarkable. Accepted views are challenged and there is a major indictment of the scheme of things, of Mrs. Grundy, and of all that she stands for. The true marriage is what Jude calls 'Nature's own marriage', while Heaven's marriage is one in which Sue can regard it as a blessed thing to have brought her body into complete subjection to a man who physically repels her. Conventional values are inverted and the living together 'in sin' of Sue and Jude is seen as something far preferable to the 'holy matrimony' experienced by Arabella and Jude and by Sue and Phillotson. But perhaps Hardy, to some extent a D. H. Lawrence born out of his due time, felt that, even so, he had been unable to say exactly what he wanted to say. It is even possible that the deep emotional disturbance and sexual frustration which he was feeling at the time, and his growing awareness of life's ambivalence, made him unsure what he was trying to say. Certainly there is for me about *Jude* an air of frustration in the writing which shows itself partly in an uncertainty of tone and in a personal distress felt by Hardy which finds no adequate objective correlative; that is to say, Hardy's vehicle is not equal to what it has to carry. The tragic tone of *Tess* has been replaced by bitterness, and its richness of texture is missing from *Jude*. The perceptive reader of Hardy's novels is aware of the moral ambiguities and the ambivalent attitudes which exist and are part of their greatness, but in *Jude* there is an artistic uncertainty which for many of us is a flaw. There is something almost crudely satirical, for example, in the throwing of the pig's pizzle at Jude at the very moment when his wishful thinking has reached the ludicrous 'Yes, Christminster shall be my Alma Mater; and I'll be her beloved son, in whom she shall be well pleased.' And for the modern reader what worries is not Hardy's morality but the whole concept of Father Time, his murders and his suicide. Did Hardy realize, one wonders, that he had reached the end of his struggle with Grundyism and that he could go no further without loss, that his victory was in at least one sense a defeat? No one can really accept Hardy's statement that he gave up novel writing just because of the hostile reception of *Jude the Obscene*, as one reviewer called it. He was sensitive about the reviews, but then he always had been, and he had that great consolation of writers, that both *Tess* and *Jude* were selling extremely well. In considering the influence of Hardy on his readers, we need to remember that the total sales of his books were, by Victorian standards, comparatively small until the 1890s, when the publicity given to *Tess* and *Jude* and the publication of cheap paperback editions led to a rapid acceleration. In his letter of 22 March 1902 to Macmillan, Hardy gives the sales of *Tess* for the year 30 June 1900 to 30 June 1901 in the 6d. edition as 100,000 copies. *Far from the Madding Crowd* sold 45,016 copies at 6d. during the same period. Sales of this size meant contact with a wide circle of readers.

When Hardy in the mid-1890s decided to return to his first love, the writing of poetry, he was shrewd enough to know that the skills he had developed over twenty-five years of novel writing, his ability to use word and image in a highly creative, intense and imaginative way, were exactly those which a good poet needs. He tells us that in returning to poetry he hoped that he might be able to

> express more fully in verse ideas and emotions which run counter to the inert crystallized opinions — hard as a rock — which the vast body of men have vested interests in supporting. (*Life*, 284)

Even a cursory look at the poetry will show that it contains the strong sensual notes we have seen in the novels and that there is a real frankness about sexual, religious and social matters. And yet, as he expected, there was very little adverse criticism about the content of his books of verse.

In one of his earliest poems, published in 1898, 'At a Bridal', he is concerned with the difference between the stolid offspring of a conventional marriage and the rare forms that might have graced a union based on natural love. 'The Fire at Tranter Sweatley's' is a particularly interesting poem. It first appears in a bowdlerized version in a journal in 1875, but on its next appearance in Lionel Johnson's *The Art of Thomas Hardy* in 1894 there is a substantial change in the story and a marked increase in the sensuality. Thus in 1875 we are told that

> *Her form in these cold mildewed tatters he views*

whereas in 1894

> *Her cold little buzzoms half naked he views.*

Throughout *Time's Laughingstocks* (1909) there is an emphasis on the falseness of so much that is conventional and formal in the man-woman relationship. In 'The Conformers' it is suggested that marriage is the end of

> *those night-screened, divine,*
> *Stolen trysts of heretofore.*

In 'The Dawn after the Dance' the lovers return to parents whose

> *slumbers have been normal after one day more of formal*
> *Matrimonial commonplace and household life's mechanic gear.*

In 'After the Club-Dance' the girl wonders why she should

> *sink with shame*
> *When the birds a-perch there eye me?*
> *They, too, have done the same.*

A wife waits, in the poem of that name, for her newly married husband, who is already off dancing with a new love. In 'The Dark-Eyed Gentleman' Hardy writes an excellent pastiche of a typical folk-song in which a maiden meets a handsome gentleman who ties up her garter for her and gets her with child. The barrows in 'By the Barrows' are likened to bulging bosoms, and in the poem, 'One Ralph Blossom Soliloquizes', the seven women who have been brought on the rates by the fornication of that virile gentleman think of the past and decide by a majority of five to two that it was worth it. Cicily will not reproach because 'it was to be'. Rosa feels no hostility, 'For I must own I lent facility', Lizzy has at least known love and all its gloriousness, Patience has a son to be proud of, and Anne bursts out:

> 'O the time was fair,
> So wherefore should you burn down there?
> There is a deed under the sun, my Love,
> And that was ours. What's done is done, my Love.
> These trumpets here in Heaven are dumb to me
> With you away. Dear, come, O come to me!'

Publishing such a poem in 1909, Hardy could not have been surprised to find that he was never offered the post of Poet Laureate. Yet the book was well reviewed, was reprinted within two months, and caused no outcry from its readers.

Even in his last book of verse, *Winter Words* (1928), much of which must have been written when he was in his middle eighties, there is a touch of spring in the recurring emphasis on sexual matters. There is a translation from Meleager in which all girls yet virgin are exhorted to

> have constant care you
> Become not staled by use as she has, ere you
> Meet your most-loved; lest, tumbled, you should lose him.

There is the confession of a woman who, losing at cards, pays with her body. In another poem a pregnant wife who has been amorously involved with 'Will Peach' and 'Waywell' and 'Nobb' and 'Knight' kills herself when she discovers her husband is coming home after two years with the army in France. In yet another, a wife sews up her drunken husband in a sheet to protect herself from his sexual attentions when he wakes – and kills him in doing so. The discovery of clasped skeletons in an ancient British barrow near Max Gate inspires a poem about the great lovers of history. Hardy thinks of Paris lying with Helen,

David 'bedding' Bathsheba, and of the insatiate Cleopatra. And there is the frank outburst of 'A Practical Woman',

> *'O who'll get me a healthy child: —*
> *I should prefer a son —*
> *Seven have I had in thirteen years,*
> *. Sickly every one!'*

At the end of the poem she returns with 'a blooming boy', saying,

> *'I found a father at last who'd suit*
> *The purpose in my head,*
> *And used him till he'd done his job. . . .*

What would have been the reaction of Leslie Stephen's three respectable ladies to that?

Those three respectable ladies take us back to 1874 and almost to where we began. This is an exploration rather than an attempt to reach conclusions, a questioning of such solidly held critical opinions as that serial writing was necessarily a thoroughly bad thing and that Hardy in his writing is always naïvely direct and explicit, or worse, an awkward amateur. Space will not allow me to look at novels important to my subject, such as *Two on a Tower* and *The Well-Beloved*, nor have I said anything about Hardy's essay of 1890, 'Candour in English Fiction', with his attack on the 'They married and were happy ever after' school of writers. Much of that essay is an attack on what Hardy then saw as the pernicious influences of the family magazine on serious writers. But Hardy did not *have* to write *Tess* and *Jude* as magazine serials, and even in their magazine form *A Pair of Blue Eyes*, *The Return of the Native*, *The Mayor of Casterbridge*, *Tess of the d'Urbervilles* and *Jude the Obscure* can hardly be said to have conventional happy endings. Ironically, Hardy was too humble to realize that he had got the better of Mrs. Grundy, and that, like Dickens, he had both entertained his readers and influenced their moral attitudes. If he could look back now on his years as a writer, he might see it as one of life's big ironies that the very limitations which he found so irksome were paradoxically one cause of his greatness as a writer. He might see that some of his power to clutch at our hearts and work on our imagination is the result of the discipline he had to submit to in an adverse situation, and he might recognize that the constant struggle with language, the never-ending revision, was to provide the foundation of his greatness as a poet, that Ezra Pound was indeed right when he said of Hardy's *Collected Poems*, 'There *is* the harvest of having written 20 [*sic*] novels first.' And, looking back as he so often did, might he not wonder whether the freedom which writers enjoy today may not have led to a concentration on fact rather than spirit, and to an over-explicitness in which a drab kind of factual realism has taken the place of evocation and imaginative suggestion, and in which, because there is nothing left to feed it, the imagination withers and dies?

NOTES

1. Alexander Macmillan to Hardy, 10 August 1868; Charles Morgan, *The House of Macmillan 1843–1943*, 1943, 90.
2. *Ibid.*, 93–4.
3. Unsigned review in *The Athenaeum*; Cox, 1.
4. Unsigned review in *The Spectator*; Cox, 3.
5. Cf. *Henry IV Part 2*, where Doll Tearsheet is referred to (II, 2, 159) as 'some road'. M. P. Tilley, *A Dictionary of the Proverbs in England in the Sixteenth and Seventeenth Centuries*, Ann Arbor, 1950, mentions the proverb 'as common as the highway' as having a sexual meaning.
6. Leslie Stephen to Hardy, 12 March 1874; Purdy, 338–9.
7. F. W. Maitland, *Life and Letters of Leslie Stephen*, 1906, 275.
8. Purdy, 32–3.
9. *Good Words*, 1880, 807.
10. F. R. Leavis, *The Great Tradition*, 1948, 124.
11. T. S. Eliot, *After Strange Gods*, 1934, 54.
12. *The Graphic*, 20 February 1886, 217.
13. *Ibid.*, 2 January 1886, 17.
14. Mowbray Morris to Hardy, 19 September 1886; MS. letter in Dorset County Museum.
15. J. T. Laird, *The Shaping of 'Tess of the d'Urbervilles'*, 1975, 4.
16. *The Graphic*, 26 December 1891, 761.
17. *Ibid.*, 14 November 1891, 574.
18. Professor Norman Page has pointed out that this phrase occurs in Browning's 'A Toccata of Galuppi's'.
19. D. Hawkins, *Hardy: Novelist and Poet*, 1976, 138.

20. Mowbray Morris to Hardy, 25 November 1889; MS. letter in Dorset County Museum.

21. M. Millgate, *Thomas Hardy: His Career as a Novelist*, 1971, 292.

22. *Harper's New Monthly Magazine*, January 1895, 198.

9: Thomas Hardy: A Reader's Guide

RICHARD H. TAYLOR

'CRITICISM IS SO EASY, and art so hard: criticism so flimsy, and the life-seer's voice so lasting,' wrote Hardy in September 1908. He added that since 'the history of criticism is mainly the history of error, which has not even, as many errors have, quaintness enough to make it interesting, we may well doubt the utility of such writing on the sand.'[1] Hardy's hostility towards critics was deeply rooted. He felt ill served by contemporary reviewers and at the end of his long life was equally disturbed by biographical intrusions. Unlike many Victorian writers he never supplemented his income by writing reviews and in 1921 told Robert Graves that 'he regarded professional critics as parasites'.[2] Yet while no one would dispute the paramountcy of creative art, and we can all share his anguish over reviews as crushing as that of *Desperate Remedies* which in 1871 provoked Hardy to sit on a stile and wish he were dead, it has to be said that he was on balance very favourably reviewed. Not all critics saw him as just a chronicler of sheepfarming and even the reception of his controversial later works (*Jude* included) was by no means so uniformly damning as he would have us believe. His reputation was established quickly (he was a distinct 'name' when his third novel appeared in 1874) and never seriously challenged. During this century Hardy's work has provoked an ever-growing *corpus* of criticism of astonishing breadth of approach and subject-matter. The eclectic range of attempts to define his achievement is hardly surprising for an author self-described in a poem as 'so various' in pith and plan. For all this, Hardy's Protean qualities have proved hard to define adequately and no

---

* For the sake of brevity critical journals and, where appropriate, titles of novels are represented by acronyms or abbreviations, an index to which appears at the head of the select bibliography. *Life* indicates the one volume edition of Hardy's disguised autobiography: F. E. Hardy, *The Life of Thomas Hardy*, 1962. DCM indicates the Dorset County Museum.

real consensus has emerged. The Hardy so excellently encapsulated in Molly Holden's poem 'T. H.',[3] the elusive and secretive countryman, has proved elusive to the end.

Part of the problem is the duality of Hardy's achievement as a poet of the first rank as well as a novelist. The qualities of his fiction are different from those which make the novels of Henry James or George Eliot so highly valued. They were professionals in the sense that they believed in the novel and regarded it as a vocation or mission. It is not a lack of seriousness (his claim to have wished to be no more than 'a good hand at a serial' has been divorced from its original context and seriously abused – it was never intended as a definitive statement) or an unwillingness to theorize that distinguishes Hardy. Though he was a professional writer, in the sense that he lived (and lived well) by fiction, he remained a poet by vocation and belief. An intuitive poet lives within, behind, beyond the fiction; the novels are shot through with peculiar poetic intensity. It is no accident that in attempting to define the novels, Virginia Woolf invokes the title of one of Hardy's volumes of poetry: 'His own word, "moments of vision", exactly describes those passages of astonishing beauty and force which are to be found in every book that he wrote.'[4]

The division of Hardy's canon into discrete historical periods, an accident of publication dates, has led to a serious undervaluation of the poetry and a misunderstanding of its basic interpenetration with the novels. Only comparatively recently has proper critical attention begun to be paid to Hardy as a *poet*-novelist and this cumulative awareness may prepare the way for the definitive work that has yet to appear.

COLLECTED EDITIONS AND TEXTUAL STUDIES

There has been a series of collected editions of Hardy's works but only two are textually important. *The Wessex Novels* (16 vols., 1895–6) is necessarily incomplete but incorporates more thorough textual revisions than any other edition. Many chapters are retitled and a new Preface is attached to each novel. It is *The Wessex Edition* (24 vols., 1912–31), however, that has for over half a century been regarded as the standard, authoritative text. It incorporates Hardy's last complete revision of his novels and his thoroughness is suggested in a letter of 22 April 1912 (*Life*, 357–8), but the revisions are minor. Apart from some postscripts to Prefaces the most interesting feature of the Wessex Edition is Hardy's addition of a 'General Preface to the Novels and Stories' (October 1911) in Vol. I. Hardy classifies his fiction in four telling categories: (i) Novels of Character and Environment [*Tess, FFMC, Jude, RN, MC, The W, UGT, LLI, WT*]; (ii) Romances and Fantasies [*PBE, TM, TT, WB, GND*]; (iii) Novels of Ingenuity [*DR, HE, AL*]; (iv) Mixed Novels [*CM*]. The implications of these divisions must direct our understanding of Hardy's aims, and concomitantly perhaps the nature of his achievement, in different modes of fiction. More generally, the essay is essential reading if we are to read Hardy aright. Subsequent editions, such as the *Mellstock Edition* (37 vols., 1919–20), are of no profound textual importance but are generally perpetuations of the Wessex Edition text. R. L. Purdy's *Thomas Hardy: A Bibliographical Study* (1954) is an invaluable guide to Hardy's publishing history, from serial versions and *editiones principes* onwards (see under 'Bibliographies and Handbooks').

The latest collected edition is the first to be equipped with introductions and notes. The *New Wessex Edition* of the novels (14 vols., 1974–5), under the general editorship of P. N. Furbank, is commendable (see below). Its main defect is its failure to grasp the textual nettle. An ideal opportunity to confront some of the deficiencies of textual scholarship on Hardy has been missed, even though a definitive (and preferably variorum) edition is sorely needed. The New Wessex Edition too readily follows the earlier text, of which both substantives and accidentals need careful critical attention. Purdy's contention that 'the Wessex Edition is in every sense the definitive edition of Hardy's work and the last authority in questions of text' has recently been challenged, notably by Robert C. Schweik in 'Current Problems in Textual Scholarship on the Works of Thomas Hardy' (*ELT*, XIV, 1971). Schweik argues that Purdy's assumption is unjustified (for example, Hardy made some nine pages of corrections and additions for the Mellstock Edition as late as 1920) and presents an unanswerable case for the re-editing of Hardy's texts.

The New Wessex Edition is otherwise admirable. Hardy's idiosyncratic and sometimes self-conscious cultural erudition, an essential component of the texture of his style, has long demanded exegesis; thorough annotations bring these references comfortably within the grasp of the modern reader. The introductory essays maintain a consistently high standard and faithfully reflect a central enigma in the study of Hardy: the apprehension that despite the unifying cohesiveness of Hardy's fiction (in style, in the fusion of realism and symbolism, in the tension between his Victorian and modern instincts) there are a freshness and variety that make each novel distinct in tone, emphasis and even theme. Consequently, although Hardy's work is stimulatingly related to moral, intellectual and social traditions by different contributors, the essays are complementary rather than repetitious. It is healthy, for example, to find Barbara Hardy's association of Hardy with the moral assumptions of Dickens and Eliot [*TM*] being elsewhere rejected by P. N. Furbank [*Tess*]. But a common general introduction might have usefully integrated this series of individual case studies, some of which are distinguished (especially Furbank, Hardy, David Lodge [*The W*], John Bayley [*FFMC*], and Ian Gregor [*MC*]). Only Geoffrey Grigson, dyspeptically ungenerous about *UGT*, and J. Hillis Miller, stylized and self-indulgent on *WB*, do their novels less than justice. Not the least virtue of the New Wessex Edition is its disinterment of the lesser novels, long denied the critical attention (and paperback publication) they deserve. Apart from *WB*, they are gratifyingly reinstated by C. J. P. Beatty [*DR*], Ronald Blythe [*PBE*], Barbara Hardy [*AL*], Robert Gittings [*HE*], and F. B. Pinion [*TT*].

The New Wessex Edition has been confusingly followed by the *Macmillan Students' Hardy* (10 vols., 1975), advisory editor James Gibson, an edition including *Chosen Poems* and *Chosen Short Stories* with the major novels for students with no previous knowledge of Hardy, with useful notes and careful introductions. The inclusion of photographs of 'originals' of Hardy's fictive locations is, though understandable, unfortunate. It is the sort of thing that leads to the blurring of the distinction between Wessex and Dorset, the fictional and the real world, that bedevils serious study of what Hardy actually wrote. A coach-trip to Dorchester is no substitute for imaginative transportation into Casterbridge; each experience is quite distinct. Location-spotting is a delightful and diverting pastime, and we all do it, but to elevate topographical identification higher is to commit the same sort of error as recent publicity posters defining Hardy's novels as 'an enduring memorial to English country life'. They may be, but to leave it at that is seriously to belittle his achievement as a novelist. D. H. Lawrence writes of Hardy's characters wanting to burst out of Wessex and do extraordinary things, and this is to recognize Wessex for what it is, a psychic entity, the objective correlative of the author's imagination. Hardy *is* a novelist of place but only because he knows well enough that there is 'quite enough human nature in Wessex for one man's literary purpose' ('General Preface', 1911). The real Hardy country is off the map and in the mind. It is the psychic life of its inhabitants, not just a delightful country tradition, that he celebrates. It is with this perspective in mind that the illustrations in the Students' Hardy must be seen and all the guidebooks must be read. The younger students at whom this series is aimed are arguably the least well equipped to make this distinction. The cautionary note in all this is important since it is an error into which we are all liable to be seduced by Hardy's fictive realism.

Two works of fiction remain uncollected. *An Indiscretion in the Life of an Heiress*, the remains of Hardy's first and unpublished novel (*The Poor Man and the Lady*) after it had been dismembered and its segments fed into other early novels, appeared as a serial in 1878 but was not published separately until Florence Hardy's private edition in 1934; it was reprinted in America, ed. C. J. Weber (1935), and has now been revived, ed. Terry Coleman (1976). *Our Exploits at West Poley*, a story for boys, appeared in an obscure Boston journal in 1892–3 and was published separately, ed. R. L. Purdy, in 1952, and reprinted in 1978.

Collected editions of Hardy's poetry have until now fared less well than the fiction, partly because of his testamentary request 'in respect of my complete poems that an edition if not already in existence shall be produced and on sale at a reasonable price so as to be within the reach of poorer readers' (24 August 1922). The first *Collected Poems* appeared in 1919 and subsequent volumes of verse were bound into it as they appeared in 1923, 1928 and 1930. Since 1930 the *Collected Poems* has been simply a collocation of the eight separate volumes, continuously reprinted to meet Hardy's intentions yet in a cramped typeface and with errors intact. At last the poems have been entirely revised and reset, with twenty-nine previously uncollected poems added, in James Gibson (ed.) *The Complete Poems* (1976). The editing is scrupulous and the notes useful (though too restricted) and it is reassuring to know that Mr. Gibson has in hand the much needed variorum edition.

This is all the more encouraging since textual study is the one major area in Hardy scholarship which remains strangely neglected, and this goes beyond the failure to establish a definitive text. Most of Hardy's manuscripts are readily available for textual examination and he was an assiduous reviser, not only of these but of printed versions of his work from serial publication onwards. The successive interlineations, transpositions, deletions and additions provide a fascinating insight into the artist in his workshop as shaper and maker, and into his enforced deference to currently acceptable beliefs (it is arguable that even now some of Hardy's most important fiction remains bowdlerized). John Paterson, in 'RN as an Anti-Christian Document' (*NCF*, XIV, 1959), shows how Hardy retreated from his original explicit attack on orthodox Christianity, while Otis B. Wheeler's 'Four Versions of *RN*' (*NCF*, same issue) discusses Hardy's extensive amendment of details and reveals that social changes enabled Hardy to confront issues more directly in later revisions. Other studies show that Hardy was much more seriously concerned with the tone and texture of his style than his own deprecatory comments imply. An excellent example of what close textual study can reveal is Dale Kramer's 'Revisions and Vision: Thomas Hardy's *The W*' (*BNYPL*, LXXV, 1971).

Surprisingly, there are only three full-length textual examinations. A lucid early study is Mary Ellen Chase's *Thomas Hardy from Serial to Novel* (1927), which examines *MC*, *Tess* and *Jude* but unfortunately not their manuscripts. John Paterson, in *The Making of 'The Return of the Native'* (1960), examines the textual variants that reveal Hardy's gradually altering conception of the story and its characters and his adjustment of the tone through intensification of imagery. (Paterson's shortcomings, notably his faulty reading of the evidence, are suggested by Schweik in *ELT*, XIV, 1971.) J. T. Laird's *The Shaping of 'Tess of the d'Urbervilles'* (1975) similarly traces the novel from the Ur-version through manuscript drafts and printed editions; though some interpretations may be controversial the textual account is excellent. Laird and Paterson reveal some consistency in Hardy's methods of composition and revision, the refinement of character and imagery being a major preoccupation as well as the ever-present process of bowdlerization (Hardy's genuflection to contemporary *mores* is one of the most important forces operating on his art). A more distinct awareness of Hardy's craftsmanship (as opposed to the view of him as an instinctive and helplessly uneven writer) is beginning to emerge through such desirable studies.

BIBLIOGRAPHIES AND HANDBOOKS

Hardy's readers are exceptionally fortunate in having at their disposal the painstaking work of Richard L. Purdy, whose *Thomas Hardy: A Bibliographical Study* (1954) could hardly be superseded. The work describes the composition and publication of all Hardy's works, giving scrupulous details of manuscripts, serial versions, first and collected editions, uncollected contributions to periodicals and some important revisions. Purdy enjoyed the confidence of Florence Hardy before her death in 1937. The result is an essential reference work which is even more valuable than its title implies: in Purdy's own words it is almost 'a biography of Hardy in bibliographical form'.

   Works *about* Hardy now by many times exceed his own works and as if by fission their number rapidly increases each year, so that reliable listings are now of the essence. Carl J. Weber's *The First Hundred Years of Thomas Hardy, 1840–1940: A Centenary Bibliography of Hardiana* (1940), thorough and the first major listing, has now been superseded. Hardy's work has inspired so much research that (in the words of its publisher) a 'mighty tome' has,been published, running to 841 pages and 3,153 entries and five indexes: H. E. Gerber and W. E. Davis (eds.) *Thomas Hardy: An Annotated Bibliography of Writings About Him* (1973) lists criticism 1871–1969, and a supplement is promised. It is a massive and valuable work, though not entirely complete (Hardy's own books of press notices could have been consulted). The stamina of its editors is enviable but attempts to summarize books and articles are not uniformly successful, and not all of these responses to Hardy are equally important. Brief abstracts would have sufficed: the reader needs signposts to the real thing rather than extended paraphrase in such a listing, and this would have resulted in a much more economical and much less discursive account of ninety-eight years of the Hardy industry. Readers seeking more selective guidance into this mass of secondary material will find 'Criticism of Thomas Hardy: A Selected Checklist' (*MFS*, VI, 1960) very helpful, and for subsequent years this should be supplemented by annual serial bibliographies (comprehensive rather than selective, however) such as *M.H.R.A. Annual Bibliography of English Language and Literature*, *M.L.A. International Bibliography* or the 'Victorian Bibliography' in *Victorian Studies*. The *Thomas Hardy Catalogue*, ed. K. Carter and J. M. Whetherly (1968, rev. ed. 1973), lists materials in Dorset County Library (*not* the museum) and is an invaluable guide for researchers there; though its local origin and purpose deny it comprehensiveness it is a sectional general bibliography of a wider usefulness than its full title implies. The best annotated guides to Hardy scholarship are Lionel Stevenson's essay in *The Victorian Poets: A Guide to Research* (1956, rev. ed. 1968) and the essay in *Victorian Fiction: A Guide to Research* (1964) by George S. Fayen, Jr., now revised (1978) by Michael Millgate.

Handbooks to Hardy's works have taken two forms: those concerned with scenes and characters and those with a broader critical view. Hermann Lea's *Handbook to the Wessex Country of Mr. Thomas Hardy's Novels and Poems* (1905) and its successor, *Thomas Hardy's Wessex* (1913), both benefited from Hardy's active co-operation, as extant correspondence shows, with the *caveat* (urged by Hardy) in the 1905 volume that 'it may be wise to state clearly at the outset that the author has never admitted more than that the places named fictitiously were *suggested* by such and such a real place'. Lea's book shows that Hardy's Wessex is conterminous with the historical Wessex (i.e. wider in area than Dorset alone) and remains a reliable detailed guide to 'Hardy country'. Denys Kay-Robinson's *Hardy's Wessex Reappraised* (1971) brings all previous information up to date and draws upon local historical records to provide a sectionally organized account of Wessex and the artistic transformation involved. Hardy thought it curious when in 1910 F. O. Saxelby proposed his *Thomas Hardy Dictionary: The Characters and Scenes of the Novels and Poems Alphabetically Arranged and Described* (1911) simply because the name of one of Hardy's characters resembled his own, and on 4 January 1911 he warned Saxelby that he would accept no responsibility. Yet later in the year he approved the proofs, so we may accept the dictionary as reasonably accurate. Glenda Leeming's *Who's Who in Thomas Hardy?* (1975) is a similar compendium though limited to a listing and brief description of the characters. It is more complete though less valuable than the 'Dictionary of People and Places' in F. B. Pinion's *A Hardy Companion* (1968, rev. ed. 1974). Pinion's is one of two invaluable major handbooks on Hardy's works, a sane and balanced guide to Hardy's art and ideas which identifies major preoccupations of the author and the influences of architecture, music, painting and literature on his work. Brief accounts of the novels, short stories and poems are given and a useful glossary illuminates Hardy's idiosyncratic vocabulary. J. O. Bailey's *The Poetry of Thomas Hardy: A*

Handbook and Commentary (1970) is an essential reference work. Bailey discusses each poem individually, identifying persons, places and ideas, and where relevant giving details of publication history and revisions. Bailey is concerned to clarify the background and meaning of each poem. Some readers may find the Ordnance Survey identification of settings finicking but it is up to the reader to use or abuse the information provided. In the handbooks of both Pinion and Bailey critical appraisal is subsidiary to other aims, yet both authors contribute some penetrating analyses and observations. Along with Purdy and Millgate they are scholars whose enthusiastic and scrupulous work on Hardy in various areas puts Hardy's readers firmly in their debt.

LIFE, LETTERS, NOTEBOOKS AND FRAGMENTS

Hardy is a conspicuously personal writer whose novels require that his readers form an unusually close relationship with the author. Throughout his work there is a uniquely pervasive sense of Hardy the man. This is not to admit the validity of T. S. Eliot's misleading charge that Hardy wrote 'as nearly for the sake of "self-expression" as a man well can' (*After Strange Gods*, 1934), but certainly Hardy would have disapproved the impossible notions of authorial detachment proclaimed by Flaubert and James, whose presence is so perceptible in their own work despite their austere theories of the novel as an art form. Since all art is created (in Goethe's phrase) 'from within outwards', no artist is capable of clinically excerpting himself from it; and as Evelyn Waugh has said, 'The novelist does not come to his desk devoid of experience and memory. His raw material is compounded of all he has seen and done' (*A Little Learning*, 1964). The personal presence of Hardy, the colour of his feelings and the rhetoric of his voice, enhances the quality and expands the significance of his fiction and poetry, and gives a fundamental unity to all his work.

The dangerous concomitant of this is the temptation to construe information about the author from his work. It is naïve to suppose that any of the novels, for example, is 'about' the facts of Hardy's life in a direct sense; they are much more diffused translations of his experience. Undeniably some of the young architects in the early novels and Jude Fawley in the last are to some extent·*doppelgänger* figures for Hardy, various life experiences furnish scenes, thoughts and characters in other fictions, and we have Hardy's own word that *A Laodicean* contains 'more of the facts of his own life'[5] than any other novel; yet biographical correspondences make no difference to the value we set upon the works as fiction – it is how Hardy transmutes his raw material that matters. The author's own disingenuous attitude has not helped him to escape a certain species of detective work – a letter written over Florence Hardy's name but dictated by Hardy himself admonished a correspondent: 'To your inquiry if *Jude the Obscure* is autobiographical, I have to answer that there is not a scrap of personal detail in it, it having the least to do with his own life of all his books' (30 October 1919; *Life*, 392), a statement remarkable for its lack of candour. But if this statement has engendered some perverse speculations about the extent to which Hardy buried his secrets in his fiction, a further remark in the same letter is disarmingly frank in its implications: 'Speaking generally, there is more autobiography in a hundred lines of Mr. Hardy's poetry than in all the novels.' It is no derogation of the self-expository quality of the poetry to admit that our understanding of many poems must in view of this be enriched by awareness of the influential biographical facts, but we must always be aware that it is imagination that animates them into art. Such caution is a vital prerequisite for any account of studies of Hardy's life because of the confusion among some of his biographers about the relationship between fact and fiction. It is quite unacceptable to hypothesize about the facts of an author's life on the basis of the text alone and to extrude biography from it, yet the subjectivity of Hardy's work has misled some of his critics and biographers into ignoring this fundamental principle.

T. S. Eliot does not construe facts about Hardy's life but his criticism is decidedly *ad hominem* when he complains that the self which Hardy had to express 'does not strike me as a particularly wholesome or edifying matter of communication'. That Eliot should be capable of so profound a misconception underlines the need for a thorough exposition of the self that Hardy is striving to express; the need, in fact, for a thorough personal, spiritual and intellectual biography. There is still no definitive biography but several complementary studies to be going on with. We have to begin with that extraordinary volume, Florence Emily Hardy's *The Life of Thomas Hardy* (1962), which combines the *Early Life* (1928) and *Later Years* (1930). It is now well known that this is one of the more curious deceptions of modern literary history since Hardy himself wrote, in the third person, all but the concluding chapters, leaving instructions for the work to be completed and published after his death. It is common enough for an inexpert writer's autobiography to be 'ghosted' but Hardy is unique among major literary figures in reversing the process: he is, in effect, 'ghost writer' of his own biography. This unusual work shows Hardy in flight from the attentions of unauthorized biographers (such as F. A. Hedgcock, whose *Thomas Hardy, penseur et artiste* (1911) offended Hardy, whose personal copy is heavily annotated with remarks like this: 'This is not literary criticism, but impertinent personality & untrue'). A private memorandum, entitled 'Information for Mrs. Hardy in the preparation of a biography', itself a document seeking to mislead readers about the true authorship, confirms this and shows Hardy's intention to exclude facts which 'should seem to be indiscreet, belittling, monotonous, trivial, provocative, or in other ways inadvisable'. Hardy willed the *Life* to posterity as the authorized version, seeking to disguise its inevitable lack of objectivity through its third-person narration and to pre-empt other biographers by the authoritative 'authorship' of his wife. The manuscript was destroyed as soon as it was typed and subsequent revisions were made by Hardy in a disguised calligraphic hand. But posterity has caught up with Hardy and discovered him doing a dance of the seven veils, wafting remnants before the reader's eyes, yet the dance is often more intriguing than what is revealed: the 'performance' is all.

The *Life* is nevertheless indispensable. What it records is largely accurate and makes full use of Hardy's copious memoranda (many of which were destroyed as the *Life* was written), and it remains a workmanlike and full account of one view of Hardy's life. It is fascinating too in so far as it implies Hardy's estimate of himself and his work and the self that he wanted to be remembered. But the very process of concealment is revealing and inevitably the work evades many issues and episodes. The original typescript is slightly more telling. It has benefited structurally but suffered as autobiography from the final revisions of Florence Hardy and J. M. Barrie, who advised her. To give just one example, Hardy is shown to be even more extremely sensitive to critics and reviewers than we already know, and in view of this the impulse to produce the disguised autobiography itself may be more clearly understood. Barrie advised excision of many passages of sardonic invective against critics since he thought that the book 'leaves too much an impression that any silly unimportant reviewer could disturb and make him angry' (letter, 3 February 1928), yet this is a true impression and their omission falsifies the record further. (All the typescript passages omitted from the published version are included in Richard H. Taylor (ed.) *The Personal Notebooks of Thomas Hardy*, 1978.)

The task of subsequent biographers has been first to repair the omissions of the *Life* and then to build on its foundations a more objective account of Hardy's life than the author himself could supply. Clive Holland's *Thomas Hardy, O.M.* (1933) depends heavily on the *Life* and adds some details not taken up later, but the first substantial biography was William R. Rutland's *Thomas Hardy* (1938). This is a succinct, carefully researched account of Hardy's life; a special virtue of this urbane study is its combination of personal and intellectual biography. For many years the standard biography was Carl J. Weber's *Hardy of Wessex* (1940, rev. ed. 1965), still an impressive record of the many new facts uncovered by Weber over years of extensive research. Weber seeks to discover 'the causes of [Hardy's] particular adjustment, or maladjustment, to his world' and to examine the release of his unrest in his writings. The book has the virtues and defects of the work of a disciple, the assiduous pursuit of miniscule details that distinguishes the true biographer, countered by difficulty in objective interpretation. Weber's biography is copious in supportive material (if casual in its attribution) but as a study of Hardy's career as a novelist it is now effectively superseded by Michael Millgate's work (see under 'Critical Studies'). Unfortunately Weber is guilty of some unjustified suppositions on textual evidence alone, and his erratic critical judgement and lapses into journalese irritate just as his research yields so much of great value. In *Hardy and the Lady from Madison Square* (1952) Weber describes Hardy's relationship with his admirer Rebekah Owen, a well-off spinster who moved from New York to England and became a friend of each of Hardy's wives as well as of the author himself. This interesting account is specially justified by Miss Owen's own memoirs of Hardy.

Edmund Blunden's *Thomas Hardy* (1942) depends more on printed sources and in this area 'a great deal of hunting has been done in outlying places'. Blunden's searches are rewarding, not least in his presentation of accounts of Hardy from those best equipped to record their impressions, other writers. (Blunden himself had been Hardy's guest in 1922.) The picture which emerges, of Hardy as 'one of the kindest and brightest of men', though challenging to some popular notions, is surely an accurate one. While Blunden provides a well-judged synthesis of previous biographical research his book is enriched by critical acumen and the sympathetic stringency of a fellow poet. The first biography to supplement Weber's work in primary source research was Evelyn Hardy's *Thomas Hardy: A Critical Biography* (1954), notable for sensitive analysis of Hardy's relationships with women either more or less central in his life, including his ambivalent emotional attachment to the lady of the manor, Julia Martin. Miss Hardy's handling of Hardy's ideas, though sometimes perceptive, is less certain, and her criticism is uneven. But this is a lucid and often agreeably intuitive biography that offers no radical reassessment of Weber's Hardy but which gives a real sense of the uncertainties and sensibility that shaped Hardy's awareness of psychic pain and left the author outside his art vulnerable to the most minor reviewer's strictures to the end of his life.

When Hardy died his heart was cut out and placed in a biscuit tin prior to its separate burial at Stinsford. It is an indication of the even tenor of Hardy's life that this was one of the most unusual things that happened to him. This curious incident, with its macabre Gothic touch, is something we feel Hardy would have appreciated ironically: a wry poem, a satire of circumstance, might have told the tale well. Hardy's was not a life brimful of external incident and it is ironic details of this kind that enliven it as a story. This presents the biographer with special difficulties, so that when allegations that Hardy had fathered the son of his cousin Tryphena Sparks, and that their relationship had been incestuous, were introduced into the marketplace, they were seized upon gratefully as high drama, a smattering of scandal to enliven a fairly pedestrian tale. The thesis was advanced in the now notorious *Providence and Mr. Hardy* (1966) by Lois Deacon and Terry Coleman. That Hardy enjoyed a close relationship with and possibly engagement to Tryphena is undisputed, but otherwise the work represents the epitome of suppositious biography. Speculation is advanced as fact, syllogisms abound, and Hardy's poems and novels are plundered for the evidence that research fails to supply.

The allegations have been demolished in a distinguished account of Hardy's early years, Robert Gittings's *Young Thomas Hardy* (1975), almost a model biography in its respect for empirical evidence painstakingly gathered, its acuity of interpretation and its lucidity of presentation. Conjecture is firmly labelled as conjecture. Gittings's study vigorously reveals the deficiencies of the *Life*, giving a full account of Hardy's formative experiences and his emergence from the lower division of the rigid social hierarchy of his youth. One of his characters, Paula Power, has 'a *prédilection d'artiste* for ancestors of the other sort': Hardy shared this intuitive feeling and in later years falsified the record of his humble origins. It is no surprise that class deracination is one of the most insistent themes of his fiction and poetry, probably not so much as an expiation of his own guilt over desertion of his class as an expression of an essential contrariety within him. Gittings objectively evokes the almost medieval village society in which Hardy was brought up, the very real talents of his parents (it is still a sometimes neglected truism that talent has nothing to do with social 'class'), his self-help education and the rural traditions operating upon him. Gittings also shows how the macabre came to have an almost erotic fascination for Hardy, a feeling transmitted into the hanging of Tess, and traces the effects of the suicide of his friend Horace Moule on the cast of the author's mind. *Young Thomas Hardy* is a major work and the most reliable biography so far.*

The 'poor man and the lady' motif interwoven into so much of Hardy's writing was inevitably inspired by his self-deluding first wife, Emma, to whose defence Gittings comes armed with evidence that she was not (as Florence alleged) 'of tainted stock'. The conventional view of Emma as a snobbish, jealous bigot is modified by Gittings, who admits her eccentricities but stresses too that the woman, who after years of

---

* Gittings's *The Older Hardy* (1978) explores Hardy's life from 1876 until his death, and it is Hardy's domestic and personal idiosyncrasies rather than the externalities of his career that hold our interest. In his middle age and in his eighties Hardy remained susceptible to the imaginative draw of attractive women, from Mrs. Florence Henniker (a good friend who did not reciprocate his near infatuation) in the eighteen nineties to Gertrude Bugler (the young Dorchester actress) in the nineteen twenties. But from this study he emerges as a man neglectful of the feelings of either his first or his second wife, a man hard to live with. Hardy's retreat into the gloom of Max Gate is described and what remains with the reader is an impression of his meanness and the vicariousness of his living through his art rather than through his demonstrable feelings. This is a surprise, if not a shock, in view of his aesthetic commitment to lovingkindness and compassion. It was, in part at least, probably a side effect of his shyness and reserve; its exposure by Gittings has certainly been regarded as heresy by some of the Hardy faithful.

estrangement re-entered Hardy's mind only when she could enter his imagination as the 'ghost-girl-rider' of the 'Poems of 1912–13', had much to endure from a difficult and negligent husband. In a brilliant phrase Gittings says that Emma had 'moments of disorganized poetry' to the end of her life. A proper understanding of Emma, the central personality of Hardy's life for so many years, is essential if we are to understand the man, and some of her 'disorganized poetry' infuses the short manuscript she completed in 1911, the year before her death, published in 1961 under her own title, *Some Recollections*, ed. Robert Gittings and Evelyn Hardy. It is a revealing and often moving document. Its final paragraph begins, after recalling her marriage to Hardy in 1874: 'I have had various experiences, interesting some, sad others, since that lovely day, but all showing that an Unseen Power of great benevolence directs my ways.' These sometimes childlike recollections and Gittings's reassessment of Emma should generate towards her some of the deserved sympathy so long withheld by tradition. (Denys Kay-Robinson is at present preparing a full-length biography of Emma Hardy.) Gittings's assertion that Florence Hardy wished to denigrate Emma's memory has been hotly denied by those who enjoyed her hospitality and help.[6] Yet Florence was moved to complain to Sydney Cockerell that 'all the poems about [Emma] are a fiction but a fiction in which their author has now come to believe':[7] perceptive irony or ungenerous assertion, this goes some way to explaining why Florence excised some of the evidence of Hardy's old affections from the *Life*, from a celebration of her chestnut hair to more signal accounts of Emma's qualities. This surely implies no derogation of Florence's loyalty but simply the human impulse of a second wife's protective jealousy: Florence too had much to put up with, sharing her husband with the Emma literally enshrined in the 'Poems of 1912–13' and being marshalled around the scenes of his first courtship, an unusual compulsory pilgrimage for a second wife.

Gittings's study is also supplemented by Harold Orel's *The Final Years of Thomas Hardy* (1976), a less ambitious but compact and penetrating analysis of Hardy's life and thought after the watershed of Emma's death. We can now await with confidence a definitive biography by Michael Millgate. F. E. Halliday's *Thomas Hardy: His Life and Works* (1972) is a readable general account with numerous illustrations, and Timothy O'Sullivan's *Thomas Hardy: An Illustrated Biography* (1975) is a handsomely produced pictorial record of Hardy's life with an unpretentious commentary. There are more than 200 illustrations (some in colour, including stirring aerial views of 'Lyonnesse' and Beeny Cliff) of people, places, and Hardy's manuscripts and drawings. There are some suggestive collocations of individual poems with drawings and photographs in this excellent, evocative compilation.

Outside the formal biographies there are some short accounts and monographs. One may be of dubious authenticity: Cyril Clemens's *My Chat with Thomas Hardy* (1944) is the record of a visit to Hardy in 1925. Mark Twain's nephew seems to be gifted with total recall and to have discovered Hardy in unusually voluble mood, holding forth at length and in measured phrases about American writers ('Cooper's dark aborigines, crafty, noble, eloquent, superseded all others') and confessing authorship of his own 'biography'. Some statements attributed to Hardy severely strain our ability to give credence to Clemens: 'In Dorchester, where I was brought up, I was the only youth who could write.' Vere H. Collins's *Talks with Thomas Hardy at Max Gate 1920–1922* (1928), cast as dialogue with Hardy, Florence and Collins as *dramatis personae*, recounts six meetings. Collins too has a remarkable talent for recalling precise conversation and he even manages 'stage directions' ('During a pause in the conversation C notices that H, who has hitherto sat erect during the whole of the interview, is leaning back with his head slightly drooping forward'). But we need not accept the book as a *verbatim* transcript to appreciate the apparent authenticity of Hardy's comments on (among other topics) his poetry, other authors and men of letters, and critical studies of his life and works. Other recollections of Hardy appear among the seventy-two monographs published by the Toucan Press (1962–71), later bound together as J. S. Cox (ed.) *Materials for a Study of the Life, Times and Works of Thomas Hardy* (Vol. I, 1968; II, 1971): most revealing are those by Edmund Blunden, May O'Rourke (Hardy's secretary), Cynthia Asquith, and two by former Hardy Players, N. J. Atkins and Gertrude Bugler ('he was not the grim, cynical man often pictured . . . I can still hear him laugh'). The range of the monographs extends beyond recollections to the annotations in Hardy's Bibles, Emma's Poems and Religious Effusions, accounts of Hardy's genealogy, etc. The quality of the monographs is very variable. Some are inconsequential ('TH at the Barber's' tells us only that Hardy was inordinately shy, refused hairclippers and would not discuss his work, and the questions directed to the barber are tonsorially esoteric: 'Q. What dressing did he prefer on his hair? A. He would have no dressing, not even brilliantine') and others unreliable: one is misleadingly titled 'Tryphena's Portrait Album' when it is no such thing. The series espouses the Tryphena story and devotes several monographs to its speculative exposition by Lois Deacon. Many of the recollections betray local gossip, unscholarly perhaps but as interesting as gossip often is. The monographs as a whole have a real value and Cox's doggedness in recording these impressions and 'Hardyana' is admirable. The findings of the first half of the series are synthesized in D. F. Barber, *Concerning Thomas Hardy* (1968). (The Cox cottage industry has now moved on to *The Thomas Hardy Year Book* (ed. J. S. and G. S. Cox, 1970–), an irregular, interesting curate's egg publication combining criticism with further research items. Transcriptions of items in the Hardy Collection must be treated with caution.) The biographical monographs show Hardy as an octogenarian: reticent, touchy, evasive, financially tight-fisted, but with his wry sense of humour intact. They should be supplemented with Virginia Woolf's vivid account of her own 1926 pilgrimage to Hardy's drawing-room in *A Writer's Diary* (1953) and then the recollection that Hardy was not always in his eighties and that these are only winter portraits.

An urgent *lacuna* in Hardy studies is the lack of a collected edition of his letters. Such a work has been in hand for many years under the editorship of R. L. Purdy, latterly in conjunction with Michael Millgate: its scholarship is thus assured. This expectation is borne out by Vol. I of *The Collected Letters of Thomas Hardy* which has now appeared (1978). C. J. Weber (ed.) *The Letters of Thomas Hardy* (1954) is too random to be of lasting importance and is limited to just over 100 letters (1873–1927) in the Colby College collection. The annotation is careful but the letters are unrevealing. Two further collections are more valuable because thematically arranged. C. J. Weber (ed.) *'Dearest Emmie': Thomas Hardy's Letters to his First Wife* (1963) contains seventy-four letters (1885–1911) which parallel the increasing estrangement of Hardy and Emma. The letters are mainly social descriptions or instructions from Hardy when away, but it is moving to see the emotional declensions from 'My dearest Emmie ... Yours affectionately ever Tom' in 1885 to 'Dear E . . T' in 1911. There is more vigour and emotional involvement implicit in Evelyn Hardy and F. B. Pinion (eds.), *One Rare Fair Woman: Thomas Hardy's Letters to Florence Henniker 1893–1922* (1972), an excellently annotated collection of 153 letters and the most interesting edition so far to appear. Hardy's almost passionate friendship with this 'charming, *intuitive* woman' (as he called her) animates the normally reticent author into diverse observations about his own work and that of others. The editors also direct our attention to poems corre-lative to this long-standing friendship; as usual, these are even more revealing than the letters. Hardy does not subscribe to Dr. Johnson's view of letters as 'epistolic art' and most of his letters are businesslike, unemotional (except when fulminating against critics), generally short and almost always undemonstrative. Literary views are scarce or per-functory. Yet his letters can be rewarding for the patient reader and the next six volumes of the projected seven volume edition of *The Collected Letters* may be anticipated with interest.

Hardy had no consistent theories of art and his most extended statements are in the 'General Preface' and other Prefaces, and three essays: 'The Profitable Reading of Fiction' (1888), 'Candour in English Fiction' (1890) and 'The Science of Fiction' (1891). These and other miscellaneous essays are collected in Harold Orel (ed.), *Thomas Hardy's Personal Writings* (1966), a most useful compilation which also includes Prefaces to the works of other writers and such essays as 'The Dorsetshire Labourer'. This supersedes Ernest Brennecke's similar *Life and Art* (1925), which contains less than half the material. Beyond these essays we need to look at the extant primary material. Much has been made of the bonfires before and after Hardy's death, when on his instructions many diaries and papers were destroyed; their contents were probably much less sensational than we might like to imagine. There remain a number of notebooks, all but one now published[8] rich in clues about Hardy's life, thought and technique.

C. J. P. Beatty (ed.), *The Architectural Notebook of Thomas Hardy* (1966) has a facsimile reproduction of Hardy's notes and raises questions about the extent to which his work was influenced by his initial profession. Lennart A. Björk (ed.), *The Literary Notes of Thomas Hardy* (Vol. I, 1974), the first of two volumes, is a first-class work of meticulous scholarship. A *literatim* transcription of Hardy's four commonplace books is accompanied by exemplary annotation identifying almost all of Hardy's sources and discussing the implications of what he copied. The literary notebooks are much more than a monument to Hardy's continuing autodidacticism (if such a term may properly be applied to a man whose capacity to assimilate ideas is as considerable as his). Hardy is a magpie, now recording factual details for potential transmission into his fiction, now keeping abreast of the latest intellectual controversies in periodicals. These notes should stimulate further study of Hardy's concern with ideological and moral aesthetics and, more generally, the interpenetration of these notes and his writing. This is a work of major importance and Björk's excellent critical introduction raises a number of issues.

Evelyn Hardy (ed.), *Thomas Hardy's Notebooks* (1955), is a selection of notes from two of Hardy's 'Memoranda' notebooks. Unfortunately the transcription is inaccurate and the annotations often misleading. Many notes are omitted entirely or so drastically abbreviated as to lose their point. Collation reveals little regard for the integrity of Hardy's holograph: punctuation is regularly and unsystematically revised and phrases are frequently added, rewritten or removed at random. All this is sad since the notebooks contain much that is of interest, in three main areas: literary and antiquarian, social, and personal, as well as some uncharacteristic flashes of passion (George Moore is dismissed as 'that ludicrous blackguard'). This material has now been re-edited, with other notebooks and the *Life* typescript passages, with introduction and annotation in Richard H. Taylor (ed.) *The Personal Notebooks of Thomas Hardy* (1978). This edition also includes some unpublished memoranda of Hardy's relating to his autobiography and some brief extracts from Florence Hardy's diary.

An author's papers are emphatically less important than his art, and scholarly mills sometimes seem to grind exceeding small. Yet Hardy's letters and few surviving notebooks are unique fragments through which we privately glimpse the man and his mind over a period of sixty years. *Valeat quantum valere potest*: Geoffrey Tillotson has given us a memorable phrase and persuasive evaluation of such things in firmly asserting that 'scraps surviving from the pen of a great genius are saint's relics'.[9]

CRITICAL STUDIES

'The worst chapter of *The Hand of Ethelberta*,' wrote Edmund Gosse, 'is recognizable, in a moment, as written by the author of the best chapter in

The Return of the Native.'[10] We can see at once what he means: a common quality informs Hardy's whole *œuvre*, the least fortunate aspects of the least regarded novels as well as the most imposing aspects of those most highly esteemed, with a stamp of 'greatness'. Among his fourteen novels, considerable in range, diverse in methods and materials and bold in idiosyncratic experiments, there is no 'failure'. The unity of his art and the self-possessed fictive world that he creates should not be underestimated, but it has not a consistency of the kind sometimes alleged and often sought. Criticism, individual and cumulative, has tried to define Hardy and his achievement more exactly than he would have wished. Hardy is quite explicit:

> Unadjusted impressions have their value, and the road to a true philosophy of life seems to lie in humbly recording diverse readings of its phenomena as they are forced upon us by chance and change.
>
> (Preface to *Poems of the Past and the Present*, August 1901)

His 'unadjusted impressions' have been knitted together into fabrics that quite often do not in any real sense exist. The network is more complex than some such studies allow, and less ingenious than others. 'The mission of poetry,' Hardy said, 'is to record impressions, not convictions' (*Life*, 377), and this stands for all his art. This is not to say that Hardy is detached or that conviction is absent, but his conviction is not set out in the form of convictions: the distinction is important. This makes him hard to isolate but the response his work provokes is all the more rewarding for its denial of ready definition.

Hardy resists classification, either in mode or literary tradition. There is no other novelist whom he is 'like'; or, to put it another way, no other novelist is like him. The unusual way in which the individual impress of Hardy's mind is made present in his work makes it distinctive, and it is this which gives inescapable unity to all his writing. Whether or not he is consistent in his ideas is a tributary issue; the values Hardy embodies are those of feeling. It matters more that he is consistent in his art; that *The Hand of Ethelberta*, for instance, whatever its rank as a novel, can be recognized as the work of a great writer. The obvious homology of Hardy's novels raises the provocative question posed by Ian Gregor in his important article, 'What kind of fiction did Hardy write?' (*EC*, XVI, 1966).

It is a question answered by contemporary reviewers with little of Gregor's subtlety. The men of letters reviewing Hardy's novels as they appeared were schooled in the Victorian fiction mill and as a partial consequence often given to periphrastic summary than rigorous analysis. Yet from an early stage Hardy's poetic qualities, scenic and atmospheric effects, evolution of character, stylized bucolic humour and tragic power were recognized. But his early rural paintings of the Dutch school soon had Hardy classified, even though 'he had not the slightest intention of writing for ever about sheepfarming' (*Life*, 102) after *FFMC*. The inevitable comparisons with George Eliot salted the wound and reviewers continued to show a determined resistance to Hardy's modernism and attempts to deal with the contemporary world or higher social classes. They were alert enough to isolate what they saw as a certain 'nastiness' in Hardy and to disapprove of his melodramatic outrages (Hardy's desire for an intelligent audience was always seasoned with popular sensationalism), while his mannerisms, cumbrous words and oddities of style were deplored. Two more spectres haunted his reviewers: Hardy's increasing 'pessimism' was unacceptable (*MC* was coolly received), and his alleged immorality led him to be pursued by a Grundyism which, although not so exclusive as he thought, did preclude a wide range of objective discussions of the literary merits of *Tess* and *Jude*. Three reception studies or anthologies have appeared. L. Lerner and J. Holmstrom (eds.) *Thomas Hardy and his Readers* (1968) is too casual a *potpourri*, and too limited in scope, to give any balanced idea of the growth of Hardy's literary reputation. (There are also some inaccuracies.) But an anthology which does just that almost immediately superseded it: R. G. Cox (ed.) *Thomas Hardy: The Critical Heritage* (1970) has a good interpretative introduction and shows that Hardy provoked some contemporary criticism of real distinction. C. J. Weber's *Hardy in America* (1946) is a careful, detailed survey of American responses to Hardy's work as it appeared. Hardy's deep emotional mistrust of his critics is suggested in this typical passage excised from the *Life* (original typescript, DCM; *Personal Notebooks*, p. 244):

It is curious to conjecture what must be the sensations of critics like the writers of these personalities in their times of loneliness, sickness, affliction, and old age, when equally with the criticized they have to pause and ask themselves: What have I been trying to do for so many years? Surely they must say, 'I withered the buds before they were blown, and turned back the feet of the morning.' Pheu, pheu! So it is and will be!

Yet for all their misjudgements of individual novels, and the changes in taste and critical priorities that render some of their evaluations eccentric to us, the Victorian reviewers did identify the major features of Hardy's art and the inequalities that flaw his fiction.

The earliest full-length studies, Lionel Johnson's *The Art of Thomas Hardy* and Annie Macdonell's *Thomas Hardy*, appeared in 1894, before Hardy's last novel. 'Both Lionel Johnsons [*sic*] books & another on my novels by Miss Macdonell were unauthorized by me, as you will suppose,' Hardy wrote to Sir George Douglas. 'While he is too pedantic, & hers too knowing, & both are too laudatory, they are not in bad taste on the whole, if one concedes that they had to be written, which I do not quite. Indeed I rather dreaded their appearance' (16 November 1894; National Library of Scotland, Edinburgh). Hardy need not have worried. Macdonell's survey is uncritical and descriptive and Johnson's is enthusiastic and intelligent. Johnson laid the foundation stone of the Hardy industry in a remarkably balanced first study that immediately apprehends the poetic nature of Hardy's Wessex and the importance of the choric characters in support of the tragic protagonists. Chapters treat discrete aspects of Hardy's fiction and its style and structure but a sense of unity and pattern emerges from consideration of the major novels. Hardy is the chronicler of rural decay and we receive from the novels 'a sense of awe, in the presence of a landscape filled with immemorial signs of age; a sense of tranquillity, in the presence of human toil, so bound up and associated with the venerable needs of human life'.

Johnson's eloquent (if verbose) and authoritative testimonial to Hardy's stature inaugurated a period during which Hardy's reputation was consolidated. Hardy abandoned novels and, in the shadow of Johnson, book-length work on Hardy was limited to topographical treatises by Wilkinson Sherren (1902), Bertram Windle (1902), C. G. Harper (1904) and Hermann Lea (1905). In 1904 Edward Wright could still describe the 'sentimental materialist' Hardy as 'a prince of modern English literature by reason of his earlier works, but in certain of his later works a misdirected force',[11] but this lingering Grundyism had been sufficiently swept away by 1910 for newer preoccupations to have set in with Hardy's assured status: 'The pessimism of Mr. Hardy resembles that of Schopenhauer in being absolutely thorough and absolutely candid,' wrote W. L. Phelps, 'it makes the world as darkly superb and as terribly interesting as a Greek drama.'[12] By the time Lascelles Abercrombie's *Thomas Hardy: A Critical Study* appeared in 1912, the apotheosis was complete. Classical tragedy was the touchstone, Abercrombie could write approvingly of 'Hardy's loving study of Sophocles', and Hardy was already seen as an irreproachable elder statesman, our greatest native tragedian.

An urbane reverence unites early studies by Harold Child (1916, rev. ed. 1925), H. C. Duffin (1916, rev. ed. 1937), Samuel Chew (1921, rev. ed. 1928) and H. B. Grimsditch (1925). These studies are discursive rather than analytical and fortified by common assumptions about the tragic grandeur of human nature as presented by Hardy. Among their mainly unexceptionable commentaries Duffin's is the most profound and Chew's the most uneven. The obsession which most distinctly characterized Hardy's other early critics was not the instinctive regard for classical aesthetics which underlies these studies but a preoccupation with Hardy's 'philosophy'. Helen Garwood's *Thomas Hardy: An Illustration of the Philosophy of Schopenhauer* (1911) led the field, though Hardy was quick to rebut her thesis: 'My pages show harmony of view with Darwin, Huxley, Spencer, Hume, Mill, and others, all of whom I used to read more than Schopenhauer', he told her in a letter.[13] The exposition which most disturbed Hardy was Ernest Brennecke Jr.'s *Thomas Hardy's Universe* (1924). Brennecke attempts a metaphysical biography of Hardy but goes beyond establishing an intellectual affinity between author and philosopher to write of 'Hardy's dependence upon Schopenhauer' and to assert that certain scenes in *The Dynasts* 'could not possibly have been composed if Schopenhauer had not previously written *Die Welt als Wille und Vorstellung*'. If Hardy disingenuously underplays his interest in Schopenhauer, Brennecke's assertion is dangerous overstatement. *The World as Will and Idea* is in any case a red herring: it was Schopenhauer's *On the Four-Fold Root of the Principle of Sufficient Reason* that Hardy carefully annotated (in 1890). Much emphasis has been placed upon the influence of Schopenhauer and Von Hartmann (whose *Philosophy of the Unconscious* was published in English in 1884), yet assigning 'influence' is a risky pursuit. What Schopenhauer amd Nietzsche call 'will' and Von Hartmann calls 'consciousness' all have something in common with Hardy's Immanent Will, a concept which Hardy regarded as a legacy from time immemorial rather than recent philosophers. The notion of 'consciousness' injects into Hardy's thought the meliorism that divides him from Schopenhauer (as in *The Dynasts*, 'Consciousness the Will informing / Till it fashion all things fair'). Hardy claimed some originality in this evolutionary element: 'That the Unconscious Will of the Universe is growing aware of Itself, I believe I may claim as my own idea solely' (2 June 1907; letter in DCM and *Life*, 335). Yet to identify exclusive influences is critically naïve. Hardy's ideas are inevitably a synthesis of his own independent apprehensions and his immersion in nineteenth-century ideas. He does not reproduce philosophical theories but responds to them.

It is the response that matters, the same process of imaginative transmutation that sometimes transforms the base metal of biographical fact into art, and that is Hardy's alone. There is honest equivocation in his thought and no logical consistency:

> Positive views on the Whence and the Wherefore of things have never been advanced by this pen as a consistent philosophy. Nor is it likely, indeed, that imaginative writings extending over more than forty years would exhibit a coherent scientific theory of the universe even if it had been attempted.
>
> ('General Preface', 1911)

In 1920 Hardy again declared in a letter: 'I have no philosophy – merely what I have often explained to be only a confused heap of impressions, like those of a bewildered child at a conjuring show' (*Life*, 410). A later reference in the same letter to 'my mood-dictated writings' is suggestive: Hardy, avowedly a feeler rather than a reasoner, is more interested in intuitive truth. Each work has its philosophical *haecceitas* but ideas are always subservient to the needs of art, aesthetic fuel for the imagination.

Other early studies, such as Harriet Lane's *Fate in the Novels of Thomas Hardy* (1925) and Patrick Braybrooke's *Thomas Hardy and his Philosophy* (1928), are misleading because they fail to appreciate this distinction. A. P. Elliott, whose *Fatalism in the Works of Thomas Hardy* (1935) is chiefly concerned with 'Hardy the artist, and with an analysis of his art in its relation to Fate as an artistic motif', is refreshingly clear in his priorities but proves unequal to the task. W. R. Rutland's *Thomas Hardy: A Study of his Writings and their Background* (1938) analyses Hardy's debt to Victorian thought in general (a wider contextual study than German philosophers alone), traces the aesthetic development of Hardy's 'Will', and is the first substantial account of Hardy's view of the relationship between man and nature. Harvey C. Webster's *On a Darkling Plain: The Art and Thought of Thomas Hardy* (1947) is a sophisticated examination of Hardy's fiction in terms of aspects of nineteenth-century thought (especially deterministic notions and evolution through natural selection) subsumed into his outlook to contribute to his individual views of chance and circumstance. In a note added to a 1964 reprint Webster admits that the novels are not an illustration of Hardy's philosophy but a dramatization of his search for one. He articulates the conventional view of Hardy's outlook:

> Tortured by natural law, unrealizable desires, Circumstance and Chance, against a background inimical to man, in a time out of joint, man is an unhappy creature. The reader feels convinced that the author, in common with Clym and Sophocles, believes that not to be born is best.

John Holloway, in *The Victorian Sage* (1953), advances this view of Hardy as a determinist and analyses Hardy's view of Nature not as a backcloth but a system that includes, modifies and at last controls human activity, through its spatial and temporal force. Hardy's characters, borne down by their natural environment and the ironical consequences of their inevitable actions, illustrate this everywhere. Human wishes are entirely disregarded by a determined system of things.

Roy Morrell's *Thomas Hardy: The Will and the Way* (1965) expresses 'complete disagreement'. His seminal study, crabbed in exposition, is intellectually bracing and rejects all received opinions of Hardy's determinism and its aesthetic implications (the novelist as cruel manipulator). Morrell argues that Hardy's characters suffer because of their misuse of the free will and choice available to them. In other words, though Hardy does not go so far as Novalis ('Character is Fate') he does show that human character is at least as influential as circumstance. Oak and Farfrae adapt to (and therefore master) their environments; Henchard is a 'man of character' whose downfall results from his own defiant intractability; Tess is never 'hopelessly trapped' but acquiescent in her fate – it is 'because she fails to control circumstances in time' that she is seduced. Lack of the will to will engenders catastrophe. Morrell's urgent and stimulating thesis deepens the resonance of Hardy's fiction. F. R. Southerington's *Hardy's Vision of Man* (1971) adds little to Morrell's view (which he endorses without explicit acknowledgement) apart from a useful chapter on *The Dynasts*. This sound enough account of freedom and responsibility in Hardy becomes tendentious when the extent of 'autobiographical features embedded deep in the fabric of the novels' becomes a major concern, especially since this aspect is infiltrated by Lois Deaconry.

The studies of determinism in Hardy and Morrell's corrective astringent have established a *status quo* worth preserving for the moment. Other aspects of Hardy's response to Victorian intellectual concerns have been examined, notably by David J. DeLaura in ' "The Ache of Modernism" in Hardy's Later Novels' (*ELH*, XXXIV, 1967). DeLaura explores Hardy's view of the modern condition (psychic dislocation, alienation, rootlessness), his attempt to endorse a Hellenic ideal and his debt to Arnold. The discussion mainly concerns *Tess* and *Jude* though DeLaura might also have invoked *A Laodicean* where Hardy's awareness of the need for a new ethical centre animates Paula's neo-Hellenic Laodiceanism and the painful exigencies of the modern spirit are made socially and psychically explicit. The consequences of 'the ache of modernism', the propulsion of characters into a catatonic condition, are discussed by Lawrence J. Starzyk, 'The Coming Universal Wish Not to Live in Hardy's "Modern" Novels' (*NCF*, XXVI, 1972).

The Hebraism-Hellenism dichotomy is part of the background to Hardy's attitude to Christian belief. Chesterton's description of Hardy as 'the village atheist brooding and blaspheming over the village idiot'[14] is as unfair as it is misleading. Hardy does show a certain animosity towards organized religion (e.g. the fraternal clergymen in 'A Tragedy of Two Ambitions', Bishop Helmsdale, some of the pointed remarks in *Tess*), and Norman Holland, in *Jude*: Hardy's Symbolic Indictment of Christianity' (*NCF*, IX, 1954), shows how Hardy uses images and symbols from the evolution of Christianity to criticize the late Victorian society that called itself Christian. The Higher Criticism he read encouraged his rejection of an anthropomorphic God but agnostic rationalism was emotionally unsatisfying. Hardy's sense of lost faith is poignantly articulated in his poetry, his experience of the numinous is manifest throughout his work, and his failure to discover a logical system of belief is neither defeatist – Morrell's reminder of Hardy's 'gaiety' is timely – nor atheistic. The denial of formal faith does not vitiate Hardy's moral and emotional endorsement of Christian sentiments. His humane values are exactly right – profound compassion, abhorrence of human and macrocosmic cruelty, and instinctive feeling that a 'way to the Better' can only be achieved by harnessing these values.

While Hardy could not accept the simple country faith of his village home, though it deeply affected him, other traditional rural values permeated his thought. His relationship with nature is almost mystical. An admirable study formed on the assumption of Hardy's 'profound spiritual sympathy with the land and the people' is Ruth Firor's *Folkways in Thomas Hardy* (1931), a thorough and fascinating account of folklore and custom and their extensive application in Hardy's work. Hardy the countryman is just as evident in minute details of visual and aural observation, reactively undervalued by A. J. Guerard who says that we are now 'repelled' by 'the regionalist's ear for dialect, the botanist's eye for the minutiae of field and tree, the architect's eye for ancient mansions, and the farmer's eye for sheepshearings'.[15] He is reacting against an earlier generation of critics who saw Hardy's countryside as pictorial evocation. We have learned that the natural descriptions are never gratuitous and that nature is reshaped to convey a mood, an imagistic pattern, a symbolic or mythical dimension. Though he is less explicit in statement, Hardy's feeling is animistic. Nature is philosophically inclusive but its narrative function remains equally important and Hardy's relationship with pastoral has been examined in several articles: Robert Drake, '*The W* as Traditional Pastoral' (*MFS*, VI, 1960) and Michael Squires, '*FFMC* as Modified Pastoral' (*NCF*, XXV, 1970) are now supplemented by Squires's full-length study, *The Pastoral Novel* (1975) (on Eliot, Hardy and Lawrence), and Charles May, '*FFMC* and *The W*: Hardy's Grotesque Pastorals' (*ELT*, XVII, 1974). Our understanding of the rustics as pastoral figures is extended by Harold E. Toliver, 'The Dance Under the Greenwood Tree: Hardy's Bucolics' (*NCF*, XVII, 1962) and modified by W. J. Hyde, 'Hardy's View of Realism: A Key to the Rustic Characters' (*VS*, II, 1958): the characters accurately but obliquely reflect real economic distress. This is not incompatible with the mode. Our view of the pastoral itself has gradually been modified to recognition that it is often a dynamic mode in which the characters set against the fundamental patterns of the created world embody a psychic, even moral, conflict between natural and man-made environments.

This raises the question of the values inherent in living close to nature. John Holloway, arguing that Hardy advocates living naturally, infers from the novels that 'to adapt one's life to one's traditional situation is good, to uproot oneself for material ends is bad' (*The Victorian Sage*). One corollary to this is to read Hardy as a social historian. Critics as early as Lionel Johnson identified the theme of agricultural decay but Douglas Brown, in his *Thomas Hardy* (1954, rev. ed. 1961), is its most persuasive apologist:

> Hardy presents his conception through the play of life in a tract of the countryside. His protagonists are strong-natured countrymen, disciplined by the necessities of agricultural life. He brings into relation with them men and women from outside the rural world, better educated, superior in status, yet inferior in human worth. The contact occasions a sense of invasion, of disturbance.

Brown's thesis is that the novels record 'Hardy's dismay at the predicament of the agricultural community in the south of England during the last part of the nineteenth century and at the precarious hold of the agricultural way of life'. His study contains some unusually distinctive criticism and sharp textual analyses, but the theme of agricultural decline, certainly one of Hardy's thematic subjects and emotional concerns, is given a quite disproportionate emphasis. It is misleading to regard it as the dominant motif of the novels and to do so extrudes an artificial chronology out of Hardy's fictional world (and discounts the lesser novels entirely). Despite his deep empathy, artistically Hardy saw Wessex and its peasantry as raw material for the portrayal of elementary passions in a circumscribed scene, and while the particularity of his use of period is important, the novels are not just constituent parts of a para-historical allegory. It is doubtfully useful to assume that the turn-of-the-century world in *TM* schematically prefigures the thirties as described in *UGT* (written eight years earlier) or the forties in *RN* (written two years earlier) and *MC* (written five years later). Hardy's imagination was readily stimulated by retrospection: it is not so much the social as the aesthetic implications of his antiquarian instinct and sense of historical perspective that are important, and R. J. White's *Thomas Hardy and History* (1974) helps to illuminate this. Some of the details in Brown's historical arguments, further developed in his incisive short study, *Thomas Hardy: The Mayor of Casterbridge* (1962), are refuted by J. C. Maxwell's 'The "Sociological" Approach to *MC*' in Maynard Mack and Ian Gregor (eds.) *Imagined Worlds* (1968). Raymond Williams (*CQ*, VI, 1964) regards the received views of the peasant in Hardy's fiction as 'absurdly misleading' and argues that the class system is already inherent in rural society, not imported from outside. This view is reinforced by Merryn Williams in her *Thomas Hardy and Rural England* (1972) which relates Hardy's conception of rural society to the facts revealed in social and economic records and identifies Hardy as an accurate (and deliberate) social historian. Emphatic left-wing subjectivity clouds interpretation of some of the evidence but this is a useful and lively empirical study.

Studies so far discussed express partial views and drive us back to the question they do not individually answer: what *kind* of fiction did Hardy write? Contrary to earlier views of Hardy as a pastoral or social realist, his aesthetic sympathies actually derive largely from the older conventions of romance. When Chew placed Hardy in the tradition of the Brontës, George Eliot, Trollope and Blackmore, Hardy wrote in the margin: '? Fielding ? Scott'.[16] Fielding felt that human nature should never be violated and Scott in 1824 defended the 'marvellous and uncommon incidents' of romance — Hardy's position is a synthesis of these attitudes: 'human nature must never be made abnormal . . . the uncommonness must be in the events, not in the characters; and the writer's art lies in shaping that uncommonness while disguising its unlikelihood' (July 1881; *Life*, 150). Hardy is a transitional figure between what Donald Davidson identifies as the 'traditional narrator' of the nineteenth century and earlier (*SR*, VI, 1940) and the symbolic modern novelist.

In an article which remains the fullest discussion of Hardy's aesthetic position, M. D. Zabel, in 'Hardy in Defence of his Art: The Aesthetic of Incongruity' (*SR*, VI, 1940), shows Hardy as 'a realist developing toward allegory . . . an imaginative artist who brought the nineteenth century novel out of its slavery to fact'. His fiction is full of modern tensions and ambiguities, standing 'in a succession of novelists . . . that has arrived at the achievements of Joyce, Proust, Gide, and Kafka'. Zabel uses Hardy's notes and practice to identify a personal aesthetic elevating instinct and emotion above intellect, grandiose symbolism over restrictive naturalism. This emergent view of Hardy as a conscious anti-realist is developed in A. J. Guerard's *Thomas Hardy: The Novels and Stories* (1949, rev. ed. 1964), a stimulating book which (like Morrell's revision of earlier philosophical assumptions) rejects 'the realistic bias and expectation of post-Victorian critics'. He shows that 'the absurd coincidences, the grotesque heightenings of reality' are symbolic and reveal Hardy's sense of the cosmic absurd and existential irrationality. T. S. Eliot, in *After Strange Gods* (1934), virtually accuses Hardy of diabolic morbidity. Certainly Hardy is fond of the macabre: we know that in 1877 (*Life*, 118) he held a candle for a doctor cutting open a boy's body to examine the heart and stomach for an autopsy. It was not necessary to be a human candlestick in such circumstances and it is the transferral of such impulses into his art that makes Eliot see him as a symptom of decadence. Guerard's book is a powerful corrective, emphasizing Hardy's role as a storyteller with melodramatic psychological curiosity and a modernist aesthetic. An earlier article by Jacques Barzun, 'Truth and Poetry in Thomas Hardy' (*SR*, VI, 1940), had also hinted at the anti-realism of this 'poet miscast as a novelist', and a good general study by Richard Carpenter, *Thomas Hardy* (1964), extends the case with attention to the archetypal and mythic dimensions of Hardy's work.

The atomic components of Hardy's aesthetic have been distinguished in a diversity of studies but some major concerns may be identified. Character has always been a preoccupation but a summary of the shifting emphases of successive full-length works would serve no valuable function. Some essential work has been done in articles, such as Ted Spivey's 'Thomas Hardy's Tragic Hero' (*NCF*, IX, 1954), which measures the tragic heroes and heroines against classical definitions. Some suggestive typologies have been defined. Guerard offers a persuasive, if over-schematic, genealogy of Hardy's female characters; Richard Beckman's 'A Character Typology for Hardy's Novels' (*ELH*, XXX, 1963) discerns a full seasonal cycle of temperaments and examines these archetypes in various novels; and J. O. Bailey's 'Hardy's "Mephistophelian Visitants"' (*PMLA*, LXI, 1946) discovers a recurrent series of interlopers (such as Venn, Farfrae, Dare) who psychically disrupt the communities they invade. A more recent tendency has been to submit such typologies, and the characters themselves, to psychological analysis, as in Geoffrey Thurley's *The Psychology of Hardy's Novels: The Nervous and the Statuesque* (1975). The apposition in the title implies that fictive tension occurs when 'a type of human being based upon flexibility, movement, rhythm, balance, is confronted, opposed or attracted by one based upon solidity, rootedness, rigidity'. Perry Meisel's *Thomas Hardy: The Return of the Repressed* (1972) is Freudian in technique and implication and a certain amount of jargon obscures some of the otherwise useful exposition of psychological tensions in Hardy's characters. Meisel's book and Terry Eagleton's account of the tragic portrayal of self-division in 'Thomas Hardy: Nature as Language' (*CQ*, XIII, 1971) contribute something towards the study of pain – Hardy's 'continual imaginative celebration of what is both the truest and most important element in life' – thus advocated by Philip Larkin (*CQ*, VIII, 1966). The most distinctive 'psychological' reading of the characters is D. H. Lawrence's 'Study of Thomas Hardy' (in *Phoenix*, 1936), a testament to the imaginative empathy between the two authors and a series of brilliant insights cemented by syllogisms into a fervent thesis. The tragedy in Hardy is always the same: those who escape from 'the walled security, the comparative imprisonment, of the established convention' – the passionate, the individual, the wilful – must die; 'the primitive, primal earth, where the instinctive life heaves up' is their champion and their burial ground. The bourgeois will flourish. Profoundly subjective as it is, Lawrence's argument yields analyses sometimes perverse, sometimes irrefutable, always enlivening, of the springs and consequences of action in the Wessex novels.

Hardy's use of imagery and symbolism deserves more extended attention than it has yet received, though several articles hint at what might be achieved, notably F. P. W. McDowell on *Jude* (*MFS*, VI, 1960), Richard Carpenter on *FFMC* (*NCF*, XVIII, 1964) and Tony Tanner on *Tess* (*CQ*, X, 1968). The influence of Hardy's interest in painting is undoubtedly far-reaching. Lord David Cecil, in *Hardy the Novelist* (1943), discusses Hardy's 'power of visualization' – the dramatic possibilities of which are realized in *The Dynasts*. The implications of Alistair Smart's important article on 'Pictorial Imagery in the Novels of Thomas Hardy' (*RES*, XII, 1961) would seem to justify a full study. Meanwhile Norman Page has made two valuable contributions in this neglected area: 'Visual Techniques in *DR*' (*Ariel*, IV, 1973) and 'Hardy's Pictorial Art in *MC*' (*EA*, XXV, 1972), where a 'vocabulary of seeing' is identified and the pictorial element in the novels is shown to be not merely decorative but 'an economical and effective narrative device', and this approach is developed (in the course of a comprehensive study of Hardy's work) in his readable full-length book, *Thomas Hardy* (1977).

That Hardy is 'supremely pictorial in an impressionistic sense' is one conclusion of Penelope Vigar's *The Novels of Thomas Hardy: Illusion and Reality* (1976), which includes an excellent analysis of his pictorial techniques and imagery. Her more general concern with Hardy's concept of style is welcome. Only in recent years has his craftsmanship rivalled broader issues as a critical concern. Victorian reviewers deplored his style, George Moore called his novels 'ill-constructed melodramas, feebly written in bad grammar' and T. S. Eliot contended that Hardy always wrote 'very badly'. It has been a commonplace to regard Hardy as an intuitive artist, a novelist by accident and immune to the prescripts of good writing. His style is laden with neologisms, provincialisms, sometimes abstruse pedantry (ably defended by C. H. Salter, who argues in 'Hardy's Pedantry' (*NCF*, **XXVIII**, 1973) that such references are not displays of otiose learning but deliberately relate Wessex to myth, literature, history and the outside world), sometimes ungainly syntax: yet he transcends all isolatable deficiencies to produce great art. His stylistic devices are analysed by Robert B. Heilman's thorough 'Hardy's *MC*: Notes on Style' (*NCF*, **XVIII**, 1963), but the answer is not here. His idiosyncrasies of style still need to be properly related to the total experience of reading Hardy and his interest in language, and all considerations of style and structure should take into account the textual studies discussed earlier.

The architectonic construction of the novels was noticed from the first. J. W. Beach, in *The Technique of Thomas Hardy* (1922), avers that the plots are 'expressible almost in algebraic formulas' but his analysis is too unsystematic and selective to be convincing. Later critics, such as McDowall (1931) and Guerard (1949), have deplored Hardy's architectonics as subversive of his spontaneity, but R. W. Stallman regards them as 'a triumph of total aesthetic effect' and in 'Hardy's Hour-Glass Novel' (*SR*, **LV**, 1947) discerns in the structure of *RN* 'a mechanical concatenation of seven hour-glass plots'. A sophisticated structural study by Dale Kramer, *Thomas Hardy: The Forms of Tragedy* (1975), stresses Hardy's interest in the naturalness or organic nature of fiction: 'Hardy in each novel uses a dominant aesthetic feature, or organizing principle, that informs the entire work and creates the peculiar quality of tragedy that distinguishes it.' After *MC* formal mechanism decreases and the last three great novels are open-ended. The dominant aesthetic features – such as cyclical pattern in *MC*, consciousness in *Tess* – imply the evolution of Hardy's tragic view.

Three important recent books all extrapolate from structural concerns a more total view of Hardy's artistry than has formerly been achieved. J. Hillis Miller's *Thomas Hardy: Distance and Desire* (1970) is as subjective, brilliant and sometimes tendentious as Lawrence's study. Rejecting extralinguistic metaphors for criticism and mimetic preoccupations, Miller insinuates himself inside the text and 'its threads and filaments' to perceive a single design uniting all Hardy's work, poetry and prose: 'Distance and desire – distance as the source of desire and desire as the energy behind attempts to turn distance into closeness.' These impulses animate Hardy's characters, most especially in his most urgent theme: love, the dance of desire doomed to failure. The temporal and spatial structures of the novels and poems are eternally recurrent: 'His writing, to give it a final definition, is a resurrection and safeguarding of the dead within the fictive language of literature.' Miller's thesis does not 'explain' Hardy but many of his insights and cross-weavings are exciting. Sharing his regard for the unity of the poetry and prose but truer to Hardy's intentions is Jean Brooks's *Thomas Hardy: The Poetic Structure* (1971), a remarkably comprehensive work which defies summary analysis but demands enthusiastic endorsement. Brooks starts from the view that 'the poetic impulse, expressing the basic but multiple faces of experience, defines the Hardeian quality' and shows how Hardy 'anticipates the modern anguish of unresolved tensions in the stylized forms which contain the undirected chaos of life'. This poetic multiplicity of perspective allows Hardy to combine 'the personal and formal vision' from the subjective to the mythopoeic. Close analysis, eclectic *exempla*, densely packed theoretical argument make this perhaps the most complete study of Hardy yet written.

Organic narrative structure is the basis of the most penetrating reading the major novels have yet received: Ian Gregor's *The Great Web: The Form of Hardy's Major Fiction* (1974), an 'extended meditation' on his important 1966 article, 'What kind of fiction did Hardy write?' We are back to that question again and here is an answer. Gregor rescues Hardy from the shadow of restrictive Jamesian precepts of form (the novel presented to the reader as a formal *fait accompli*) to demonstrate the 'gradually unfolding process which builds itself up in the reader's experience'. The filaments of Hardy's interests (ballad-writer, social historian, troubled reader of Darwin, Mill and Schopenhauer) in no way compromise coherence. Story is central to Hardy and plot is mimetic of his metaphysic. Ideas are subservient to 'the continual dialectic of feeling that is operative between the narrator and his narrative' – in other words, the teller is as vital as the tale and becomes part of the imaginative act, feeling his way with characters and readers. 'A series of seemings', Hardy's phrase for his novels, is shown to imply 'a seeking for a truth whose form is always provisional, whose dynamic is the tension between the story-teller and the sage, the author and the reader'. Narrative rhythm therefore becomes 'a provisional design flung across the vacancy of experience', a conclusion fortified by Hardy's preference for plurality of ending. Hardy's sense of form resides in process, the weaving of the cumulative web, and the novels as a whole reveal a 'coherent imaginative journey' culminating in the deeper psychic resonances and ambiguities of the modern novel. Lawrence is invoked as a touchstone and shown as the dynamic heir to Hardy's psychic process and as an exponent of techniques not available to his antecedent: 'Where *Jude* ends *The Rainbow* begins.' Gregor's rigorous, mature textual analysis is meticulously true to Hardy.

'Criticism should open more books than it closes': George Steiner's unexceptionable criterion can be applied to strike off a summary roll-call of general studies not already described but which are surely 'book-openers' and deserve more attention than space allows. Both Arthur McDowall (whose 1931 book is perhaps the most intelligent early study) and David Cecil (1943) are superbly responsive to Hardy's poetic texture: their classically informed and original analyses, deceptively simple, are amateur in the root sense of the word. Desmond Hawkins's lively study of the novels (1950), blessedly free of 'apparatus', is now fleshed out into an even livelier one treating life and poems as well (1976); it includes a useful check-list of dramatizations of Hardy's works. Irving Howe (1967) is sensitive to Hardy's interior landscape. Like Howe's, two shorter books belong to established series. Trevor Johnson (1968) eschews critical jargon and applies colloquial enthusiasm with good effect to Hardy's life and works. George Wing (1963) is author of the best brief study. Condensed criticism of the stories and poems is supplemented by ingenious division of the novels into 'outers', 'inners' and 'bulls' – the very proper implication being that they are all on target. There is more value in Wing's intensive study than in many books twice the length. J. I. M. Stewart (1971) offers a generous, methodical, relaxed and acute assessment. The best recent survey is undoubtedly Michael Millgate's (1971), the only study to incorporate much original research and unique in giving a truly balanced view of Hardy's development by devoting coextensive space to the lesser novels. Chapters on individual novels are interspersed with more general analyses of germane issues (e.g. 'The Uses of a Regional Past', 'Hardy's Laodiceanism: Politics and Ideas'). It is an excellent distillation of Hardy's fiction-writing career. Two distinguished studies have just appeared, each taking in Hardy's prose and poetry: John Bayley's *An Essay on Hardy* (1978), an urbane and sometimes delicately radical reappraisal, and F. B. Pinion's *Thomas Hardy: Art and Thought* (1977), a gathering of discrete and stimulating essays by one of Hardy's most respected critics.

There are various collections of critical essays, including those edited by A. J. Guerard (1963), Donald Davie (1972), R. P. Draper (1975) and Margaret Drabble (1976). Guerard and Draper collect some standard essays, the latter also drawing on more recent material. Davie's special issue of *Agenda* has some very good new essays (notably Thom Gunn on 'Hardy and the Ballads', Henry Gifford on revisions and Davie himself on Virgilian influences). F. R. Southerington's defence of Lois Deacon is rather cranky. Miss Deacon herself contributes to Drabble's uneven collection, in which the critical contributions (with one or two honourable exceptions) are much the best. The excellent Thomas Hardy Society, deservedly reputed for its summer schools and other activities, has now ventured into publication with two stimulating collections of essays (1974 and 1976), and a further collocation (of lectures delivered at the 1978 academic summer school) is expected shortly. These, and *The Thomas Hardy Society Review* (annual, 1975–), the first regular journal seriously devoted to 'informed critical views and inquiry', appear under the very capable editorship of F. B. Pinion.

'By the will of God some men are born poetical' (*Life*, 385): Hardy was of their number, a poet by instinct and the practice of sixty-three years, yet even now his poetry has received a dismally small portion of the critical attention afforded his work as a whole. F. R. Leavis, in *New*

Bearings in English Poetry (1932), generated the myth that Hardy's 'rank as a major poet rests upon a dozen poems'. Though this assertive hyperbole is the sheerest nonsense the notion has taken hold. Even critical admirers of his poetry sometimes fasten upon it: Hynes (1961), for example, expounds the view that Hardy has a 'severely limited range of tone and ideas' and that over 900 poems are 'monotonous'. Such Laodiceanism is rightly swept aside by the acute critical intelligence of T. R. M. Creighton (1974): 'The slightest or oddest poem he wrote has the power over language, intensity of apprehension, acuteness of observation and distinction of imagination of the greatest, and could only have been written by a great and true poet.' I urgently endorse both this and Philip Larkin's stirring call (*CQ*, VIII, 1966): 'May I trumpet the assurance that one reader at least would not wish Hardy's *Collected Poems* a single page shorter, and regards it as many times over the best body of poetic work this century so far has to show?'

Measured against these bracing assessments, Hardy's contemporary critics were extraordinarily imperceptive: 'Curious and wearisome . . . slovenly, slipshod, uncouth verses, stilted in sentiment, poorly conceived and worse wrought'[17] was a typical judgement. Many critics admonished Hardy on the grounds of its being 'a dubious experiment for a proseman to sit in the Siege Perilous of poetry',[18] regarding his venture as a novelist's capricious diversion. Hardy was incensed by 'the short-sighted belittlement of [his] art by these minor men' and remarked that 'had the criticasters . . . been minds of any great power in judgement, they would have perceived that there might be an obvious trap for their intelligence in his order of publication' (*Life* [299] original typescript, DCM). Even Pound's famous 1937 remark on Hardy's poems – 'Now *there* is clarity. There *is* the harvest of having written 20 novels first' – is, though right in essence, wrong in chronology since Hardy had regularly written poems since 1865, a fact obscured by the accident of their publication only from 1898.

We are not concerned here with the gradual, grudging recognition of Hardy's poetic genius, but the turning-point came only with the 1940 *Southern Review* special issue on the centenary of Hardy's birth, including distinguished essays on the poetry by W. H. Auden, R. P. Blackmur, John Crowe Ransom, Delmore Schwartz and Allen Tate. Auden's moving testimonial to Hardy as his own archetype of the Poetic is one of the first of many to acknowledge Hardy's major influence on twentieth-

century poetry. Donald Davie slightly botched this promising theme in
Thomas Hardy and British Poetry (1972). Excellent stylistic analyses of the
tension between the 'imperious verbal engineer' and the poet of
'cunning irregularity' (Hardy's phrase) are succeeded by identification
of a Hardy tradition – assigning more influence to Hardy than to Yeats
or Eliot. Scientific humanism is its theme and Larkin (the purest disciple),
Lawrence, Tomlinson, Auden, Betjeman, Amis are amongst those
picked out as followers. So far so good, but it is reductive to define
Hardy's poetry solely in terms of modern humanism, and other poets
who might be enrolled into a Hardy tradition – Gunn or Heaney? – are
mysteriously ignored. (One confessed disciple, C. Day Lewis, has
written the best short introduction to 'The Lyrical Poetry' (1951, repr.
1965).) One of Davie's *données*, the aesthetic interrelationship of 'Poetry
and Belief' in Hardy, is investigated discerningly in Delmore Schwartz's
1940 essay, which concludes that any genuine poetic criterion for
enjoying Hardy's poetry requires us not to violate each poem as a
concrete whole, and to do this 'it is necessary that we keep Hardy's
beliefs *in* his poetry, and our own beliefs outside'. The dangers of doing
otherwise are only too evident in J. G. Southworth's *The Poetry of
Thomas Hardy* (1947), so damning in its faintness of praise that a Leavisite
vision of occasional genius vitiated by general feebleness, and of Hardy's
inability to reach the standards set by the great Victorians, is about all
that emerges from this ideologically unsympathetic reading.

Samuel Hynes also sees Hardy as an 'artist involved with questions of
meaning and belief' but, in *The Pattern of Hardy's Poetry* (1961), his
emphasis is upon the basic antinomial structure of the poems. That the
poetry is ordered by thesis and antithesis, 'the eternal conflict between
irreconcilables', is persuasively argued, and the study yields admirable
analyses of diction and (especially) imagery. The treatment is ultimately
too schematic and Hynes's unwillingness to endorse Hardy's greatness
means that his subject emerges rather the worse for wear. Kenneth
Marsden's *The Poems of Thomas Hardy: A Critical Introduction* (1969)
proposes no profound thesis but renders an urbane and (Callooh!
Callay!) *enthusiastic* account of the poetry, its techniques, ideas,
influences and tone. In this sane survey Marsden implies that some
modern predilections (*avant-garde* structural ideas and Eliot's impersonality theory, for example) have reduced even many proponents
of Hardy's poetry to the status of fainthearts.

Two more recent studies are also unequivocally on the side of Hardy. The categoric organization of Paul Zietlow's *Moments of Vision: The Poetry of Thomas Hardy* (1974) allows poems to be excitingly juxtaposed and generic groups to be rewardingly isolated for discussion. Two revaluative judgements may be mentioned. Zietlow's view that Hardy's championship of the superiority of poetry was not a 'consistently held conviction' but a self-justifying, negative espousal of a form that 'permitted freer revelations in the guise of greater concealment' is surely wrong: he did see poetry as a more flexible mode of expression, and he had an innate impulse to concealment, but he was a poet by nature and not circumstance. On the other hand, Zietlow's stress on the positive quality of the poetry and its 'muted' optimism, set against the general ingrained conviction of Hardy's thoroughgoing pessimism, is entirely convincing. Tom Paulin's *Thomas Hardy: The Poetry of Perception* (1975) is the best critical reading yet to appear. The aesthetic of 'perception' – involving a 'stress on sight and the numerous issues implicit in it' – is more a principle of organization than a determined hobby-horse. Epistemological influences and problems are indeed elucidated but it is for the many fine, original analyses directed by Paulin's eclectic critical intelligence that this study deserves acclaim.

An outstanding critical edition of the poetry is T. R. M. Creighton (ed.) *Poems of Thomas Hardy: A New Selection* (1974). There could be no better point of embarkation, for readers old or new, than this anthology of nearly 300 poems. Creighton organizes the poems into sections, 'to allow Hardy's art to reveal itself by reducing its bulk and defining its main kinds and preoccupations', drawing upon Hardy's own tentative classifications: the effect of such groupings is very stimulating as new perceptions get jogged into the mind. Individual poems are thoroughly annotated. Creighton is Hardy's ideal apologist; his general and sectional introductions constitute a brilliantly concise account of the nature of Hardy's poetic art and thought. Valuable analyses of the poetry may also be found in the books by A. McDowall (1931), Douglas Brown (1954, rev. ed. 1961) and A. J. Guerard (rev. ed. 1964), whose title, 'The Illusion of Simplicity', is itself a rebuke to those who stress Hardy's limitations. Jean Brooks (1971) is as outstanding on the poems as on the novels and J. Hillis Miller (1970) illuminates many poems as he expounds his ingenious thesis. J. O. Bailey's *Handbook* (1970) is discussed earlier.

Hardy's longest poem, *The Dynasts*, is 'among the great eccentric works of our time' (Hynes). It is hard to endorse the view of Barrie and others that Hardy's whole life was spent in preparation for this 'great event', but the ambitious span of this vast epic-drama, often compared to *The Iliad* and *War and Peace*, and its *avant-garde* form, is clearly remarkable. Whether many people read it may be another matter. Its resilience against generic definition has not deterred the publication of some distinctive criticism in the last twenty years. Three major complementary studies have appeared. J. O. Bailey's main concern in *Thomas Hardy and the Cosmic Mind* (1956) is to examine the Spirits in the context of Von Hartmann ('influence' is not proven) and the nature of evolutionary meliorism implicit in the outcome. It includes a scholarly reappraisal of the Immanent Will. Harold Orel's *Thomas Hardy's Epic-Drama: A Study of 'The Dynasts'* (1963) shows how, like earlier epics, it is 'a poem of sublime aspect' (owing much to Burke's aesthetics – 'the disorder of these diverse materials is, and was to Hardy, *magnificent* in Burke's sense'). He invokes *Paradise Lost* as a touchstone to show how the work is 'a frank divergence from classical and other dramatic precedent'. and *The Iliad* against which to measure Hardy's horrified view of war. Walter F. Wright's *The Shaping of 'The Dynasts'* (1967) is a thorough and scholarly record of the genesis, intentional *ambience*, and composition of the work. These three works explicate many of the problems inherent in what Hardy calls this 'modern expression of a modern outlook'.

As a final judgement on the poetry, and those who deny its stature, I return to T. R. M. Creighton, since his is the only view that will do: '"Greatness" is a quality much easier to withhold than to define. It is hard to see how poetry which communicates intense and varied emotion with supreme articulacy can be anything but very great.'

In venturing a swath through the maze of professional criticism this essay has revealed generations of Hardy critics on their progress from moral stricture and classical apotheosis, via philosophical postulation and agrarian history, to psychic analysis and once again the text itself. The Protean Hardy has led us a merry dance. The poet-novelist stubbornly resists the conventional moulds and the geometric rule of easy definition. We have heard too much about his thought and of Dorset originals, too little about his style or his poetry. Other *lacunae* insistently declare themselves: the short stories, the lesser novels, his humour. But the cumulus of criticism is so immense that at the end of such a survey we need to reassert proportion and remember the man and his work at the apex of the pyramid, a Middle Eastern metaphor that may recall to us Hardy's own metaphor for criticism. If it is not exactly writing in the sand it is certainly shot through with impermanence by the side of the work itself. Criticism is a craft that implies a challenging humility. To speak of the elusive Hardy is at last ineligible, the distraught cry of the sand castle maker: Hardy declares himself on every page. Critics may and should enhance appreciation and understanding of his art, but he needs no interpreter. At the beginning and in the end, there is only one experience of remarkable reward: with the imperative urgency of Pound's exhortation for Eliot – READ HIM!

NOTES

1. Preface to *Select Poems of William Barnes*, ed. T. Hardy, 1908; reprinted in *Thomas Hardy's Personal Writings*, ed. H. Orel, Kansas, 1966, 81.
2. R. Graves, *Goodbye to All That*, 1960, 250.
3. *CQ*, XV, 1973, 101–2.
4. V. Woolf, *Collected Essays*, ed. Leonard Woolf, 1966, I, 258.
5. W. L. Phelps, *Autobiography with Letters*, 1939, 391.
6. See *TLS*, 4 July 1975 (R. L. Purdy), 25 July 1975 (H. Bliss).
7. W. Blunt, *Cockerell*, 1964, 223n.
8. A small 1865 notebook, 'Studies, Specimens &c', is privately owned by R. L. Purdy.
9. G. Tillotson, 'The English Scholars get their Teeth into Dickens', *Sewanee Review*, LXXV, 1967, 332.
10. 'Thomas Hardy', *The Speaker*, II, 1890, 295; Cox, 168.
11. 'The Novels of Thomas Hardy', *Quarterly Review*, CXCIX, 1904, 523; Cox, 365.
12. W. L. Phelps, *Essays on Modern Novelists*, 1910; Cox, 403.
13. C. J. Weber, *Hardy of Wessex*, 1965, 246–7. For an account of the influence of Darwin on Hardy, see Lionel Stevenson, *Darwin among the Poets*, 1932, and Roger Robinson's essay in the present collection.
14. G. K. Chesterton, *The Victorian Age in Literature*, 1913, 143.
15. A. J. Guerard, *Thomas Hardy: The Novels and Stories*, Cambridge, Mass., 1964, 6.
16. S. Chew, *Thomas Hardy: Poet and Novelist*, 1921, 141; Hardy's copy in DCM.
17. *Saturday Review*, LXXXVII, 1899, 19; Cox, 319.
18. *The Academy*, LVI, 1899, 43; Cox, 322.

Thomas Hardy:
A Select Bibliography

RICHARD H. TAYLOR

Note

Place of publication is London unless otherwise stated. The following
abbreviations have been used:

CQ	*Critical Quarterly*
EC	*Essays in Criticism*
ELH	*Essays in Literary History*
ELT	*English Literature in Transition*
MFS	*Modern Fiction Studies*
NCF	*Nineteenth Century Fiction*
PMLA	*Publications of the Modern Language Association of America*
PQ	*Philological Quarterly*
RES	*Review of English Studies*
SR	*Southern Review*
SP	*Studies in Philology*
THSR	*Thomas Hardy Society Review*
VP	*Victorian Poetry*
VS	*Victorian Studies*

Essays reprinted in the anthologies edited by A. J. Guerard or R. P.
Draper are indicated by [G] or [D] after the entry.

Titles of novels and short story volumes are abbreviated as follows:
*AL (A Laodicean), CM (A Changed Man), DR (Desperate Remedies),
FFMC (Far from the Madding Crowd), GND (A Group of Noble Dames),
HE (The Hand of Ethelberta), Jude (Jude the Obscure), LLI (Life's Little
Ironies), MC (The Mayor of Casterbridge), PBE (A Pair of Blue Eyes),
RN (The Return of the Native), Tess (Tess of the d'Urbervilles),*

TM (The Trumpet-Major), TT (Two on a Tower), UGT (Under the Greenwood Tree), The W (The Woodlanders), WB (The Well-Beloved), WT (Wessex Tales).

1. COLLECTED EDITIONS AND TEXTUAL STUDIES

(a) *Collected Editions*
The Wessex Novels, 16 vols. 1895–6.
The Wessex Edition, 24 vols. 1912–31.
The New Wessex Edition, ed. P. N. Furbank, 22 vols. 1974–8 [includes novels, short stories, poetry and *The Dynasts*].
The Macmillan Students' Hardy, ed. James Gibson, 10 vols. 1975.
Collected Poems, 1919, 1923, 1928, 1930.
The Complete Poems, ed. James Gibson, 1976.
[*Uncollected*:
An Indiscretion in the Life of an Heiress, privately printed by Florence Hardy, 1934; ed. Carl J. Weber, Baltimore 1935; ed. Terry Coleman 1976.
Our Exploits at West Poley, intro. R. L. Purdy, Oxford 1952.]

(b) *Textual Studies*
[See also section 6. 'Studies of Specific Works'. Essential reading for textual study includes R. L. Purdy (under 'Bibliographies') and J. O. Bailey (under 'Handbooks').]

Beach, J. W., 'Bowdlerized Versions of Hardy', *PMLA* 37, 1921.
Chase, Mary Ellen, *Thomas Hardy from Serial to Novel*, Minneapolis 1927.
Schweik, Robert C., 'Current Problems in Textual Scholarship on the Works of Thomas Hardy', *ELT* 14, 1971.

2. BIBLIOGRAPHIES AND HANDBOOKS

(a) *Bibliographies*
Beebe, Maurice, Bonnie Culotta and Erin Marcus, 'Criticism of Thomas Hardy: A Selected Checklist', *MFS* 6, 1960.
Carter, Kenneth, and June M. Whetherly (eds.) *Thomas Hardy Catalogue: A List of the Books By and About Thomas Hardy . . . in Dorset County Library*, Dorchester 1968; rev. edn. 1973.

Fayen, George S., Jr., 'Thomas Hardy' in *Victorian Fiction: A Guide to Research*, ed. Lionel Stevenson, Cambridge, Mass., 1964. [Forthcoming: revised essay by Michael Millgate in new edn., ed. George H. Ford.]

Gerber, Helmut E., and W. Eugene Davis (eds.)*Thomas Hardy: An Annotated Bibliography of Writings About Him*, DeKalb, Illinois, 1973.

Purdy, Richard Little, *Thomas Hardy: A Bibliographical Study*, Oxford 1954.

Stevenson, Lionel, 'Thomas Hardy' in *The Victorian Poets: A Guide to Research*, ed. F. E. Faverty, Cambridge, Mass., 1956; rev. ed. 1968.

Weber, Carl J., *The First Hundred Years of Thomas Hardy, 1840–1940: A Centenary Bibliography of Hardiana*, Waterville, Maine, 1942.

(b) *Handbooks*

Bailey, J. O., *The Poetry of Thomas Hardy: A Handbook and Commentary*, Chapel Hill 1970.

Kay-Robinson, Denys, *Hardy's Wessex Reappraised*, New York 1971, Newton Abbot 1972.

Lea, Hermann, *Thomas Hardy's Wessex*, 1913.

Leeming, Glenda, *Who's Who in Thomas Hardy?*, 1975.

Pinion, F. B., *A Hardy Companion*, 1968; rev. ed. 1974.

Saxelby, F. Outwin, *A Thomas Hardy Dictionary*, 1911.

3. BIOGRAPHY, LETTERS AND NOTEBOOKS

(a) *Biography*

Blunden, Edmund, *Thomas Hardy*, 1942.

Collins, Vere H., *Talks with Thomas Hardy at Max Gate 1920–1922*, 1928.

Cox, J. S. (ed.) *Thomas Hardy: Materials for a Study of his Life, Times and Works*, St. Peter Port, Guernsey, Vol. I 1968, II 1971 [monographs bound together].

Deacon, Lois, and Terry Coleman, *Providence and Mr. Hardy*, 1966 [to be read only in conjunction with the next entry].

Gittings, Robert, *Young Thomas Hardy*, 1975.

——, *The Older Hardy*, 1978.

Hardy, Emma Lavinia, *Some Recollections* [1911], ed. Evelyn Hardy and Robert Gittings, Oxford 1961.

Hardy, Evelyn, *Thomas Hardy: A Critical Biography*, 1954.

Hardy, Florence Emily, *The Life of Thomas Hardy, 1840–1928*, 1962 [combines *The Early Life of Thomas Hardy, 1840–1891*, 1928, and *The Later Years of Thomas Hardy, 1892–1928*, 1930]. Cf. Purdy (above), pp. 262–73, and Richard H. Taylor, 'Hardy's Disguised Autobiography', *THSR* 4, 1978.

Orel, Harold, *The Final Years of Thomas Hardy*, 1976.

O'Sullivan, Timothy, *Thomas Hardy: An Illustrated Biography*, 1975.

Phelps, Kenneth, *The Wormwood Cup: Thomas Hardy in Cornwall*, Padstow 1975.

Rutland, William R., *Thomas Hardy*, Oxford 1938.

Weber, Carl J., *Hardy of Wessex: His Life and Literary Career*, New York 1940; rev. ed. 1965.

——, *Hardy and the Lady from Madison Square*, Waterville, Maine, 1942. [Forthcoming: a definitive biography by Michael Millgate.]

(b) *Letters*

Hardy, Evelyn, and F. B. Pinion (eds.) *One Rare Fair Woman: Thomas Hardy's Letters to Florence Henniker, 1893–1922*, 1972.

Purdy, R. L., and Michael Millgate (eds.) *The Collected Letters of Thomas Hardy*, Vol. I (1840–1892), 1978.

Weber, Carl J. (ed.) *The Letters of Thomas Hardy*, Waterville, Maine, 1954.

—— (ed.) *'Dearest Emmie': Thomas Hardy's Letters to his First Wife*, 1963. [Some of Hardy's early letters to his publishers are quoted in Charles Morgan, *The House of Macmillan*, 1943, and a calendar of correspondence between Hardy and Tinsley, his first publisher, is given in Purdy, *op. cit.*]

(c) *Notebooks and Uncollected Writings*

Björk, Lennart A. (ed.) *The Literary Notes of Thomas Hardy*, Vol. I, Göteborg 1974.

Beatty, C. J. P. (ed.) *The Architectural Notebook of Thomas Hardy*, Dorchester 1966.

Hardy, Evelyn (ed.) *Thomas Hardy's Notebooks and Some Letters from Julia Augusta Martin*, 1955.

Orel, Harold (ed.) *Thomas Hardy's Personal Writings*, Lawrence, Kansas, 1966.

Taylor, Richard H. (ed.) *The Personal Notebooks of Thomas Hardy*, 1978, New York 1979 [also includes unpublished passages from the *Life* typescripts].

4. CRITICAL STUDIES OF THE NOVELS AND STORIES

(a) *Book-length Studies*

Abercrombie, Lascelles, *Thomas Hardy: A Critical Study*, 1912.

Bayley, John, *An Essay on Hardy*, 1978.

Beach, Joseph Warren, *The Technique of Thomas Hardy*, Chicago 1922.

Blunden, Edmund, *Thomas Hardy*, 1942.

Brennecke, Ernest, Jr., *Thomas Hardy's Universe*, Boston 1924.

Brooks, Jean, *Thomas Hardy: The Poetic Structure*, 1971.

Brown, Douglas, *Thomas Hardy*, 1954; rev. ed. 1961.

Butler, Lance St. John (ed.) *Thomas Hardy After Fifty Years*, 1977.

Carpenter, Richard, *Thomas Hardy*, New York 1964, London 1976.

Cecil, Lord David, *Hardy the Novelist*, 1943.

Cox, J. S. and G. S. (eds.) *Thomas Hardy Year Book*, 1970–.

Cox, R. G. (ed.) *Thomas Hardy: The Critical Heritage*, 1970.

Davie, Donald (ed.) *Agenda: Thomas Hardy Special Issue*, 1972.

Drabble, Margaret (ed.) *The Genius of Thomas Hardy*, 1976.

Draper, R. P. (ed.) *Thomas Hardy: The Tragic Novels*, 1975.

Duffin, Henry C., *Thomas Hardy: A Study of the Wessex Novels*, Manchester 1916; 3rd rev. ed., 1937, adds *The Poems*, and *The Dynasts*.

Firor, Ruth A., *Folkways in Thomas Hardy*, Philadelphia 1931.

Gregor, Ian, *The Great Web: The Form of Hardy's Major Fiction*, 1974.

Guerard, Albert J., *Thomas Hardy: The Novels and Stories*, Cambridge, Mass., 1949; rev. ed., Norfolk, Conn., 1964, includes chapter on the poetry.

—— (ed.) *Hardy: A Collection of Critical Essays*, Englewood Cliffs, N.J., 1963.

Hawkins, Desmond, *Hardy the Novelist*, 1950.

——, *Hardy: Novelist and Poet*, Newton Abbot 1976.

Hornback, Bert G., *The Metaphor of Chance: Vision and Technique in the Works of Thomas Hardy*, Athens, Ohio, 1971.

Howe, Irving, *Thomas Hardy*, New York 1967.

Johnson, Lionel, *The Art of Thomas Hardy*, New York 1894; rev. ed. 1923.

Johnson, Trevor, *Thomas Hardy*, 1968.

Kramer, Dale, *Thomas Hardy: The Forms of Tragedy*, Detroit 1975.

McDowall, Arthur, *Thomas Hardy: A Critical Study*, 1931.

Meisel, Perry, *Thomas Hardy: The Return of the Repressed*, New Haven 1972.

Miller, J. Hillis, *Thomas Hardy: Distance and Desire*, Cambridge, Mass., 1970.

Millgate, Michael H., *Thomas Hardy: His Career as a Novelist*, 1971.

Morrell, Roy, *Thomas Hardy: The Will and the Way*, Kuala Lumpur 1965.

Page, Norman, *Thomas Hardy*, 1977.

Pinion, F. B., *Thomas Hardy: Art and Thought*, 1977.

—— (ed.) *Thomas Hardy and the Modern World*, Dorchester 1974.

—— (ed.) *Budmouth Essays on Thomas Hardy*, Dorchester 1976.

—— (ed.) *The Thomas Hardy Society Review*, 1975–.

Rutland, William R., *Thomas Hardy: A Study of His Writings and Their Background*, Oxford 1938.

Stewart, J. I. M., *Thomas Hardy: A Critical Biography*, 1971.

Thurley, Geoffrey, *The Psychology of Hardy's Novels: The Nervous and the Statuesque*, 1975.

Vigar, Penelope, *The Novels of Thomas Hardy: Illusion and Reality*, 1974.

Weber, Carl J., *Hardy in America: A Study of Thomas Hardy and his American Readers*, Waterville, Maine, 1946.

Webster, Harvey Curtis, *On a Darkling Plain: The Art and Thought of Thomas Hardy*, Chicago 1947.

White, R. J., *Thomas Hardy and History*, 1974.

Williams, Merryn, *Thomas Hardy and Rural England*, 1972.

Wing, George, *Thomas Hardy*, Edinburgh and London, 1963.

(b) *Articles, Essays and Parts of Books*

Bailey, J. O., 'Hardy's "Mephistophelian Visitants"', *PMLA* 61, 1946.

——, 'Hardy's Visions of the Self', *SP* 56, 1959.

——, 'Hardy and the Modern World' in *Thomas Hardy and the Modern World*, ed. F. B. Pinion, Dorchester 1974.

Barzun, Jacques, 'Truth and Poetry in Thomas Hardy', *SR* 6, 1940.

Beckman, Richard, 'A Character Typology for Hardy's Novels', *ELH* 30, 1963.

Carpenter, Richard C., 'Hardy's Gurgoyles', *MFS* 6, 1960.

Chapman, Frank, 'Revaluations, IV: Hardy the Novelist', *Scrutiny* 3, 1934.

Davidson, Donald, 'The Traditional Basis of Hardy's Fiction', *SR* 6, 1940 [G].

DeLaura, David J., ' "The ache of modernism" in Hardy's Later Novels', *ELH* 34, 1967.

Eagleton, Terry, 'Thomas Hardy: Nature as Language', *CQ* 13, 1971.

Eliot, T. S., in *After Strange Gods*, 1934.

Friedman, Alan, 'Hardy: Weddings be Funerals' in *The Turn of the Novel*, 1966.

Gregor, Ian, 'What kind of Fiction did Hardy write?', *EC* 16, 1966.

Hardy, Barbara, in *The Appropriate Form*, 1964.

Holloway, John, in *The Victorian Sage*, 1953.

——, 'Hardy's Major Fiction' in *From Jane Austen to Joseph Conrad*, ed. R. Rathburn and M. Steinmann, Jr., Minneapolis 1959.

Huss, Roy, 'Social Change and Moral Decay in the Novels of Thomas Hardy', *Dalhousie Review* 47, 1967.

Hyde, W. J., 'Hardy's View of Realism: A Key to the Rustic Characters', *VS* 2, 1958.

Larkin, Philip, 'Wanted: Good Hardy Critic', *CQ* 8, 1966.

Lawrence, D. H., 'Study of Thomas Hardy' in *Phoenix: The Posthumous Papers of D. H. Lawrence*, ed. Edward D. McDonald, 1936.

Murry, John Middleton, 'Thomas Hardy' in *Katherine Mansfield and Other Literary Portraits*, 1949.

Newton, William, 'Chance as employed by Hardy and the Naturalists', *PQ* 30, 1951.

Page, Norman, 'Hardy's Short Stories: A Reconsideration', *Studies in Short Fiction* XI, 1974.

Pinion, F. B., 'Chance, Choice, and Charity: Hardy and the Future of Civilisation' in *Thomas Hardy and the Modern World*, ed. F. B. Pinion, Dorchester 1974.

Porter, Katharine Anne, 'Notes on a Criticism of Thomas Hardy', *SR* 6, 1940.

Salter, C. H., 'Hardy's "Pedantry" ', *NCF* 28, 1973.

Sankey, Benjamin, 'Hardy's Plotting' and 'Hardy's Prose Style', *Twentieth Century Literature* 11, 1965.

Scott, James F., 'Thomas Hardy's use of the Gothic: An Examination of Five Representative Works', *NCF* 17, 1962.

Scott-James, R. A., and C. Day Lewis, *Thomas Hardy* (British Council pamphlet), 1951; rev. ed. (incl. Day Lewis) 1965.

Smart, Alistair, 'Pictorial Imagery in the Novels of Thomas Hardy', *RES*, n.s. 12, 1961.

Spivey, Ted R., 'Thomas Hardy's Tragic Hero', *NCF* 9, 1954.

Starzyk, Lawrence J., 'The Coming Universal Wish not to Live in Hardy's "Modern" Novels', *NCF* 26, 1972.

Toliver, Harold E., 'The Dance Under the Greenwood Tree: Hardy's Bucolics', *NCF* 17, 1962.

Williams, Raymond, 'Thomas Hardy', *CQ* 6, 1964 [D].

Woolf, Virginia, 'Novels of Thomas Hardy' in *The Second Common Reader*, 1932; repr. in *Collected Essays*, ed. Leonard Woolf, 1966.

Yuill, W. E., '"Character is Fate": a note on Thomas Hardy, George Eliot and Novalis', *Modern Language Review* 57, 1962.

Zabel, Morton Dauwen, 'Hardy in Defence of his Art: The Aesthetic of Incongruity', *SR* 6, 1940 [G].

5. CRITICAL STUDIES OF THE POETRY

Auden, W. H., 'A Literary Transference', *SR* 6, 1940 [G].

Bailey, J. O., 'Evolutionary Meliorism in the Poetry of Hardy', *SP* 60, 1963.

——, *The Poetry of Thomas Hardy: A Handbook and Commentary*, Chapel Hill 1970.

Bartlett, Phyllis, 'Hardy's Shelley', *Keats–Shelley Journal* 4, 1955.

Blackmur, R. P., 'The Shorter Poems of Thomas Hardy', *SR* 6, 1940.

Bowra, C. M., *The Lyrical Poetry of Thomas Hardy*, Nottingham 1947; repr. in *Inspiration and Poetry*, 1955.

Brooks, Jean R., *Thomas Hardy: The Poetic Structure*, 1971.

Brown, Douglas, in *Thomas Hardy*, 1954; rev. edn. 1961.

Casagrande, Peter J., 'Hardy's Wordsworth: A Record and a Commentary', *ELT* 20, 1977.

Creighton, T. R. M. (ed.) *Poems of Thomas Hardy: A New Selection*, with Introduction and Notes, 1974.

Daiches, David, in *Poetry and the Modern World*, 1940.

Davie, Donald, *Thomas Hardy and British Poetry*, 1972.

——, 'Hardy's Virgilian Purples', *Agenda* 10, 1972.

Gibson, James, 'The Poetic Text' in *Thomas Hardy and the Modern World*, ed. F. B. Pinion, Dorchester 1974.

Gunn, Thom, 'Hardy and the Ballads', *Agenda* 10, 1972.

Hickson, E. C., *The Versification of Thomas Hardy*, Philadelphia 1931.

Hornback, Bert G., 'Thomas Hardy: The Poet in Search of his Voice', *VP* 12, 1974.

Hynes, Samuel, *The Pattern of Hardy's Poetry*, Chapel Hill 1961.

Lewis, C. Day, 'The Lyrical Poetry of Thomas Hardy', *Proceedings of the British Academy* 37, 1951; also in *Thomas Hardy* (British Council pamphlet), rev. edn. 1965.

Leavis, F. R., 'Hardy the Poet', *SR* 6, 1940.

Marsden, Kenneth, *The Poems of Thomas Hardy: A Critical Introduction*, 1969.

Morgan, William W., 'Form, Tradition, and Consolation in Hardy's "Poems of 1912–13"', *PMLA* 89, 1974.

Paulin, Tom, *Thomas Hardy: The Poetry of Perception*, 1975.

Perkins, David, 'Hardy and the Poetry of Isolation', *ELH* 26, 1959 [G].

Pinion, F. B., *A Commentary on the Poems of Thomas Hardy*, 1976.

Quinn, Marie A., 'The Personal Past in the Poetry of Thomas Hardy and Edward Thomas', *CQ* 16, 1974.

Ransom, John Crowe, 'Honey and Gall', *SR* 6, 1940.

———, 'Thomas Hardy's Poems, and the Religious Difficulties of a Naturalist', *Kenyon Review* 22, 1960.

Salter, C. H., 'Unusual Words beginning with *un*, *en*, *out*, *up* and *on* in Thomas Hardy's Verse', *VP* 11, 1973.

Schwartz, Delmore, 'Poetry and Belief in Thomas Hardy, *SR* 6, 1940 [G].

Siemens, Lloyd, 'Parody in the Poems of Thomas Hardy', *Dalhousie Review* 52, 1972.

Stevenson, Lionel, 'Thomas Hardy' in *The Victorian Poets: A Guide to Research*, ed. F. E. Daverty, Cambridge, Mass., 1956; rev. edn. 1968.

Tate, Allen, 'Hardy's Philosophic Metaphors', *SR* 6, 1940.

Taylor, E. Dennis, 'The Riddle of Hardy's Poetry', *VP* 11, 1973.

Zietlow, Paul, *Moments of Vision: The Poetry of Thomas Hardy*, Cambridge, Mass., 1974.

6. STUDIES OF SPECIFIC WORKS

[Arranged alphabetically with a section on lesser novels at the end. This listing does not include detailed readings of specific works in studies already mentioned.]

The Dynasts

Bailey, J. O., *Thomas Hardy and the Cosmic Mind*, Chapel Hill 1956.

Baker, Donald, 'Thomas Hardy: Prophet of Total Theatre', *Comparative Drama* 7, 1973.

Chakravarty, Amiya C., *The Dynasts and the Post-War Age in Poetry*, 1938.

Clifford, Emma, '*War and Peace* and *The Dynasts*', *Modern Philology* 56, 1956.

——, '"The Trumpet-Major Notebook" and *The Dynasts*', *RES*, n.s. 13, 1957.

——, 'Thomas Hardy and the Historians', *SP* 56, 1959.

Dobrée, Bonamy, '*The Dynasts*', *SR* 6, 1940.

Garrison, Chester A., *The Vast Venture: Hardy's Epic-Drama The Dynasts*, Salzburg 1973.

Horsman, E. A., 'The Language of *The Dynasts*', *Durham University Journal* 41, 1949.

Laird, John, 'Hardy's *The Dynasts*' in *Philosophical Incursions into English Literature*, 1946.

Orel, Harold, *Thomas Hardy's Epic-Drama*, Lawrence, Kansas, 1963.

Wright, Walter F., *The Shaping of The Dynasts*, Lincoln, Nebraska, 1967.

Far from the Madding Crowd
Babb, Howard, 'Setting and Theme in *FFMC*', *ELH* 30, 1963.

Carpenter, Richard C., 'The Mirror and the Sword: Imagery in *FFMC*', *NCF* 18, 1964.

May, Charles E., '*FFMC* and *The W*: Hardy's Grotesque Pastorals', *ELT* 17, 1974.

Pettit, Charles, 'Narrative techniques in *FFMC*', *THSR* 1, 1975.

Schweik, Robert C., 'A First Draft Chapter of Hardy's *FFMC*', *English Studies* 53, 1972.

Squires, Michael, '*FFMC* as Modified Pastoral', *NCF* 25, 1970.

Sullivan, Tom R., 'The Temporal Leitmotif in *FFMC*', *Colby Library Quarterly* 10, 1974.

Jude the Obscure
Alexander, B. J., 'Thomas Hardy's *Jude*: A Rejection of Traditional Christianity's "Good" God Theory', *Southern Quarterly* 3, 1964.

Burstein, Janet, 'The Journey Beyond Myth in *Jude*', *Texas Studies in Literature and Language* 15, 1973.

Clifford, Emma, 'The Child: The Circus: and *Jude*', *Cambridge Journal* 7, 1954.

Heilman, R. B., 'Hardy's Sue Bridehead', *NCF* 20, 1966.

Holland, Norman, Jr., '*Jude*: Hardy's Symbolic Indictment of Christianity', *NCF* 9, 1954.

Hoopes, Kathleen R., 'Illusion and Reality in *Jude*', *NCF* 12, 1957.

Hyde, William J., 'Hardy's Response to the Critics of *Jude*', *Victorian Newsletter* 19, 1961.

——, 'Theoretic and Practical Unconventionality in *Jude*', *NCF* 20, 1965.

McDowell, Frederick P. W., 'Hardy's "Seemings or Personal Impressions": The Symbolical Use of Image and Contrast in *Jude*', *MFS* 6, 1960.

Mizener, Arthur, '*Jude* as a Tragedy', *SR* 6, 1940.

Paterson, John, 'The Genesis of *Jude*' *SP* 57, 1960.

Slack, Robert C., 'The Text of Hardy's *Jude*', *NCF* 11, 1957.

Steig, Michael, 'Sue Bridehead', *Novel* 1 and 2, 1968.

Sutherland, John, 'A Note on the Teasing Narrator in *Jude*', *ELT* 17, 1974.

The Mayor of Casterbridge

Brogan, Howard O., ' "Visible Essences" in *MC*', *ELH* 17, 1950.

Brown, Douglas, *Thomas Hardy: MC*, 1962.

Dike, D. A., 'A Modern Oedipus: *MC*', *EC* 2, 1952.

Heilman, Robert B., 'Hardy's *MC* and the Problem of Intention', *Criticism* 5, 1963.

——, 'Hardy's *MC*: Notes on Style', *NCF* 18, 1963.

Karl, Frederick R., '*MC*: A New Fiction Defined', *MFS* 6, 1960.

Kiely, Robert, 'Vision and Viewpoint in *MC*', *NCF* 23, 1968.

Lerner, Laurence, *Thomas Hardy's MC: Tragedy or Social History?*, Sussex 1975.

Maxwell, J. C., 'The "Sociological" Approach to *MC*' in *Imagined Worlds: Essays . . . in Honour of John Butt*, 1968 [D].

May, Derwent, 'The Novelist as Moralist and the Moralist as Critic', *EC* 10, 1960.

Moynahan, Julian, '*MC* and the Old Testament's First Book of Samuel: A Study of Some Literary Relationships', *PMLA* 71, 1956.

Page, Norman, 'Hardy's Pictorial Art in *MC*', *Etudes Anglaises* 25, 1972.

Paterson, John, 'MC as Tragedy', *VS* 3, 1959 [G].
Schweik, Robert C., 'Character and Fate in Hardy's MC', *NCF* 21, 1966 [D].

The Return of the Native

Bailey, J. O., 'Temperament as Motive in RN', *ELT* 5, 1962.
Benvenuto, Richard, 'RN as a Tragedy in Six Books', *NCF* 26, 1971.
Björk, Lennart A., ' "Visible Essences" as Thematic Structure in Hardy's RN', *English Studies* 53, 1972.
Deen, Leonard W., 'Heroism and Pathos in Hardy's RN', *NCF* 15, 1961 [D].
Eggenschwiler, David, 'Eustacia Vye, Queen of Night and Courtly Pretender', *NCF* 25, 1971.
Evans, Robert, 'The Other Eustacia', *Novel* 1, 1968.
Goldberg, M. A., 'Hardy's Double-Visioned Universe', *EC* 7, 1957.
Hagan, John, 'A Note on the Significance of Diggory Venn', *NCF* 16, 1961.
McCann, E., 'Blind Will or Blind Hero: Philosophy and Myth in Hardy's RN', *Criticism* 3, 1961.
Paterson, John, *The Making of The Return of the Native*, Berkeley 1960.
——, 'RN as an Anti-Christian Document', *NCF* 14, 1959.
——, 'The "Poetics" of RN', *MFS* 6, 1960.
Schweik, Robert C., 'Theme, Character and Perspective in Hardy's RN', *PQ* 41, 1962.
Stallman, Robert W., 'Hardy's Hour-Glass Novel', *Sewanee Review* 55, 1947.
Wheeler, Otis B., 'Four Versions of RN', *NCF* 14, 1959.

Tess of the d'Urbervilles

Brick, Allan, 'Paradise and Consciousness in Hardy's Tess', *NCF* 17, 1963.
Gose, Elliott B., Jr., 'Psychic Evolution: Darwinism and Initiation in Tess', *NCF* 18, 1963.
Gregor, Ian, and Brian Nicholas, 'The Novel as Moral Protest: Tess' in *The Moral and the Story*, 1962.
Griffith, Philip M., 'The Image of the Trapped Animal in Hardy's Tess', *Tulane Studies in English* 13, 1963.

Hildick, Wallace, in *Word for Word: A Study of Author's Alterations*, New York 1965.

Holloway, John, 'Tess and the Awkward Age' in *The Charted Mirror*, 1960.

LaValley, Albert J. (ed.) *20th Century Interpretations of Tess*, Englewood Cliffs, 1969.

Laird, J. T., *The Shaping of Tess of the d'Urbervilles*, 1975.

Lodge, David, 'Tess, Nature and the Voices of Hardy' in *The Language of Fiction*, 1966 [D].

Tanner, Tony, 'Colour and Movement in Hardy's *Tess*', CQ 10, 1968 [D].

Van Ghent, Dorothy, 'On *Tess*' in *The English Novel: Form and Function*, New York 1953 [G].

The Woodlanders

Casagrande, Peter J., 'The Shifted "Centre of Altruism" in *The W*: Hardy's third "Return of a Native"', *ELH* 38, 1971.

Drake, Robert Y., Jr., '*The W* as Traditional Pastoral', *MFS* 6, 1960.

Fayen, George S., Jr., 'Hardy's *The W*: Inwardness and Memory', *Studies in English Literature* I, 1961.

Kramer, Dale, 'Revisions and Vision: Thomas Hardy's *The W*', *Bulletin of the New York Public Library* 75, 1971.

Matchett, William H., '*The W*, or Realism in Sheep's Clothing', *NCF* 9, 1955.

May, Charles E., '*FFMC* and *The W*: Hardy's Grotesque Pastorals', *ELT* 17, 1974.

Steig, Michael, 'Art Versus Philosophy in Hardy: *The W*', *Mosaic* 4, 1971.

Lesser Novels

Jones, Lawrence O., '*Desperate Remedies* and the Victorian Sensation Novel', *NCF* 20, 1965.

Page, Norman, 'Visual Techniques in Hardy's *DR*', *Ariel* 4, 1973.

Short, Clarice, 'In Defence of *Ethelberta*', *NCF* 13, 1958.

Drake, Robert Y., Jr., '*A Laodicean*: A Note on a Minor Novel', *PQ* 40, 1961.

Amos, Arthur K., 'Accident and Fate: The Possibility for Action in *A Pair of Blue Eyes*', *ELT* 15, 1972.

Bebington, W. G., *The Original Manuscript of The Trumpet-Major*,
   Windsor 1948.

Thomson, George H., 'The *TM* Chronicle', *NCF* 17, 1962.

Danby, John F., 'Under the Greenwood Tree', *CQ* 1, 1959.

Gerber, Helmut E., 'Hardy's *The Well-Beloved* as a Comment on the
   Well-Despised', *English Language Notes* 1, 1963.

Priestley, Alma, 'Hardy's *WB*: A Study in Failure', *THSR* 2, 1976.

Index